Focused Issues in Family T

MW00677793

Series editor

D. Russell Crane
School of Family Life
Brigham Young University
Provo, Utah, USA

More information about this series at http://www.springer.com/series/13372

Valentín Escudero • Myrna L. Friedlander

Therapeutic Alliances with Families

Empowering Clients in Challenging Cases

 Springer

Valentín Escudero
University of A Coruña
A Coruña, Spain

Myrna L. Friedlander
University at Albany/SUNY
Albany, New York, USA

ISSN 2520-1190   ISSN 2520-1204   (electronic)
Focused Issues in Family Therapy
ISBN 978-3-319-86609-3   ISBN 978-3-319-59369-2   (eBook)
DOI 10.1007/978-3-319-59369-2

This Springer imprint is published by Springer Nature
The registered company is Springer International Publishing AG
The registered company address is: Gewerbestrasse 11, 6330 Cham, Switzerland

To our own families, with whom we have shared some challenging situations but, above all, much unconditional love

Foreword

This book should come with a warning: *Be careful when you pick it up, because you won't be able to put it down.*

Escudero and Friedlander have succeeded royally in tackling a difficult genre of books for mental health professionals: highly readable *and* informed by clinical experience *and* research-based and constructed and written in a manner that seamlessly stitches these elements together and engages the reader from the start. The focus of the book is on challenging family cases (not challenging *families*). The cases are highly challenging indeed, e.g., multi-problem families with multi-agency involvements, clients who are therapy "hostages" (including couples in which one partner is initially passively or actively resistant to treatment and families with reluctant adolescents), cases of abuse and neglect in the family system, and "parenting in isolation," i.e., in situations in which one of the parents is absent physically or psychologically and/or obstructing the other's parenting efforts.

These are the most daunting kinds of cases for experienced therapists as well as therapists in training. To be honest, treating families of *any* kind is often daunting for experienced therapists and therapists in training. Most training programs in psychotherapy focus on individual treatment, and many therapists have not been trained to think systemically or to work conjointly with families, let alone those in very difficult circumstances. Thus, despite the fact that family therapy has been shown to be efficacious and even preferable to individual therapy for a wide range of problems (Heatherington, Friedlander, Escudero, Diamond, & Pinsof, 2015), there is an unfortunate dearth of family therapy providers in the USA and internationally.

This work has the potential to make significant progress on that front by informing, empowering, and encouraging readers at all levels in their work with families. It addresses the reader directly, with engaging chapter titles that are packed richly with case material and thorough, practical answers to the complex question: *What do I do now!?* Their answers are informed by a combined 60+ years of experience in treating families themselves, training and supervising others, and consulting, as well as by a well-established and ongoing program of research on creating therapeutic alliances in family therapy. This book represents the integration of clinical wisdom and clinical science at its best and in service of those who need it the most: families in great need and the therapists who are courageously helping them.

Reference

Heatherington, L., Friedlander, M. L., Escudero, V., Diamond, G., & Pinsof, W. M. (2015). 25 years of family therapy research: Progress and promise. *Psychotherapy Research (25th Anniversary Special Issue), 25*, 348–364.

Williams College   Laurie Heatherington,
Williamstown, MA, USA

About the Authors

Valentín Escudero, PhD, is a professor of psychology at the University of A Coruña, Spain, and director of the Family Intervention and Care Research Unit (UIICF). The UIICF is a family therapy center, where four prestigious programs of family therapy research and family therapy training have taken place from 1999. A psychotherapist and family therapist widely recognized by European institutions, Escudero is also an adjunct clinical professor at the University at Albany, State University of New York, USA. He was a visiting professor for 3 years at the Vrije Universiteit Brussel (2007–2011) and a visiting researcher at the Centre for Family Policy and Child Welfare at the University of Bristol, UK (2006–2007). Escudero is co-author with M. Friedlander and L. Heatherington of the *SOFTA (System for Observing Family Therapy Alliances)*. An associate editor of the *Journal of Family Therapy*, he has published in the *Journal of Family Therapy*, the *Journal of Marital and Family Therapy*, *Psychotherapy*, *Psychotherapy Research*, and the *Journal of Counseling Psychology*. Aside from his respected profile as researcher, Escudero is the director of the Therapy Program for Vulnerable Children and Families, which is the primary program of psychotherapy for the Child Protective Services of the Xunta de Galicia in Spain (a program that includes seven therapy centers).

Myrna L. Friedlander, PhD, is a professor in the counseling psychology PhD program at the University at Albany, State University of New York, where she served as training director from 1999 to 2016. She has supervised master's and doctoral students for over 35 years and published more than 140 book chapters and journal articles, including several self-report instruments and observational coding systems, primarily related to the processes of psychotherapy and supervision. She has co-authored three books published by the American Psychological Association: *Therapeutic Alliances in Couples and Families: An Empirically Informed Guide to Practice* (Friedlander, Escudero, & Heatherington, 2016), *Critical Events in Psychotherapy Supervision: An Interpersonal Approach* (Ladany, Friedlander, & Nelson, 2005), and *Supervision Essentials for the Critical Events Model of Psychotherapy Supervision* (Ladany, Friedlander, & Nelson, 2016). A Fellow of the

American Psychological Association, she has served on the editorial boards of six journals and received awards for her lifetime contribution to research by the University at Albany, the Society of Counseling Psychology (within the American Psychological Association), and the American Family Therapy Academy. A licensed psychologist in New York State, she has been in independent practice for over 30 years.

Acknowledgments

Many people have profoundly influenced our work in recent years, and we would like to acknowledge their influence. First, we must thank all the couples and families who trusted us with their hopes and dreams, sharing their difficulties and their suffering with us and giving us the opportunity to learn as professionals and to grow as people.

Additionally, we would like to express our appreciation to our graduate students and colleagues, particularly Laurie Heatherington and Marilyn Wheeler, who inspired our thinking about the alliance, our research, and our clinical work. In particular, Valentín Escudero wants to thank his team of therapists at the UIICF for their unwavering support: Alberto Abascal, Carlos de Francisco, Iria García, Raquel García, Naiara González, Belén López, Emma R. Maseda, Lucia Pérez, and Nuria Varela. Working with them is always stimulating, and each challenging case has provided us with the stimulus to learn and improve our skills along with helping clients change. Working with the UIICF team is a real privilege and an inexhaustible source of good humor. Valentín also wishes to thank all the coordinators and therapists in the Program of Therapeutic Treatment for Children at Risk and Foster Care, which he has been directing since 2012 for the Xunta de Galicia (Spain). The clients in that program are vulnerable children and families who cope every day with enormous difficulties. Working with them is a great honor. Similarly, Valentín wants to acknowledge 10 years of collaboration and learning with the Family and Children Care Program of the Junta de Castilla y León (Spain), which has been one of the most enjoyable and productive learning and research experiences of his professional life.

Contents

Chapter 1
Using the Therapeutic Alliance to Empower Couples and Families

Although Lily Goddard, a 44-year-old mother, smiled somewhat nervously, her expression suggested that she was ready to participate in her family's first conjoint therapy session. Rob, her 51-year-old husband, had a serious expression that was much less transparent. Their son Michael (15) seemed distracted as he made a visual sweep of the office, while Pamela (18) was highly attentive and seemed eager to get started.

After introducing herself, the therapist invited the family members to explain their ideas about how therapy could be beneficial for them. The response to her invitation was quite different from what she expected based on her first impression of the family:

Michael (to the therapist):   I don't know about your idea or what my parents told you, but I don't need therapy, and nobody can force it on me.

Hearing this comment, both parents squirmed in their chairs—Rob looked resigned and Lily looked uncomfortable. Immediately, Michael's sister interjected:

Pamela:	Can I tell her, Michael? I took some notes (opening a notebook) to explain what's happening with him. I think we need to explain it clearly.
Michael (to Pamela):	Now *you're* a psychologist?! So are you gonna run the therapy?! This is the last straw! Are you also gonna mention that you have anorexia?
Pamela:	I do *not* have anorexia!
Lily (starting to cry):	Please, please … don't start, you two… I beg of you…

© Springer International Publishing AG 2017
V. Escudero, M.L. Friedlander, *Therapeutic Alliances with Families*, Focused Issues in Family Therapy, DOI 10.1007/978-3-319-59369-2_1

Father (sarcastically, to Lily):	Here we go again with "I beg of you." We're already letting Michael do whatever he wants. Don't even think about crying!
Michael (to the therapist):	My father's always like this with my mother.
Therapist:	Well, I'm going to ask you all to show some respect for each other. Please make an effort so I can get an idea of how to help you.
Pamela (to the therapist):	Who should start talking?
Rob (to Lily):	I can't believe your daughter came with notes about what's happening in this family!
Lily (to Rob):	*My* daughter!
Therapist:	Michael…
Michael (interrupting, defiantly to Rob):	You want to explain how you want a psychiatric evaluation of me? All for smoking weed …?
Lily:	Please, I'm begging you, don't talk like that.
Pamela:	Michael, we're not here because of your weed. You don't get what's happening to you.
Rob (furious):	Pamela, would you let me or your mother describe the situation?
Pamela:	I just want to help. I can't stand it anymore. I don't even have to be here, but I came 'cause no one else tells the truth in this family.
Michael (to the therapist):	Pamela's planning to leave home, but my mother doesn't know. And my parents are talking about separating.
Lily:	That's not true, Michael!
Rob:	Michael, we're only here to talk about your problems.
Michael (angrily):	*My* problems? You're not going to talk about *your* problems too?
Lily (crying, to Rob and Michael):	I ask you both…don't do this to me!

At this point, the therapist realizes she needs to turn around this chaotic conversation and contain the emotional volatility that could easily derail the entire session. She knows she has to organize all the information, apparently contradictory, that the family just revealed. She also needs to foster a less hostile climate and provide space for each family member to express his or her unique perspective. And she needs to intervene quickly!

Let's consider the options. Should the therapist impose a structure so that everyone has a turn to speak? Should she inquire about the most immediate problem that led the family to seek help at this time? Should she focus on the person who made the initial request for therapy? Should she start with Michael, as he was the one identified as having the problem? Or should she respect the family hierarchy by asking the parents to explain their concerns and reasons for making the appointment? Should she explore all the problems already mentioned, or should she focus on the conflict that is unfolding in front of her? Is it a good idea to speak to the parents (or the teenagers) alone? Would doing that calm everyone down, or would separating the family members wind up frustrating them even more?

For any therapist, regardless of theoretical orientation, these questions are likely to come to mind in a chaotic situation like this one. Our therapist might decide that the priority is to explore Michael's risk behaviors, as his problems are what led the family to seek help. However, no matter where she starts, the conflicts already played out in front of her need to be addressed. It is quite possible that any intervention could further heighten the tension.

If the therapist decides that the first priority is to attend to her working alliance with the Goddard family, she will focus on identifying the family's goals and eliciting an agreement about the specific tasks of conjoint therapy. She will also try to foster an emotional bond with each family member. After all, Bordin (1979) described the emotional bond and agreement on goals and tasks as the three essential components of the working alliance, and research amply supports this model (for individual therapy). Nonetheless, our therapist still has an immediate decision in front of her: Where should she start? What should be her priority with this family?

As in this case, there are some therapeutic contexts that by their very nature pose a challenge to the working alliance. In this book, we describe a conceptual model of the alliance that embraces the unique aspects of conjoint psychotherapy. Our premise is that by paying attention to the specific aspects of this treatment format, therapists can select alliance-enhancing interventions that have the best chance of empowering family members to collaborate with one another in seeking solutions to their difficulties.

To illustrate, let's return to the case at hand. We realize that the brief excerpt you just read is insufficient for deciding which path to take with the Goddard family, but often we have little else to guide us through a first session. We suggest you try answering the following questions:

- What seems to be driving the chaos in this initial therapy session?
- Who is afraid of participating in the therapy?
- Who feels identified as the cause of the family's problems?
- Who feels shame about the situation that brought the family to therapy?
- Who feels accused by the other family members?
- Who is afraid of what the others might say about him or her?
- Who is afraid that a secret will be revealed that he or she cannot face?
- Who is afraid the conflict will turn violent?
- Who is convinced that he or she will derive some personal benefit from taking part in the therapy?

- Who has an idea of what he or she would like to achieve as a result of therapy?
- Who thinks it makes sense for the other members of the family to be a part of the therapy?
- Who is prepared to like the therapist?
- Who thinks the therapist will understand him/her?
- Who thinks the therapist will understand the other family members?
- Who is afraid the therapist will take sides?

In posing these questions, we hope you will realize that to some extent, the four members of the Goddard family are feeling similarly about participating with each other in a conjoint therapy format. If you understand the opening of the session this way, rather than focusing on each person's individual goal for the therapy, you might take an alternate route by asking yourself the following additional questions:

- How can I foster a minimum level of safety to get the process off to a better start?
- How can I frame my understanding of the problem(s) so that no one feels excluded or accused?
- How can I convey my awareness that each member of the family is suffering?
- Can I unite these family members by helping them recall the love they have for each other?

We hope these questions make sense to you. All of them are in the service of one objective: to select interventions that will build safety, foster an emotional connection with each client, and promote meaningful engagement and within-family collaboration in the therapy process. Put simply, in particularly challenging contexts, the therapist needs to build a strong, personal alliance with each family member and expand the alliance within the family to identify and work on shared goals. (Note: We deliberately use the word *challenging* to refer to the case, i.e., the therapeutic context as a whole, not the family itself.)

The unique challenge of couple and family therapy is the need to purposefully balance alliances with multiple family members in order to help each individual and family subsystem achieve therapeutic goals. The more a family is complex and reluctant or resistant to change, the more essential it is to decisively create and maintain strong alliances with each person and with the family unit as a whole.

We wrote this book to be eminently practical. Drawing on our conceptual, empirically-supported model of the therapeutic alliance, the System for Observing Family Therapy Alliances or SOFTA (Friedlander, Escudero, & Heatherington, 2006), we describe various ways to help couples and families find unique solutions and renew close attachments. We developed the SOFTA specifically to attend to the unique aspects of conjoint work with couples and families as well as to the aspects of psychotherapy that are common across treatment modalities.

Each chapter in the book discusses a specific challenge to conjoint couple or family therapy. Specifically, the chapters address complex difficulties in couples (Chap. 2), conflicts between adolescents and parents (Chap. 3), various contexts of parenting in isolation (Chap. 4), and specialized work with survivors of relational trauma (Chap. 5) and with disadvantaged, multi-stressed families (Chap. 6). Within each chapter we describe unique challenges, summarize relevant clinical and empirical literature, and provide guidelines for working with the kinds of cases that pose the greatest risk of therapeutic failure. The chapters are abundantly illustrated with case material. Within extended case examples, we explain the intent of each alliance-related intervention. The final chapter (Chap. 7) pulls the foregoing ideas together in an overarching framework for leveraging family alliances to empower change.

Our perspective is based on our research and clinical experience—both of us have worked extensively as family therapists, researchers, and as trainers/supervisors of novice therapists. The practice recommendations in each chapter are informed by theory and research, thereby providing readers an evidence-based approach to practice. Our premise is that regardless of the therapist's theoretical approach to couple and family therapy, building and monitoring multiple therapeutic relationships simultaneously is of paramount importance.

In the remainder of this chapter, we introduce our pan-theoretical, systemic perspective on couple and family therapy (CFT), the distinguishing feature of which is a primary concern with shifting the interpersonal (as opposed to intrapersonal) dynamics that maintain psychosocial problems and family dysfunction. Next, we describe the four-dimensional SOFTA, its measures, and practical applications. In doing so, we discuss how individual differences, both clients' and therapists', come into play when building strong therapeutic alliances. Finally, we highlight three aspects of the alliance that, if not attended too closely, can lead to a rupture—specifically, (1) a lack of safety that compromises family members' engagement in the therapeutic process, especially when they are in conflict with one another, (2) a clinical context in which partners or family members have differing motivations for seeking help, and (3) distinct variability in family members' emotional connections with the therapist.

Alliances in Couple and Family Therapy

As a concept, the *therapeutic* or *working* alliance is well known to mental health practitioners. Over the past 25 years, theory and research on the alliance has established it as a clearly important factor in successful therapy across treatment modalities, with meta-analyses showing that self-reported and observed alliances account for roughly 5–7% of the variability in therapeutic outcomes in CFT (Friedlander, Escudero, Heatherington, & Diamond, 2011), similar to the alliance-outcome association in individual psychotherapy (Horvath, Del Re, Flückiger, & Symonds, 2011).

This similarity in importance does not imply that the therapeutic alliance in CFT is identical to the alliance in individual treatment. Rather, despite some common aspects, CFT alliances have some aspects that make it fundamentally different from the working alliance in individual psychotherapy. The similar aspects are those conceptualized by Bordin (1979): a strong emotional bond and agreement between therapist and client(s) on the goals and tasks of the therapy. The dissimilar aspects have to do with the uniqueness of the CFT context. Since clients are seen conjointly in therapy with other family members, a strong alliance in this treatment modality requires a within-system agreement on the problems, goals, and value of therapy, which can only be accomplished if partners or family members feel comfortable speaking openly with one another in the therapy context.

Indeed, the conjoint context is particularly challenging for clients as well as for therapists. For some clients, exposing their most intimate and vulnerable relationships to a stranger can feel threatening, almost like a betrayal of those relationships. The expectation of seeing one's partner or parent diminished in the eyes of a therapist can be particularly distressing, even if the client herself has a poor opinion of that family member. Moreover, unlike in individual therapy, clients in CFT are not entirely in control of what is revealed to the therapist, since the point of a conjoint context is for family members to discuss how they view one another and their relationships. Anticipating an unflattering portrayal of the family can prompt the fear—hopefully unfounded—that the therapist will pass judgment. For most people, an unfavorable judgment from an authority figure can be hard to discount even if the family ultimately decides not to engage in treatment.

For CFT therapists, secrets and hidden agendas can be a minefield. Although couples and families often seek help with a circumscribed problem, such as to make a decision (e.g., to relocate, to have a baby) or to cope with an illness or an external stressor, it is more typically the case that people come to therapy when they are at odds with one another. If all of the family members are emotionally mature, they are likely to expect the therapist to be caring and respectful of everyone. If, on the other hand, a family member cannot see any perspective other than her own, she may feel personally threatened when the therapist seems to encourage a point of view that she does not share. Even parents who are eager for their adolescent to like the therapist can feel uncomfortable when their teenager develops a strong bond with him (Friedlander, Kivlighan, & Shaffer, 2012).

It is not always smooth sailing even when all of the family members who attend therapy sessions are emotionally capable of handling the challenges of a conjoint treatment context, since the therapist still needs to develop and balance multiple alliances simultaneously. Doing so requires paying close attention to existing and shifting alliances between and among family subsystems, as well as considering how her individual alliance with each client affects alliances with all of the other family members. After all, clients in CFT not only engage directly with the therapist but also indirectly, through observation. Consider, for example, the effect on a mother who hears the therapist ask her 19-year-old daughter, "How do you think your relationship with your mom will change once she starts to really see you as a grown up?" The indirect message to this mother is a directive to start respecting her daughter's maturity.

Notwithstanding all of these challenges, conducting conjoint CFT can be immensely rewarding. The dramatic shifts in people's closest relationships that take place in the therapist's office have no parallel in individual or group therapy. These real-time changes have the power to improve clients' personal lives in ways that may have seemed unimaginable to them before seeking the help of a therapist.

The SOFTA Model and Measures

Our primary intention in creating the SOFTA was to develop a conceptual model of alliance, with corresponding observer (SOFTA-o) and self-report (SOFTA-s) instruments that incorporate elements of CFT that both align with and distinguish it from individual psychotherapy. When a therapist works conjointly with partners or other family members, the clients' attachments with one another necessitate creating and maintaining multiple alliances simultaneously. Alliances that already exist within the family affect how the clients behave in therapy and if and how they value the therapist and the therapeutic process.

Secondarily, in creating the SOFTA-o we wanted to identify in-session behaviors that reflect how clients behave when they view the alliance as strong and, conversely, when they see the alliance as problematic or faltering. Similarly, we were interested in identifying how therapists behave so as to contribute positively to their alliances with individuals and with families as systems. Just as a client's observable behavior reveals a weak alliance, so can a therapist's behavior detract from the alliance when, for example, he imposes goals or tasks without seeking the clients' input or when he fails to attend to the internal experience of every participant.

Our intent to identify clients' alliance-related behaviors had a twofold objective. The first objective was theoretical and empirical. In terms of theory, despite a plethora of books and articles about how therapists should approach couples and families, we found almost no literature on how clients are expected to behave in a conjoint context. Clients in psychoanalysis are expected to free associate, to suspend judgment, and to report their dreams, memories, and fantasies. Clients in cognitive-behavioral therapy are expected to try out new behaviors, dispute their irrational beliefs, accept their personal limitations, and so on. Yet little is written about what clients in conjoint therapy are expected to do. Even in describing theoretically rich CFT approaches like structural therapy, emotion-focused couple therapy, and Bowen family systems therapy, authors tend to focus exclusively on therapeutic strategies and interventions, paying little or no attention to how clients behave when the therapy is either going well or poorly.

In terms of relevant previous research, the available alliance measures lacked behavioral specificity. The observer version of the Working Alliance Inventory for couples (Symonds & Horvath, 2004), for example, has items that require subjective inference so that, for example, the observer needs to judge the degree to which "the client trusts the therapist." In contrast, we constructed low-inference behavioral indicators that could readily be identified even by clinically inexperienced observers, e.g., "The client verbalizes trust in the therapist." We reasoned that clearly observable behaviors would be easily recognized by therapists in the process stream, especially when they are specifically trained to look for and discern these important alliance-related behaviors.

Moreover, low-inference behaviors are those that are readily noticed by the family members themselves. When, for example, a father sees his daughter's reluctance to answer the therapist's question, he gets the clear sense that she is uncomfortable with what is occurring in that moment. In other words, we reasoned that if trained observers (researchers and therapists) look for the same kinds of behaviors that readily stand out as meaningful to clients, we have a good chance of creating an empirical model of alliance that would accurately reflect how family members are thinking and feeling about what is occurring during their therapy sessions.

Indeed, some research suggests that client behavior, as rated by the SOFTA-o observer measure, is closely aligned with clients' perceptions of the alliance, as reported to an interviewer (Beck, Friedlander, & Escudero, 2006) and as rated on questionnaires filled out immediately following the session (e.g., Friedlander, Bernardi, & Lee, 2010; Friedlander, Lambert, Escudero, & Cragun, 2008). Moreover, we now have evidence that SOFTA-o behavior, even alliance ratings in the first therapy session, is predictive of perceived "improvement-so-far" rated later on in treatment (Friedlander, Lambert, & Muñiz de la Peña, 2008). Client outcomes in general are also associated with in-session alliance behavior as rated on the SOFTA-o (Escudero, Friedlander, Varela, & Abascal, 2008; Isserlin & Couturier, 2012; Smerud & Rosenfarb, 2008).

But where does the therapist's theoretical approach fit in? The alliance is a common or theoretically nonspecific treatment factor that cuts across therapy approaches. Actually, meta-analyses indicate that the alliance contributes more to treatment success than theoretical orientation, which accounts for at most 1% of the variability in outcomes (Wampold & Imel, 2015). Increasingly, in CFT as in individual therapy, the boundaries between theories seem to have become blurred (Friedlander & Diamond, 2011; Lebow, 2016), as therapists increasingly draw on diverse intervention strategies in their work with couples and families.

Theoretical allegiance aside, our perspective on CFT alliances is decidedly systemic. That is, we assume that symptoms and life problems result from multiple interacting and reciprocal forces within and outside a family. Moreover, when a couple or family seeks help from a therapist to facilitate a change, the entry of this authoritative "other" invariably affects existing family relationships. The most powerful individual in the family, the mother for example, may well be viewed differently by family members after she is seen relating with deference to a therapist. The least powerful family member may well be viewed with more respect after the therapist demonstrates respect for her opinion. These dynamics play out regardless of whether the therapist approaches the family with advice on behavioral change or explores the clients' deepest attachments to one another.

Based on this reasoning, we created behavioral indicators for the client version of the SOFTA-o that reflect multiple theoretical approaches, such as "client agrees to do homework assignments" (cognitive-behavioral), "client complies with therapist's request for an enactment" (structural), and "client shows vulnerability, e.g., discusses painful feelings, cries" (emotion-focused). As for the therapist SOFTA-o, the behavioral indicators are theoretically generic enough (e.g., "therapist discloses some fact about his or her personal life") to be relevant to any and all theoretical approaches.

We see alliance and technique as intertwined (Friedlander, Heatherington, & Escudero, 2016; Heatherington, Escudero, & Friedlander, in press). Thus, for example, when a therapist expresses confidence or trust in a couple, it can be confidence in their ability to change a dysfunctional behavior pattern ("I'm sure that, with time, you will both learn to fight fair when you have a strong disagreement about something") or to take a significant emotional risk with one another ("I feel certain that you'll take this chance to find true intimacy in a way you've never before experienced it"). As another example, when the therapist is negotiating a specific in-session task, the task might be a client enactment ("How would you feel about trying to resolve that conflict right here and now?") or a particular kind of discussion ("Would it be all right with you if your son and I had a little chat, with you looking on, about his priorities for his life, now that he's turned 18?"). In other words, we do not discount theory in our alliance model. Rather, we believe in using specific kinds of alliance-related interventions for therapeutic ends, be they systemic, cognitive-behavioral, or emotion-focused in nature.

Description of the SOFTA Dimensions and Behaviors

The SOFTA conceptual model, developed simultaneously in English (Friedlander, Escudero, Horvath, et al., 2006) and Spanish (El Sistema de Observación de la Alianza Terapéutica en Intervención Familiar, or SOATIF; Escudero & Friedlander, 2003), was created inductively. First, we constructed a large pool of items from our clinical experience and an extensive review of the CFT literature. Additionally, we reviewed archived videotaped CFT sessions for which we had the clients' self-reported perceptions of the therapeutic alliance, administered via questionnaires immediately following the sessions in question. From this archival set, we selected specific sessions in which the clients had either highly favorable or highly problematic alliance perceptions in order to identify within-session behaviors, nonverbal as well as verbal, that seemed to reflect these clients' favorable (+) versus problematic (−) alliance perceptions. Examples included open body posture (+) and lengthy arguments between the client and therapist (−). Then, each member of the team independently clustered behaviors from the item pool that seemed to go together and wrote a description of the concept that seemed to underlie each cluster. The resulting comparison of independently developed clusters and definitions resulted in four SOFTA dimensions, which we named *Engagement in the Therapeutic Process* (ENGAGE), *Emotional Connection with the Therapist* (CONNECTION), *Safety Within the Therapeutic System* (SAFETY), and *Shared Sense of Purpose Within the Family* (SHARED PURPOSE). Behavioral indicators clustered within each dimension are listed in Tables 1.1 and 1.2; they are also available for download

Table 1.1 SOFTA-o: client version

Indicator	Valence
Engagement in the therapeutic process	
Client indicates agreement with the therapist's goals	+
Client describes or discusses a plan for improving the situation	+
Client introduces a problem for discussion	+
Client agrees to do homework assignments	+
Client indicates having done homework or seeing it as useful	+
Client expresses optimism or indicates that a positive change has taken place	+
Client complies with therapist's requests for enactments	+
Client leans forward	+
Client mentions the treatment, the therapeutic process, or a specific session	+
Client expresses feeling "stuck," questions the value of therapy, or states that therapy is not/has not been helpful	−
Client shows indifference about the tasks or process of therapy (e.g., paying lip service, "I don't know," tuning out)	−
Emotional connection to the therapist	
Client shares a lighthearted moment or joke with the therapist	+
Client verbalizes trust in the therapist	+
Client expresses interest in the therapist's personal life	+
Client indicates feeling understood or accepted by the therapist	+
Client expresses physical affection or caring for the therapist	+
Client mirrors the therapist's body posture	+
Client avoids eye contact with the therapist	−
Client refuses or is reluctant to respond to the therapist	−
Client has hostile or sarcastic interactions with the therapist	−
Client comments on the therapist's incompetence or inadequacy	−
Safety within the therapeutic system	
Client implies or states that therapy is a safe place	+
Client varies his/her emotional tone during the session	+
Client shows vulnerability (e.g., discusses painful feelings, cries)	+
Client has an open upper body posture	+
Client reveals a secret or something that other family members didn't know	+
Client encourages another family member to "open up" or to tell the truth	+
Client directly asks other family members for feedback about his/her behavior or about herself/himself as a person	+
Client expresses anxiety nonverbally (e.g., taps or shakes)	−
Client protects self in nonverbal manner (e.g., crosses arms over chest, doesn't take off jacket or put down purse, sits far away from group, etc.)	−
Client refuses or is reluctant to respond when directly addressed by another family member	−
Client responds defensively to another family member	−
Client makes an uneasy/anxious reference to the camera, observation, supervisor, or research procedures	−

(continued)

Table 1.1 (continued)

Indicator	Valence
Shared sense of purpose within the family	
Family members offer to compromise	+
Family members share a joke or a lighthearted moment with each other	+
Family members ask each other for their perspective	+
Family members validate each other's point of view	+
Family members mirror each other's body posture	+
Family members avoid eye contact with each other	−
Family members blame each other	−
Family members devalue each other's opinions or perspective	−
Family members try to align with the therapist against each other	−
Client makes hostile or sarcastic comments to family members	−
Family members disagree with each other about the value, purpose, goals, or tasks of therapy or about who should be included in the sessions	−

© Friedlander, Escudero, & Heatherington, 2001. Reproduced by permission of the authors
Note. Positive indicators reflect favorable thoughts and feelings about each dimension of the alliance, whereas negative indicators reflect unfavorable thoughts and feelings about each dimension

free of charge from our website, www.softa-soatif.com. Operational definitions for each of the client and therapist indicators are listed in the Appendix A.

SOFTA-o, Client Version The first dimension, Engagement in the Therapeutic Process, reflects Bordin's (1979) conceptualization of the working alliance in terms of client and therapist agreement on goals and tasks. Specifically, ENGAGEMENT reflects the alliance-related behavior of each client in the system in terms of the extent to which he negotiates the goals of treatment with the therapist, agrees to do specific in-session and/or homework tasks, and is generally involved in the therapeutic process. Some of the positive behavioral indicators include introducing a new problem for discussion, agreeing to do a homework assignment, and indicating agreement with the therapist's goals. In contrast, the negative ENGAGEMENT indicators are behaviors that reflect a lack of involvement or a refusal to participate in the process, such as showing indifference, "tuning out," and so on. ENGAGEMENT is defined in the SOFTA as:

> the client viewing treatment as meaningful; a sense of being involved in therapy and working together with the therapist, that therapeutic goals and tasks in therapy can be discussed and negotiated with the therapist, that taking the process seriously is important, that change is possible. (Friedlander, Escudero, & Heatherington, 2006, p. 270)

The second dimension, Emotional Connection to the Therapist, which is similar to Bordin's (1979) description of the emotional bond between client and therapist, is defined in the SOFTA as:

> the client viewing the therapist as an important person in his/her life, almost like a family member; a sense that the relationship is based on affiliation, trust, caring, and concern; that

Table 1.2 SOFTA-o: therapist version

Indicator	Valence
Engagement in the therapeutic process	
Therapist explains how therapy works	+
Therapist asks client(s) what they want to talk about in the session	+
Therapist encourages client(s) to articulate their goals for therapy	+
Therapist asks client(s) whether they are willing to do a specific in-session task (e.g., enactment)	+
Therapist asks client(s) whether they are willing to follow a specific suggestion or do a specific homework assignment	+
Therapist asks client(s) about the impact or value of a prior homework assignment	+
Therapist expresses optimism or notes that a positive change has taken place or can take place	+
Therapist pulls in quiet client(s) (e.g., by deliberately leaning forward, calling them by name, addressing them specifically)	+
Therapist asks if the client(s) have any questions	+
Therapist praises client motivation for engagement or change	+
Therapist defines therapeutic goals or imposes tasks or procedures without asking the client(s) for their collaboration	−
Therapist argues with the client(s) about the nature, purpose, or value of therapy	−
Therapist shames or criticizes how clients did (or did not do) a prior homework assignment	−
Emotional connection to the therapist	
Therapist shares a lighthearted moment or joke with the client(s)	+
Therapist expresses confidence, trust, or belief in the client(s)	+
Therapist expresses interest in the client(s) apart from the therapeutic discussion at hand	+
Therapist expresses caring or touches client(s) affectionately yet appropriately (e.g., handshake, pat on the head)	+
Therapist discloses his or her personal reactions or feelings toward the client(s) or the situation	+
Therapist discloses some fact about his or her personal life	+
Therapist remarks on or describes how his or her values or experiences are similar to the clients'	+
Therapist (verbally or nonverbally) expresses empathy for the clients' struggle (e.g., "I know this is hard," "I feel your pain," crying with client)	+
Therapist reassures or normalizes a client's emotional vulnerability (e.g., crying, hurt feelings).	+
Therapist has hostile, sarcastic, or critical interactions with the client(s)	−
Therapist does not respond to clients' expressions of personal interest or caring for him or her	−
Safety within the therapeutic system	
Therapist acknowledges that therapy involves taking risks or discussing private matters	+
Therapist provides structure and guidelines for safety and confidentiality	+
Therapist invites discussion about intimidating elements in the therapeutic context (e.g., recording equipment, reports to third parties, treatment team observation, one-way mirror, research, etc.)	+

(continued)

Table 1.2 (continued)

Indicator	Valence
Therapist helps clients to talk truthfully and nondefensively with each other	+
Therapist attempts to contain, control, or manage overt hostility between clients	+
Therapist actively protects one family member from another (e.g., from blame, hostility, or emotional intrusiveness)	+
Therapist changes the topic to something pleasurable or non-anxiety arousing (e.g., small talk about the weather, room decor, TV shows, etc.) when there seems to be tension or anxiety	+
Therapist asks one client (or a subgroup of clients) to leave the room in order to see one client alone for a portion of the session	+
Therapist allows family conflict to escalate to verbal abuse, threats, or intimidation	−
Therapist does not attend to overt expressions of client vulnerability (e.g., crying, defensiveness)	−
Shared sense of purpose within the family	
Therapist encourages clients to compromise with each other	+
Therapist encourages clients to ask each other for their perspective	+
Therapist praises clients for respecting each other's point of view	+
Therapist emphasizes commonalities among clients' perspectives on the problem or solution	+
Therapist draws attention to clients' shared values, experiences, needs, or feelings	+
Therapist encourages clients to show caring, concern, or support for each other	+
Therapist encourages client(s) to ask each other for feedback	+
Therapist fails to intervene when family members argue with each other about the goals, value, or need for therapy	−
Therapist fails to address one client's stated concerns by only discussing another client's concerns	−

© Friedlander, Escudero, & Heatherington, 2001. Reproduced by permission of the authors
Note. Positive indicators reflect therapists' behavioral contributions to each dimension of the alliance, whereas negative indicators reflect therapist behaviors that detract from each dimension
See www.softa-soatif.net for versions in other languages

> the therapist genuinely cares for and "is there" for the client, that he/she is on the same wavelength as the therapist (e.g., similar life perspectives, values), that the therapist's wisdom and expertise are valuable. (Friedlander , Escudero, & Heatherington, 2006, p. 270)

Positive behavioral indicators in this dimension reflect trusting, valuing, and feeling a closeness with the therapist, including, for example, stating a feeling of being understood or accepted by the therapist, sharing a lighthearted moment with the therapist, or mirroring the therapist's body posture. On the other hand, negative CONNECTION indicators reflect the opposite feeling, with behaviors like avoiding eye contact or interacting sarcastically with the therapist.

The third SOFTA dimension, Safety within the Therapeutic System, contains elements that cut across therapy modalities. It goes without saying that clients in individual and group therapy also need to feel safe in order to do the difficult work required of them in order to achieve desired outcomes. In conjoint CFT, however, safety has a unique flavor, simply because partners and family members participate in the process together. Hence, safety in the CFT context has to do with feeling comfortable not only with the therapist but also with everyone else in the session and, potentially, even with people who are not present but who are likely to be informed about what took place in the therapy, such as court officials, protective services, and so on. In the SOFTA, SAFETY indicators include showing vulnerability (+), encouraging another family member to open up or tell the truth (+), or responding defensively to another family member (−). In our model, this dimension is defined as:

> the client viewing therapy as a place to take risks, be open, flexible; a sense of comfort and an expectation that new experiences and learning will take place, that good can come from being in therapy, that conflict within the family can be handled without harm, that one need not be defensive. (Friedlander, Escudero, & Heatherington, 2006, p. 270)

The fourth SOFTA dimension, also unique to conjoint CFT, is called Shared Sense of Purpose Within the Family, otherwise known as the *within-family alliance* (cf. Pinsof, 1995). This dimension is complex in that it reflects the engagement of the couple or family as a whole in defining the problem, setting goals, agreeing on tasks, and feeling a sense of value and unity in doing so. We defined the SHARED PURPOSE dimension as:

> family members seeing themselves as working collaboratively to improve family relations and achieve common family goals; a sense of solidarity in relation to the therapy ("we're in this together"); that they value their time with each other in therapy; essentially, a felt unity within the family in relation to the therapy. (Friedlander, Escudero, & Heatherington, 2006, p. 270)

Positive behavioral manifestations of a strongly shared sense of purpose include clients' valuing each other's point of view, sharing a lighthearted moment with one another, and offering to compromise. In contrast, negative manifestations include cross-blaming and one client trying to align with the therapist against another client.

The 44 client behaviors, 10 or 11 per dimension (see Table 1.1 and Appendix A), in our model and accompanying observer rating system, the SOFTA-o (Friedlander, Escudero, and Heatherington, 2006), are neither exhaustive nor mutually exclusive. That is, depending on the characteristics of the individuals involved, there may be other important ways in which a strong or a weak alliance is manifested. Moreover, in the same speaking turn, a client might show a sense of unease by, for example, having a self-protective body posture (negative SAFETY) while nonetheless complying with the therapist's request for an enactment (positive ENGAGEMENT).

SOFTA-o, Therapist Version The four SOFTA dimensions are defined identically in the therapist version of the model, but rather than reflecting private thoughts and feelings about the alliance, the therapist indicators, listed in Table 1.2 and Appendix A, represent behaviors that either contribute to or detract from the client's engagement, emotional connection, sense of safety, and within-family alliance. Thus, for example, a behavior that contributes to a client's engagement is pulling a quiet or reluctant client into the conversation, and a behavior that contributes to the family's sense of comfort is providing structure and guidelines for safety and confidentiality.

In fact, several of the 43 therapist behaviors parallel those of the client, such as "therapist asks client(s) whether they are willing to do a specific in-session task (e.g., enactment)" and "client complies with therapist's request for an enactment" (ENGAGEMENT) or "client expresses interest in the therapist's personal life" and "therapist discloses some fact about his or her personal life" (CONNECTION). Other complementary behaviors are not quite as parallel but, rather, are likely to follow one another in succession, such as "therapist helps clients to talk truthfully and not defensively with each other" and "client encourages another family member to 'open up' or to tell the truth" (SAFETY; Friedlander, Escudero, & Heatherington, 2006, pp. 271–279).

In designing the SOFTA-o, we found it difficult to identify negative therapist behaviors, i.e., observable behaviors that would definitively detract from the alliance. Aside from blatantly problematic behavior such as engaging in hostile interactions with a client, negative therapist behavior tends to be subtle, such as ignoring a quiet client throughout the session, or failing to intervene when family members threaten one another. Consequently, as shown in Table 1.2, we only listed a few negative therapist behaviors, ones that we believed most skilled therapists would avoid. In fact, our research with the SOFTA-o has shown that it is common for there to be few or no readily observable therapist behaviors. Rather, there are missed opportunities for enhancing the client's alliances that cannot reliably be identified by observers (Friedlander, Lambert, Escudero, et al., 2008; Lambert, Skinner, & Friedlander, 2012; Sheehan & Friedlander, 2015). One example is when a therapist fails to encourage parents to support their adolescent's active involvement in the therapeutic process (Higham, Friedlander, Escudero, & Diamond, 2012).

SOFTA-s Parallel, 16-item questionnaires (see Appendix B; also available in Spanish, French, Swedish, Italian, and Hebrew on our website, www.softa-soatif. com), designed to be filled out by the therapist and each family member (over age 10) after a session, were written to reflect each of the four SOFTA dimensions. In the client version of the questionnaire, 12 of the 16 items reflect the individual's personal experience of the alliance in terms of ENGAGEMENT (e.g., "The therapist and I work together as a team"), CONNECTION (e.g., "The therapist understands me"), and SAFETY (e.g., "There are some topics I am afraid to discuss in therapy," reverse scored). The remaining four items reflect the client's experience of the within-family alliance on the SHARED PURPOSE dimension (e.g., "Each of us in the family helps the others get what they want out of therapy") (Friedlander, Escudero, & Heatherington, 2006, p. 298). The therapist's version of the SOFTA-s (also in Appendix B) asks for her perspective on what Pinsof (Pinsof, 1995; Pinsof & Catherall, 1986) called the *group* alliance on each of the four SOFTA dimensions. All 16 items on the therapist version are parallel to the corresponding client items, e.g., "The family and I are working together as a team" (ENGAGEMENT) and "I understand this family" (CONNECTION; Friedlander, Escudero, & Heatherington, 2006, p. 299). We have also used shortened versions of the SOFTA-s, one item per dimension for a total of four items (noted in Appendix B).

In several case studies, we found a correspondence between observers' alliance ratings (SOFTA-o) and the self-reported alliance perceptions of individual family members on the SOFTA-s (Friedlander, Lambert, Escudero, et al., 2008; Friedlander, Lee, Shaffer, & Cabrera, 2014; Heatherington et al., in press; Lambert et al., 2012). In a large, as yet unpublished outcome study, we found that adolescents' views of the alliance on the shortened SOFTA-s significantly predicted changes in their level of functioning as reported by their therapists.

Using the SOFTA-o and SOFTA-s in Practice and Training

The SOFTA model and measures were developed not only to provide a theoretical understanding of alliance in CFT but also to draw therapists' attention to in-session behaviors and post-session perceptions that reflect clients' private experience of their alliance with the therapist and with each other in the therapeutic context. As mentioned above, the self-report measure tends to mirror clients' alliance-related behavior as identified by observers using the SOFTA-o, and SOFTA-s scores predict treatment outcomes. For this reason, we recommend regular use of the SOFTA-s to provide therapists with feedback about how individual family members are experiencing the unfolding therapeutic process. Armed with this information, a therapist can address a faltering alliance with an adolescent, for example, or pay closer attention to a husband's relative lack of safety in sessions with his wife.

Two alliance dimensions, SAFETY and SHARED PURPOSE, appear to be the most sensitive to variations in family attendance in therapy. It is common for different family members to attend sessions at various times, and the entrance of a stepparent or an older sibling, for example, in the middle of treatment has the potential to affect a vulnerable client's experience in a dramatic way, positively or negatively. Similar shifts in SAFETY and SHARED PURPOSE are observed when the focus of discussion changes from outside influences to within-family conflicts. In one case (Friedlander, Lambert, Escudero, et al., 2008), for example, mother and children experienced a particularly strong alliance in the first six sessions as they were discussing the father's drug use and absence from the family, but when the topic shifted in a later session to conflicts between the mother and one of the daughters, the daughter's SOFTA-s SAFETY perception plummeted, as did the family's SHARED PURPOSE behavior.

Aside from our use of the SOFTA measures in research, we have trained numerous graduate students in the model. One empirical study (Carpenter, Escudero, & Rivett, 2008) mirrored our teaching experience in that in the absence of specific alliance training, novice therapists had a difficult time accurately identifying clients' alliance-related behaviors. After training, however, these trainees' performances improved notably. The results of this study and another, more recent one (Sheehan & Friedlander, 2015) suggest that CFT therapists naturally become more attuned to clients' alliance-related behaviors as they gain clinical experience.

In using the SOFTA-o, observers should focus either on the clients' behaviors or on those of the therapist. (That is, rating both simultaneously is not recommended.) The first step is to identify each family member's (or therapist's) behavior in the stream of a session, either during a live observation or by reviewing a previously recorded session on a scoring sheet, like the one in Appendix C. After becoming familiar with the operational definitions of each SOFTA-o item (listed in www. softa-soatif.com), observers take note of the occurrence of each behavior as it occurs in the session. The operational definitions (see Appendix A) were written to reduce observer subjectivity. An example is the operational definition of the SAFETY item, "client states or implies that therapy is a safe place":

> The client might not necessarily use the word "safe," but the implication in his/her words is that he/she feels safe. This item requires some kind of verbal indicator; nonverbal indicators are *not* sufficient for this item to be checked. Implicit examples are when someone says he/she decided to wait until the therapy session to discuss something with a family member or says something like, "It's okay to cry in here" or "I didn't know whether I would have the courage to tell you, but…" or "I'm glad we finally made it here." The point is that the client suggests that the therapeutic environment is valued for its safety, not only as a place to solve problems. At times the indicator may be quite subtle, as "I don't know quite how to say this, but I'll just take the plunge," or "I hope you [*other family members*] don't mind my saying this, but …." (Friedlander, Escudero, & Heatherington, 2006, pp. 53–54)

After an entire session has been reviewed, the rater considers the tallied indicators in terms of their valence (positive or negative), frequency of occurrence, intensity, and clinical meaningfulness in context and in light of the dimension's general definition in order to make a global alliance rating. These global ratings, which can vary from −3 to +3, reflect each client's individual ENGAGEMENT, CONNECTION, and SAFETY in the session and the couple's or the family unit's SHARED PURPOSE or within-system alliance. Specific rating guidelines (see Appendix C) are to be followed. For example, when considering a global rating for a client whose behavior in the session is both positive and negative, the rating must be −1, 0, or +1. The seven ratings are anchored as follows:

−3 = extremely problematic
−2 = moderately problematic
−1 = somewhat problematic
0 = unremarkable or neutral
+1 = somewhat strong
+2 = moderately strong
+3 = extremely strong

To facilitate the rating process, we developed a software program, e-SOFTA, which is available free of charge on our website (www.softa-soatif.com) in Spanish as well as English. In this program users can observe some training vignettes in order to learn the SOFTA-o and familiarize themselves with the software. Then, users can download their own videos into the program for rating. Figure 1.1 shows an e-SOFTA screen with a family therapy session (actors; Escudero & Friedlander, 2016, p. 235) for the analysis of the therapist's contributions to the SAFETY

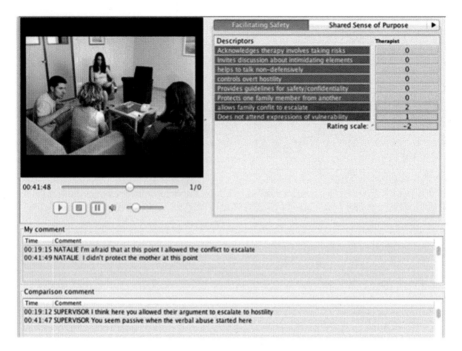

Fig. 1.1 Sample screen in e-SOFTA

dimension. Detailed explanations for downloading and learning the e-SOFTA are available on the website and described in detail in Escudero et al. (2011) and Escudero and Friedlander (2016).

As explained in these publications, the e-SOFTA is not only useful for research on the alliance, but also can facilitate a therapist's review of his own sessions and a supervisor's review of a trainee's session, for the clients' indicators as well as for the therapist's contributions to the alliance. The program automatically time-stamps the tallied behavior as the user identifies them. In Fig. 1.1, for example, the analysis of the therapist's contributions to facilitate SAFETY includes one negative instance ("does not attend expressions of vulnerability") and two negative instances of "allows family conflict to escalate."

A space at the bottom of the screen allows two users to write detailed notes about their observations, also time-stamped. In the figure, the video is poised at minute 00:41:47, and the therapist ("Natalie") as well as the supervisor wrote comments that show a similar perception that Natalie was passive with respect to conflict escalation and failed to protect the mother from the verbal abuse of the father.

The time stamps allow users to review each moment in the session when a behavior has been tallied and a comment is written. In this way, a supervisor can easily review a previously rated session by a supervisee and add her own commentary beneath the supervisee's original one.

Note, also, that underneath the list of SOFTA-o items there is space for a global rating. In Fig. 1.1, the user gave a rating of −2 for the therapist's contributions to SAFETY. (By selecting different tabs above the items, the user can switch between the four SOFTA dimensions.) e-SOFTA provides graphical displays of these global ratings.

Alliance and Individual Differences

In our society, three sociodemographic characteristics play an important role in how people interact and perceive one another: gender, race, and social class. Despite the privacy of the consulting room, the therapeutic context is not immune to these perceptions and their behavioral consequences.

In the case of gender, for example, some research with heterosexual couples suggests that a woman tends to be the partner who demands change, with the man tending to be the partner who withdraws in face of that demand (Christensen & Heavey, 1990). Despite this common pattern, in some studies heterosexual couple therapy outcomes were best predicted when the man's alliance with the therapist was relatively stronger than the woman's (e.g., Knobloch-Fedders, Pinsof, & Mann, 2004; Symonds & Horvath, 2004). Other studies, however, found that the relationship between gender and therapeutic outcomes was not altogether clear (e.g., Anker, Owen, Duncan, & Sparks, 2010).

Therapy with heterosexual couples can pose a particular dilemma for a therapist, who is the same gender as only one of the partners. Sometimes it occurs that the therapist is seen as favoring the same-gender partner, while at other times the therapist is seen as "playing up to" the opposite gender partner. For this reason, therapists need to be particularly cognizant of gender dynamics, especially when working with highly distressed couples in conflict.

With very distressed couples, indirect communication is one way to create emotional connections without suggesting alignment or flirtatiousness. Examples may be something like, "Jackie, your husband had a sparkle in his eyes when he told me about how you two met. I think that despite it all, his heart is still on fire for you… maybe you're too hurt to see it…?" or "Don, if Alice gave you the benefit of the doubt, would that encourage you to spend the kind of quality time with her that she's been longing for?" In other words, an indirect challenge that suggests deep understanding and empathy can influence change in a way that does not suggest a stronger emotional bond with one partner or the other.

In the case of race, social class, and other aspects of diversity, especially sexual orientation and religion, contemporary therapists have become sensitized to how these sociodemographic characteristics can affect the power dynamics in the consulting room. It has been shown, for example, that many African-American clients (Constantine, 2007) as well as other clients of color (e.g., Chang & Berk, 2009) tend to perceive white therapists who avoid discussing race as either not capable or as unwilling to understand their lived experience. We have little theoretical or empirical literature, however, on how therapists of color tend to experience their work with white clients, but it is quite likely that racial dynamics, like dynamics around gender and social class, influence the quality of the alliance in these clinical contexts.

Of course, demographic characteristics aside, personality plays an important role in how therapeutic alliances are created and sustained. In conjoint therapy, however, systemic interaction trumps individual personality. A mother who is deferential to the therapist when seen alone may be quite dictatorial with her children and husband in a family session. Not surprisingly, people who can readily view a situation from another person's point of view are most capable of therapeutic change. In alliance terms, family members who encourage one another to be authentic in the therapy (a positive SAFETY indicator) or who offer to compromise (a positive SHARED PURPOSE indicator) are easy to work with. In the language of family systems theorist Murray Bowen (Bowen, 1978; Kerr & Bowen, 1988), these kinds of clients are highly differentiated, that is, they are able to balance thinking and feeling on the *intra*personal level and closeness and separateness on the *inter*personal level.

Indeed, one study showed that the relatively more differentiated parents in family therapy tended to view the alliance more favorable than their less differentiated counterparts (Lambert & Friedlander, 2008). More specifically, over half of the variability in alliance perceptions was accounted for by self-reported differentiation, and the aspect of self-differentiation that was most problematic for the alliance was their level emotional reactivity. That is, parents who saw themselves as highly reactive tended to have a particularly difficult time feeling safe in conjoint family therapy (Lambert & Friedlander, 2008).

Consider how difficult it is for parents to sit in a room with their belligerent (or sullen, or symptomatic) teenager who has become very emotionally connected to the therapist, an adult like themselves. Parents who are capable of seeing the potential benefit of their child having a strong alliance with the therapist are less likely to feel threatened than parents whose self-esteem is largely wrapped up in the degree to which their child is a reflection of themselves. Parent-child relationships that are highly reactive tend to be particularly challenging in conjoint family therapy, as adolescents often need the therapist to be a personal ally in order to take the risk to open up to their parents (e.g., Diamond, Liddle, Hogue, & Dakof, 1999).

Another important individual difference factor that affects alliance building is the clients' relative comfort with closeness, which is related to their characteristic attachment style (Johnson & Whiffen, 1999). Indeed, insecure attachment is closely linked with relationship dissatisfaction (Pistole, 1989), which in turn is closely linked with depression, especially for women in distressed marriages (Brock, Kroska, & Lawrence, 2016). The pursue-distance dynamic also raises its head as children mature if adolescents' and young adults' desire to stay close to their family of origin differs from their parents' expectations.

Not surprisingly, this reciprocal pursue-distance dynamic can also play out between clients and therapist. An emotionally rough session that seemed particularly valuable to the partner who is more comfortable with intimacy could very well be the last session that the couple attends if the other partner felt too uncomfortable to tolerate the process. For this reason, therapists must carefully assess family members' comfort with intimate disclosures before encouraging enactments or other kinds of emotional risk taking in a session.

This discussion is by no means meant to discount the effects of therapist characteristics on the alliance. Personality plays a role in the kinds of therapeutic strategies and interventions that family therapists are most comfortable with (Heatherington, 1987). Therapists who are not comfortable with the expression of strong feelings are unlikely to adopt a highly emotion-focused approach to their work. As with clients, however, the therapist's personality may be less of a factor in alliance building than how she interacts with others. After all, therapists were raised in families, just like their clients. In our experience supervising psychotherapy trainees, countertransferential feelings with couples and families have a greater potential to be stirred up in conjoint than in individual treatment. The therapist whose early life was scarred by child abuse is likely to find it quite difficult to work therapeutically with maltreating or neglectful parents. Conversely, the therapist who was raised in a stable, loving, financially secure (i.e., privileged) family may find it difficult to empathize with an overburdened single parent who has little energy for his or her children.

This discussion of individual differences in the context of CFT alliances frames the remainder of this chapter, in which we discuss, first, how to use the SOFTA model with not-so-challenging couple and family cases. This section is followed by a description of alliance ruptures, particularly two common alliance patterns, the problematic within-family alliance and the split alliance.

Building Alliances in Not-so-Challenging Cases

Not-so-challenging cases have certain characteristics that are readily apparent at the start of therapy. In these kinds of cases, clients decide together to seek professional help, have similar motives for seeking treatment, and believe that therapy is a valuable way to address their interpersonal difficulties. When the "problem" is defined as a person ("his mother") or as a stressor outside the family ("her work schedule"), or when the goal is to "improve" rather than to "fix" a relationship, alliance building is likely to be smooth from the start.

Alliances begin from the first contact, usually by phone, when a family member makes the initial request for help. How the request is phrased reveals a good deal about how difficult or easy it will be to establish a working alliance with everyone in the family who decides to take part in the initial session.

In the first contact, many couples and families often formulate their desire for therapy in terms of "we" (e.g., "My partner and I want to see someone" or "We seem to be having some difficulties with our daughter"). Having a relational frame of reference from the outset suggests that the therapist need not spend a great deal of energy establishing a systemic frame of reference (Sluzki, 1992) or mitigating blame (Coulehan, Friedlander, & Heatherington, 1998). Blame—or at least responsibility for the problem—is reflected in clients' comments like "My children lack respect" or "He's just been a tough kid all around since he turned 14."

When a child or adolescent is viewed by the parents as the cause of their misery, the challenge is to reframe the presenting complaint in ways that the parents come to see themselves as clients, rather than as co-therapists who are helping the therapist fix their "bad" or "sick" child. On the other hand, alliance building in these kinds of situations may go smoothly when the parent who calls for help indicates that the other parent is also available—or willing to become available—for conjoint sessions. As discussed in depth in Chap. 4, a parent who is not present in the session is not truly absent from the therapeutic process.

Alliance Rupture and Repair

The concept of *alliance rupture*, having originated in research on individual psychotherapy, refers to a moment or an event in the therapeutic process when a client and therapist are having a difficult time collaborating effectively (e.g., Safran, Crocker, McMain, & Murray, 1990). The rupture may have been caused by differences in goals, tasks, or a break in the emotional bond, such as when a client indicates a lack of trust in the therapist or comments on a lack of progress in therapy. According to theorists, ruptures are common and their repair offers a client the opportunity for important interpersonal learning (Safran et al., 1990; Safran & Muran, 2000). Therapists who are relationally oriented are more likely than cognitive-behavioral therapists to repair a rupture by discussing the impasse directly with the client (Muran et al., 2009). Research suggests that regardless of therapeutic approach, the process is enhanced—and premature termination can be forestalled—when ruptures are recognized and addressed, whether directly by exploring the difficulty or indirectly by, for example, changing the topic or reframing the goals and tasks to be more in line with the client's perspective (Safran & Muran, 2000).

Although theorists and researchers have paid a fair amount of attention to the rupture repair process in individual psychotherapy (e.g., Safran & Muran, 2000), the concept has only minimally been applied to the process of conjoint couple and family therapy (Escudero et al., 2012; Rait, 2000). It is not that alliance ruptures do not occur in CFT, but rather the terminology is different. Authors have written about and studied *problematic alliances* (e.g., Friedlander, Escudero, & Heatherington, 2006; Lambert et al., 2012), *noncompliance* (e.g., Patterson & Forgatch, 1985), *disengagement* (e.g., Friedlander, Heatherington, Johnson, & Skowron, 1994; Higham et al., 2012) *resistance to engagement* (e.g., Santisteban et al., 1996), or *split* (e.g., Pinsof & Catherall, 1986) and *unbalanced alliances* (Robbins, Turner, Alexander, & Perez, 2003). Drop out, the inevitable outcome of a seriously ruptured alliance, has consistently been of concern in CFT, due to the fact that it is common for family members to differ in their motivations for staying in therapy and have varying interpersonal resources for tolerating and benefiting from the difficult process of conjoint treatment.

In our view (Escudero et al., 2012), CFT ruptures share some features with alliance ruptures in individual therapy, namely, their defining characteristics: withdrawal and confrontation (Safran & Muran, 2000). Withdrawal is the more passive kind of rupture, characterized by an apparent lack of engagement, whereas confrontation ruptures are signaled by active disengagement or disagreement with the therapist. Whereas these kinds of ruptures can and do take place in conjoint therapy with couples and families, ruptures also occur between and among family members. In the language of SOFTA, problematic within-family alliances occur when clients' interactions with each other indicate a resistance to collaboration in the therapy and/or a lack of attachment, which hinders the therapeutic process (Friedlander, Escudero, & Heatherington, 2006; Lambert et al., 2012).

In SOFTA terms, withdrawal and confrontation are evident when clients display negative alliance-related behaviors on any of the four dimensions (the italicized items in Table 1.1) (Escudero et al., 2012). On the ENGAGEMENT dimension, tuning out or showing indifference is a withdrawal indicator, whereas directly questioning the value or purpose of therapy is a confrontation marker. Confrontation can also occur in terms of CONNECTION or SAFETY when, for example, a client challenges the therapist's competence or leaves the room. Withdrawal indicators include a reluctance to respond, defensive body posture in response to a question, and avoidance of eye contact when addressed, either when the client is relating to the therapist or to other family members. On the SHARED PURPOSE dimension, these kinds of behaviors directed toward family members signal ruptures to the within-family alliance.

Like individual therapists, CFT therapists can initiate alliance ruptures when, for example, they fail to respond to a client's apparent distress (CONNECTION) or they impose goals or tasks without first seeking the client's input (ENGAGEMENT). Therapist-initiated ruptures can also occur in CFT when the therapist fails to protect a vulnerable client from hostility or abuse from other family members (SAFETY) or focuses uniquely on one client's stated concerns and ignores those of another family member (SHARED PURPOSE).

Many SOFTA behaviors are used by CFT therapists to forestall alliance ruptures or to repair them once they become evident. We have found that SAFETY behaviors, such as discussing confidentiality and explaining that therapy involves taking risks, or normalizing painful feelings, tend to be positively associated with client ENGAGEMENT. On the SHARED PURPOSE dimension, inviting family members to consider a compromise or to respect one another's point of view can be considered repair initiatives. Escudero et al. (2012) defined a rupture as having been repaired when "(a) the family member in question demonstrates positive alliance-related behavior, including positive within-family behavior, (b) therapist and client discuss the rupture directly or indirectly, and (c) then move past it with productive collaboration on the goals or tasks of treatment" (p. 27).

Poor Engagement in the Process: Safety First

Naturally, the first concern of CFT therapists in terms of therapeutic process is the degree to which each client is engaged. When, however, there are "therapy hostages"—clients who participate unwillingly—collaboration tends to be rough going (Friedlander, Escudero, & Heatherington, 2006).

In conjoint therapy, ideally every client should "sign on" to the proposed goals and tasks. Quiet family members need to be actively pulled into the conversation, and any comments that question the value of therapy need to be taken seriously. If not, these behaviors could signal an alliance rupture.

Indeed, engagement ruptures may have several causes. In family work, the parents may not have adequately explained the purpose or the context of therapy to the children or adolescents before therapy began. One or more clients may have little hope for the possibility of change, or one person may have privately decided to go along with the others' agenda, taking a sort of "wait and see" attitude. Alternately, the therapist's behavior may contribute to an engagement rupture if, for example, she imposes goals or tasks without asking the clients for their input or if she fails to explain sufficiently how therapy might "work" to resolve the family's concerns.

When poor engagement is evident from the very outset of treatment, the problem may be due to a prior disagreement within the family about the need to seek professional help, i.e., low SHARED PURPOSE. Alternately, the primary reason for poor engagement may be a lack of safety. Unlike clients in individual therapy who can dismiss what occurs in a session if it was not to their liking, clients in conjoint therapy have witnesses to what took place. Moreover, family therapy discussions sometimes have irrevocable consequences, especially when secrets are revealed or other frank disclosures have repercussions on family relationships. A man might find out, for example, that his wife is having an "emotional affair" with someone else and she has no intention of ending it, even if divorce is the inevitable outcome. A woman might learn that her teenage stepson hates her and always has. A father might find out that his ex-wife's boyfriend has been abusing their daughter. An adolescent might discover that her father, who she previously thought had died of cancer, actually committed suicide.

In our research with the SOFTA-o, we have fond a negative association between therapists' SAFETY interventions and clients' levels of ENGAGEMENT. That is, therapists tend not to rely on safety promoting behaviors when client engagement is high. This empirical association suggests that in problematic engagement contexts, enhancing safety by emphasizing confidentiality, explaining that therapy involves taking risks, protecting vulnerable family members, and so on, is the optimal way to enhance client engagement.

When all clients are actively engaged in the therapeutic process, they bring up new problems for discussion, they agree with the therapist's suggested goals, they suggest alternative solutions to their problems, and they indicate having thought about the therapy between sessions (e.g., "We were about to get into the same old fight and then we remembered how we learned in here to first actively listen to each other before jumping in to disagree"). A case that has been proceeding smoothly, with many of these kinds of positive ENGAGEMENT behaviors, may nonetheless experience a rupture when what is being asked of family members exceeds the level of risk that they are willing to take with one another.

One discovery-oriented study (Friedlander et al., 1994) focused on client disengagement, which was defined as implicit or explicit resistance on the part of two or more family members to engaging in an enactment, requested by the therapist, to discuss a specific topic with a view toward problem solving. In SOFTA-o terms, the rupture involved a failure to comply with the therapist's request for an enactment, i.e., an indicator of negative ENGAGEMENT. Repair of this engagement rupture was defined as at least eight consecutive speaking turns in which the clients engaged with each other on the specified topic.

Sessions from eight cases were compared and contrasted qualitatively. Results of the analysis of these sessions showed that in four of the cases the families did move from disengagement to sustained engagement when five specific process elements were evident: recognition of one's personal contribution to the engagement impasse, communication about the impasse, acknowledgement of one another's feelings about the impasse, having a new construction about the impasse, and recognition of a motivation for resolving the impasse (Friedlander et al., 1994). In one poignant session, a mother and adolescent son openly and emotionally discussed changes in their relationship due to his growing need for autonomy. In another case, a teenage boy moved from indifferent engagement ("I'm tired, Mom" and, later, "I want a pizza"; p. 43) to a disclosure about something his mother hadn't previously known (a positive SAFETY behavior) that he felt threatened by her plans to remarry.

By contrast, in the four cases in which the ENGAGEMENT rupture was not repaired, at least one of the five process elements was not present. In some of the cases, the therapists simply shifted the focus, giving up on the enactment. In one session, however, the husband finally blurted out his hopelessness about his marriage and his disdain of therapy as a way to save it (Friedlander et al., 1994).

Not surprisingly, a fair amount of attention has been paid in the literature to the problem of engaging and retaining adolescents in conjoint family therapy (Sheehan & Friedlander, 2015). Arguably, family therapy with adolescents tends to pose the greatest challenge to engagement, possibly because more often than not, the parents view their adolescents as the "problem." For this reason, many adolescents expect the therapist, who is after all an adult authority figure, to like their parents and take their parents' side. It is not that a strong alliance with the therapist is irrelevant to teenagers. Rather, just like adult clients, adolescents need to see the therapist as their ally who takes their personal goals and concerns seriously (Diamond et al., 1999; Higham et al., 2012). In one SOFTA study, the adolescents, as well as their parents, had significantly positive alliance-related behavior (ENGAGEMENT, CONNECTION, and SAFETY) in sessions that both they and their therapist viewed as more valuable than in sessions that they and the therapist saw as relatively less valuable (Friedlander et al., 2010).

In other research (Muñiz de la Peña et al., 2012), we found that in cases in which an adolescent had a problematic SOFTA-o alliance, the therapist related in a significantly more competitive way, a finding that replicated a study by Cabero Alvarez (2004). Compared to cases in which the adolescent/therapist alliance remained problematic from Session 1 to Session 3, the alliance repair was evident only in cases in which the therapist began relating to the adolescent in a less domineering fashion.

Finally, we designed a qualitative investigation to discover how therapists were able to repair problematic involvement on the part of an adolescent (Higham et al., 2012). To do so, we analyzed sessions in which the adolescent demonstrated an ENGAGEMENT rupture, mostly through indifferent responding or inattentiveness. In two of the cases, the ruptures were repaired, while in the other two cases, the rupture persisted throughout the session. Six elements were present in both of the repaired sessions: the therapist's "structuring the therapeutic conversation, fostering autonomy, building systemic awareness, rolling with resistance, and focusing on the adolescent's subjective experience" (p. 36). By contrast, in one session in which the engagement rupture was not repaired, none of the six elements was present, and in the other session only two elements were observed. Notably, the more effective therapists also probed for, clarified, and reflected the adolescents' feelings, empathized with them, and structured their comments in a one-down way through open-ended questions (Higham et al., 2012). Perhaps even more notably, only in the repaired cases did the parents encourage their teenagers to become involved in the process, a behavioral indicator of SAFETY as well as SHARED PURPOSE.

We have noted in the course of our work that when more than one family member demonstrates a low level of engagement, it is quite likely that the SHARED PURPOSE aspect of the alliance, which reflects within-family relationships, is highly problematic. Ruptures on this important SOFTA dimension are discussed in the next section.

Problematic Within-Family Alliances

Of the four SOFTA dimensions, Shared Sense of Purpose Within the Family is the only one that develops even before therapy begins, when a couple or family first considers the need for professional help. When SHARED PURPOSE is strong, family members agree on (1) the nature of their problem(s), (2) the anticipated goal(s) of therapy, and (3) the need or value of treatment for resolving the identified concerns. When these three aspects of the within-family alliance are in alignment, the initiation of treatment tends to go smoothly, especially if there are no hidden agendas and the problems are construed relationally rather than as residing within one individual who is blamed, directly or indirectly.

Research with the SOFTA measures suggests that this alliance dimension tends to be the most sensitive to change over time, not surprisingly because it is present in the family's discussions (or non-discussions) between sessions at home. Our analyses suggest that the SHARED PURPOSE aspect of the alliance tends to improve as treatment progresses (e.g., Escudero et al., 2008), its quality distinguishes better from worse outcome cases (Beck et al., 2006; Friedlander, Lambert, Escudero, et al., 2008), and the observed SHARED PURPOSE even in the first session predicts client-reported early improvement (Friedlander, Lambert, & Muñiz de la Peña, 2008).

However, due to the multidimensional nature of SHARED PURPOSE, family members do not always view their within-family alliance similarly. One study (Lambert et al., 2012) compared and contrasted sessions from five cases in an archival data set in which (a) the SOFTA-o observed SHARED PURPOSE score indicated a problematic within-family alliance (i.e., −1, −2 or −3), but (b) two or more family members' self-reported SHARED PURPOSE scores on the SOFTA-s differed by at least one standard deviation from the full sample's mean score. The purpose of this discovery-oriented study was to determine what accounts for a problematic within-family alliance. Qualitative analyses of the five sessions showed that the various families had one of three different rupture patterns. In one family, the clients disagreed about whether there was a problem and whether participating in therapy was worthwhile. In two families, despite dissimilar perspectives on the problem and the goals, therapy was considered valuable. In the remaining two families, there were similar views on the problem but a disagreement about the nature of the goals for treatment and whether seeking help was worthwhile (Lambert et al., 2012).

Of particular importance was the therapists' failure to address the rupture, despite perceiving its existence (as noted by their SOFTA-s scores). Rather, the therapists tended to persist in focusing on individuals (rather than the family as a whole), seemingly trying to clarify individuals' goals and perspectives on therapy (Lambert et al., 2012). Two of the therapists did, however, attempt a repair by pointing out family members' shared feelings and experiences (a positive SHARED PURPOSE behavior). As the authors noted, "although none of the therapists exhibited negative alliance-related SOFTA-o behaviors, the relative absence of positive contributions suggests that there may have been some missed opportunities" (p. 426) for repairing the within-family alliance.

In each of these five cases, the therapy apparently got off the ground without a strong within-family alliance. Yet a rupture on this alliance dimension can occur at any point along the way and, if not effectively addressed (i.e., repaired), can derail the treatment. In one successful case, mentioned earlier in this chapter (Friedlander, Lambert, Escudero, et al., 2008), a mother and two daughters came to therapy to cope with the father's absence and the girls' feelings about his unrelenting drug use and time spent in prison. Each family member made a strong individual connection with the therapist, so that when the older daughter and mother began addressing conflicts between them—and their SHARED PURPOSE dipped, both observationally and in the daughter's SOFTA-s score—they were able to weather the storm and ended their ten-session course of therapy on a positive note.

Not every SHARED PURPOSE rupture is successfully repaired in such short order. Consider the case of Era and Jack Tolliver, who were married six "blissful" years before they sought help for a single purpose, one that they had discussed and agreed upon before contacting a therapist: to decide whether or not to start a family. Having married in her mid-30s, Era's biological clock was advancing rapidly, and she had increasingly become determined to birth a child, contrary to her previous expectation. Jack's feelings swung the other way, however, and the more determined Era became, the more resistant he became to the idea of parenthood.

Both partners indicated that their marriage was strong, that each of them was independent and successful, and that both sets of parents and all their siblings were close. Their sole intention in seeking help was to make decision "one way or the other" so that they could "move on" with their lives. Neither partner considered divorce as an acceptable solution to their dilemma. Secretly, however, Era believed that remaining childless for the rest of her life would be an intolerable outcome.

In the first two therapy sessions, Jack spoke at length about how adamant he was that fatherhood was not and *should not* be in his future. In Session 3, when the therapist remarked that up until that point Era had only minimally expressed her feelings on the issue, the within-couple alliance ruptured dramatically. Apparently feeling supported by the therapist's comment, Era turned on Jack and began voicing strong resentments about how everything in their lives went his way, that she was expected to be "the silent partner," and that in this decision, like all others they'd previously made, he seemed to expect her to "cave in, shut up, and smile sweetly."

Era's revelation was a profound shock to Jack. With the therapist's help, the couple was able to repair the ruptured alliance with each other, largely because of their strong and enduring attachments. After several tense sessions, they told the therapist that as difficult as it had been to uncover this "communication problem," their therapeutic experience had brought them closer. They decided to spend the next year strengthening their marriage and making some critical decisions about employment, geographic location, and so on, before deciding whether or not to start a family. Era stated that she had found her "voice" in the marriage and was grateful that Jack seemed "to appreciate the real me."

In this case the therapist was blindsided by the alliance rupture, since the couple had presented their problem as circumscribed and disconnected from their otherwise strong and committed relationship. But in other cases, when therapists take calculated risks to shift the focus of treatment in service of strengthening the family system, a problematic SHARED PURPOSE can develop. For example, in a case study of alliance rupture and repair (Escudero et al., 2012), a severe rupture began with the clients' cross-blaming and then heightened when the therapist attempted to renegotiate the treatment contract. A depressed single mother, "Ms. M.," had sought help for her adolescent daughter, "Rosa," who had multiple behavioral problems at home, with peers, and at school. After three sessions focused on Rosa's difficulties, it became apparent to the therapist that the important changes that the girl had made since therapy began would likely be fleeting unless Ms. M. was willing to work on her own emotional issues, which were quite manifest in her continued blame and criticism of her daughter. When, however, the therapist offered Ms. M. an individual session to discuss how her continued frustration with Rosa was related to her own emotional issues, Ms. M. exploded with anger, now with a rupture on the ENGAGEMENT dimension ("But I'll be honest with you, it [therapy] seems to be a waste of time") (p. 32) and renewed her blame of Rosa.

To repair the rupture, the therapist first focused on the daughter's sense of safety. After asking Ms. M. to leave the room briefly (a positive SAFETY behavior), the therapist questioned Rosa about her experience of the proposed new focus on her mother's personal issues. In doing so, the therapist simultaneously strengthened his bond with the adolescent and gave the mother some private time to calm down and reflect.

It was not until the very end of that session that the extreme rupture was repaired. Returning to the consulting room, Ms. M. continued to resist the implication that she could benefit from some individual help, with continued negative CONNECTION (sarcasm, hostility toward the therapist) and SHARED PURPOSE (blaming Rosa). When in ending the session the therapist stood up and offered Ms. M. a positive CONNECTION remark:

Psychotherapist:	You're feeling a sort of helplessness, you are burned out. Try a little to put all the things that are happening in your life into quarantine.
Ms. M.:	I just can't anymore. I can't. I can't. I don't know what to do. What could we do?
Psychotherapist:	Let me say this: Rosa needs therapy, YOU need therapy.
Ms. M. (crying and laughing):	Yes, we all need therapy. Even our cat needs therapy!

The therapist responded to this outburst with a positive SHARED PURPOSE behavior—sharing a lighthearted moment with the family:

Psychotherapist (humorously, offering her a tissue):	Unfortunately, the cat can't come to the hospital!
Ms. M. (smiling):	That's too bad.
Psychotherapist:	I don't know if you know the book, a short story, called, "The story of a seagull and the cat who taught her to fly."
Rosa:	Yes.
Psychotherapist:	Have you read it?
Rosa:	No, but I will read it now.
Psychotherapist:	It's very interesting, because you'll discover that some cats can talk. It's a very short novel—you can read it in an evening. I sincerely recommend it to you. (Escudero et al., 2012, p. 32)

In making these remarks, the therapist helped Ms. M. save face while indirectly communicating his positive feelings toward her. This positive CONNECTION behavior—speaking about something unconnected to the family's problems when the tension mounted—was one of several remarks in which the therapist enhanced his personal bond with Ms. M. (Escudero et al., 2012).

The remainder of this case was highly successful, as attested to by the mother's and daughter's scores on the SOFTA-s and items related to therapeutic progress. The repair to this extreme rupture was also evident in the dialogue of the subsequent session, in which the mother alluded to what had occurred the previous week ("I know I am [burned out], honestly, but it annoyed me that you said it in front of her last week. I know that I'm not well. That's obvious, but I've always been unwell. I have moments that I feel good and others when I feel bad, like everyone"), to which the therapist apologized ("I shouldn't have said this in front of her [Rosa], that I was afraid you were burned out. And now you've said it yourself: 'I'm burned out.'") (Escudero et al., 2012, p. 34).

As illustrated in these two cases, a problematic within-family alliance may or may not be experienced only on the SHARED PURPOSE dimension. The Tolliver couple remained engaged in the therapeutic process, connected with the therapist, and felt safe enough to take a close, hard look at their relationship. Ms. M. and Rosa, however, experienced a rupture that strained all of the SOFTA dimensions.

One unfortunate outcome of a problematic within-family alliance can be a split alliance with the therapist. The next section describes this all-too-common alliance rupture.

Split Alliances: Emotional Bonds in Disarray

The concept of a *split alliance*, also called an *unbalanced alliance* (e.g., Robbins et al., 2003), was first suggested by Pinsof and Catherall (1986), who introduced a multidimensional set of alliance measures for individuals, couples, and families. Using these measures, Heatherington and Friedlander (1990) operationalized a split alliance as occurring when two (or more) partners or family members report alliance perceptions that deviate from one another by at least one standard deviation from the sample mean. Based on this decision rule, the authors found that a sizable percentage of clients in both treatment formats had divergent alliance perceptions, a finding that was subsequently replicated in other studies (e.g., Mamodhoussen, Wright, Tremblay, & Poitras-Wright, 2005), with the additional finding that a greater difference in partners or family members' alliance scores often, but not invariably, predicts less favorable therapeutic outcomes (e.g., Knobloch-Fedders et al., 2004; Knobloch-Fedders, Pinsof, & Mann, 2007; Robbins et al., 2003, 2006; Symonds & Horvath, 2004).

To date, a fair amount of research has accumulated on the split alliance, although authors differ on how best to define a "split" based on self-report questionnaires administered immediately following a conjoint session (Bartle-Haring, Glebova, Gangamma, Grafsky, & Delaney, 2012). In the SOFTA we defined split alliance only as divergent scores (observer or self-reported) on the Emotional Connection with the Therapist dimension in order to distinguish this type of alliance rupture from a problematic within-family alliance. This more specific definition of split alliance seemed necessary because it commonly occurs that all family members have a strong bond with the therapist yet feel quite at odds among themselves about the need for treatment, about the problem definition, or about their attachments to one another (cf. Friedlander, Lambert, Escudero, et al., 2008).

In several studies, we found that family members' split alliances with the therapist, as measured by their self-report, tend to correspond with their observed, in-session CONNECTION behaviors (Beck et al., 2006; Muñiz de la Peña et al., 2009). Moreover, split alliances vary in intensity. That is, the discrepancy between two clients' bonds with the therapist can vary from mild to moderate or severe, and only the most severe splits are likely to precede drop out (Muñiz de la Peña et al., 2009).

It is not hard to understand the basis for a split alliance. When a family member attends therapy sessions under duress from another family member ("This is your last chance to keep our marriage together!") or from an authority ("Your children will be removed from your care unless you can work out your problems in couples therapy"), feelings about the therapy mandate can easily color the clients' perceptions of the therapist's level of skill or compassion for their situation.

In a couple, partners often expect the therapist to take sides and may even challenge the therapist to do so. In families, parents generally hope that their child will create a connection with the therapist but may nonetheless be wary when this does happen (Friedlander et al., 2012). Indeed, we found in a Spanish sample as well as a US sample that it was just as likely for the adolescent's bond with the therapist to be stronger than that of the parents as it is for the opposite pattern to occur (Muñiz de la Peña et al., 2009).

In general, CFT therapists tend to take their emotional connections with clients seriously, by paying close attention to their relationships with each partner or family member. Often, seeing the more disaffected client alone for a session, or for a portion of a conjoint session, is all that's needed to repair a split alliance. The CONNECTION behavior can also take the form of lighthearted banter about something unrelated to family problems or dynamics. Doing so is particularly effective with children, who tend to respond well to off-topic digressions, especially when they feel uncomfortable in the treatment context or disconnected from the therapist.

Consider the Buckley family, for example. Arnold, an intellectually precocious 11-year-old, was the focus of his parents' intense concern. He felt badgered by them in every aspect of his life—his school grades, his lack of friends, his self-esteem, his weight, his eating habits, and his hygiene. Name any potential problem a child could have, and Arnold had it in his parents' eyes. Largely compliant with their wishes, Arnold came to the family sessions but saw the therapist as just one more adult in a long line of "helpers" who found him lacking. The more his parents, particularly his father, seemed pleased with the therapist, the more reluctant Arnold became to respond to the therapist's questions (a negative CONNECTION behavior).

Noticing that in the waiting room Arnold regularly hid his head in an iPad, the therapist began the session by asking Arnold if he was familiar with a particular app that she was having trouble with on her own device. Arnold's eyes sparkled when he asked to see the therapist's notebook. He then proceeded to explain some technical features about the app in great detail. Warmly encouraging, the therapist drew out the conversation when she saw Arnold become more animated. They laughed together, particularly when the therapist did something wrong with her app.

Arnold's father, Warren, grew restless and frowned. Seeing this reaction, the therapist turned to Warren and said:

Therapist:	Warren, Arnold seems to be a whiz at computer stuff!
Warren:	Yea, well…too bad that doesn't translate to anything that's worthwhile.
Therapist (ignoring the implicit blame):	Are you able to keep up with him, though? I know I'm stymied by some of what he's just been showing me.
Warren:	No, I can't keep up with him for that. You're right.
Therapist:	If he keeps this up, he's got a great potential career ahead of him in IT.
Warren (clearly uncomfortable):	Hmm…

After this interchange, the boy became more visibly attentive than in the past. He asked the therapist if she had children (a positive CONNECTION indicator) and seemed pleased with her response. Then, with the therapist's support and encouragement, Arnold began telling his parents how he felt about their endless "picking" at him. When the therapist ended the session by asking father and son to "figure out something to do together that will be fun" over the next week, Warren suggested a trip to a computer museum. Arnold seemed thrilled.

This was not an easy case given how entrenched the parents were in their negative views of their son. On the other hand, the split alliance was repaired, and over the next few weeks the parents began to appreciate their son in a new way.

Moving Forward

The multiple alliances in conjoint couple and family therapy offer opportunities as well as challenges. As with the Buckley family, a skilled therapist can enhance one alliance dimension with an individual client (ENGAGEMENT, CONNECTION, and/or SAFETY), and the effects will reverberate throughout the therapeutic system. In the remainder of this book, we take a look at four particularly complex couple and family situations and offer suggestions for empowering clients to risk changing their most intimate relationships.

References

Anker, M. G., Owen, J., Duncan, B. L., & Sparks, J. A. (2010). The alliance in couple therapy: Partner influence, early change, and alliance patterns in a naturalistic sample. *Journal of Consulting and Clinical Psychology, 78*, 635–645.

Bartle-Haring, S., Glebova, T., Gangamma, R., Grafsky, E., & Delaney, R. O. (2012). Alliance and termination status in couple therapy: A comparison of methods for assessing discrepancies. *Psychotherapy Research, 22*, 502–514.

Beck, M., Friedlander, M. L., & Escudero, V. (2006). Three perspectives on clients' experiences of the therapeutic alliance: A discovery-oriented investigation. *Journal of Marital and Family Therapy, 32*, 355–368.

Bordin, E. S. (1979). The generalizability of the psychoanalytic concept of the working alliance. *Psychotherapy, 16*, 252–260.

Bowen, M. (1978). *Family therapy in clinical practice*. New York: Jason Aronson.

Brock, R. L., Kroska, E., & Lawrence, E. (2016). Current status of research on couples. In T. L. Sexton & J. Lebow (Eds.), *Handbook of family therapy* (4th ed., pp. 409–433). New York: Routledge.

Cabero Alvarez, A. (2004). *Patrones de interacción y relación terapéutica: Control de la relación y clima afectivo en la interacción terapeutapaciente* [Patterns of interaction and the therapeutic relationship: Relationship control and affect climate in the therapist–patient interaction]. Unpublished doctoral dissertation, University of Salamanca, Spain.

Carpenter, J., Escudero, V., & Rivett, M. (2008). Training family therapy students in conceptual and observational skills related to the therapeutic alliance: An evaluation. *Journal of Family Therapy, 30*, 409–422.

Chang, D. F., & Berk, A. (2009). Making cross-racial therapy work: A phenomenological study of clients' experiences of cross-racial therapy. *Journal of Counseling Psychology, 56*, 521–536.

Christensen, A., & Heavey, C. L. (1990). Gender and social structure in the demand/withdraw pattern of marital conflict. *Journal of Personality and Social Psychology, 59*, 73–81.

Constantine, M. G. (2007). Racial microaggressions against African American clients in cross-racial counseling relationships. *Journal of Counseling Psychology, 54*, 1–16.

Coulehan, R., Friedlander, M. L., & Heatherington, L. (1998). Transforming narratives: A change event in constructivist family therapy. *Family Process, 37*, 17–33.

Diamond, G. M., Liddle, H. A., Hogue, A., & Dakof, G. A. (1999). Alliance building interventions with adolescents in family therapy: A process study. *Psychotherapy, 36*, 355–368.

Escudero, V., Boogmans, E., Loots, G., & Friedlander, M. L. (2012). Alliance rupture and repair in conjoint family therapy: An exploratory study. *Psychotherapy, 49*, 26–37.

Escudero, V., & Friedlander, M. L. (2003). El sistema de observación de la alianza terapeutica en intervención familiar (SOATIF): Desarrollo trans-cultural, fiabilidad, y aplicaciones del instrumento. *Mosaico (Journal of the Spanish Federation of Family Therapy Associations), 25*, 32–36. (Reprinted in *Perspectivas Systemicas*, Vol. 15, Issue 77, 2003).

Escudero, V., & Friedlander, M. L. (2016). E-SOFTA: A video-based software for observing the working alliance in clinical training and supervision. In T. Rousmaniere & E. Renfro-Michel (Eds.), *Using technology to enhance clinical supervision*. (pp. 223–238). American Counseling Association: Alexandria, VA.

Escudero, V., Friedlander, M. L., & Heatherington, L. (2011). Using the e-SOFTA for video training and research on alliance-related behavior. *Psychotherapy, 48*, 138–147.

Escudero, V., Friedlander, M. L., Varela, N., & Abascal, A. (2008). Observing the therapeutic alliance in family therapy: Associations with participants' perceptions and therapeutic outcomes. *Journal of Family Therapy, 30*, 194–204.

Friedlander, M. L., Bernardi, S., & Lee, H. H. (2010). Better versus worse family therapy sessions as reflected in clients' alliance-related behavior. *Journal of Counseling Psychology, 57*, 198–204.

Friedlander, M. L., & Diamond, G. M. (2011). Couple and family therapy. In E. Altmaier & J. Hansen (Eds.), *Oxford handbook of counseling psychology* (pp. 647–675). New York: Oxford University Press.

Friedlander, M. L., Escudero, V., & Heatherington, L. (2006). *Therapeutic alliances with couples and families: An empirically-informed guide to practice.* Washington, DC: American Psychological Association.

Friedlander, M. L., Escudero, V., Heatherington, L., & Diamond, G. M. (2011). Alliance in couple and family therapy. *Psychotherapy, 48*, 25–33.

Friedlander, M. L., Escudero, V., Horvath, A. S., Heatherington, L., Cabero, A., & Martens, M. P. (2006). System for observing family therapy alliances: A tool for research and practice. *Journal of Counseling Psychology, 53*, 214–225.

Friedlander, M. L., Heatherington, L., & Escudero, V. (2016). Research on change mechanisms: Advances in process research. In T. Sexton & J. Lebow (Eds.), *Handbook of family therapy* (4th ed., pp. 454–467). New York: Routledge.

Friedlander, M. L., Heatherington, L., Johnson, B., & Skowron, E. A. (1994). "Sustaining engagement": A change event in family therapy. *Journal of Counseling Psychology, 41*, 438–448.

Friedlander, M. L., Kivlighan, D. M., & Shaffer, K. (2012). Exploring actor-partner interdependence in family therapy: Whose view (parent or adolescent) best predicts treatment progress? *Journal of Counseling Psychology, 59*, 168–175.

Friedlander, M. L., Lambert, J. E., Escudero, V., & Cragun, C. (2008). How do therapists enhance family alliances? Sequential analyses of therapist → client behavior in two contrasting cases. *Psychotherapy: Theory, Research, Practice, Training, 45*, 75–87.

Friedlander, M. L., Lambert, J. E., & Muñiz de la Peña, C. (2008). A step toward disentangling the alliance/improvement cycle in family therapy. *Journal of Counseling Psychology, 55*, 118–124.

Friedlander, M. L., Lee, H. H., Shaffer, K. S., & Cabrera, P. (2014). Negotiating therapeutic alliances with a family at impasse: An evidence-based case study. *Psychotherapy, 51*, 41–52.

Heatherington, L. (1987). Therapists' personalities and their evaluations of three family therapy styles: An empirical investigation. *Journal of Marital and Family Therapy, 13*, 167–178.

Heatherington, L., Escudero, V., & Friedlander, M. L. (in press). Where systems theory and alliance meet: Relationship and technique in family therapy. In O. Tishby & H. Wiseman (Eds.), *Developing the therapeutic relationship: Integrating case studies, research and practice.* Washington, DC: American Psychological Association.

Heatherington, L., & Friedlander, M. L. (1990). Couple and family psychotherapy alliance scales: Empirical considerations. *Journal of Marital and Family Therapy, 16*, 299–306.

Higham, J., Friedlander, M. L., Escudero, V., & Diamond, G. M. (2012). Engaging reluctant adolescents in family therapy: An exploratory study of in-session processes. *Journal of Family Therapy, 34*, 24–52.

Horvath, A. O., Del Re, A. C., Flückiger, C., & Symonds, D. (2011). Alliance in individual psychotherapy. *Psychotherapy, 48*, 9–16. doi:10.1037/a0022186

Isserlin, L., & Couturier, J. (2012). Therapeutic alliance and family-based treatment for adolescents with anorexia nervosa. *Psychotherapy, 49*, 46–51.

Johnson, S. M., & Whiffen, V. E. (1999). Made to measure: Adapting emotionally focused couple therapy to partners' attachment styles. *Clinical Psychology: Science and Practice, 6*, 366–381.

Kerr, M. E., & Bowen, M. (1988). *Family evaluation.* New York: Basic Books.

Knobloch-Fedders, L. M., Pinsof, W. M., & Mann, B. J. (2004). The formation of the therapeutic alliance in couple therapy. *Family Process, 43*, 425–442.

Knobloch-Fedders, L. M., Pinsof, W. M., & Mann, B. J. (2007). Therapeutic alliance and treatment progress in couple therapy. *Journal of Marital and Family Therapy, 33*, 245–257.

Lambert, J. E., & Friedlander, M. L. (2008). Relationship of differentiation of self to adult clients' perceptions of the alliance in brief family therapy. *Psychotherapy Research, 43*, 160–166.

Lambert, J. E., Skinner, A., & Friedlander, M. L. (2012). Problematic within-family alliances in conjoint family therapy: A close look at five cases. *Journal of Marital and Family Therapy, 38*, 417–428.

Lebow, J. (2016). Integrative approaches to couple and family therapy. In T. L. Sexton & J. Lebow (Eds.), *Handbook of family therapy* (4th ed., pp. 205–227). New York: Routledge.

Mamodhoussen, S., Wright, J., Tremblay, N., & Poitras-Wright, H. (2005). Impact of marital and psychological distress on therapeutic alliance in couples undergoing couple therapy. *Journal of Marital and Family Therapy, 31*, 159–169.

Muñiz de la Peña, C., Friedlander, M. L., & Escudero, V. (2009). Frequency, severity, and evolution of split family alliances: How observable are they? *Psychotherapy Research, 19*, 133–142.

Muñiz de la Peña, C., Friedlander, M. L., Escudero, V., & Heatherington, L. (2012). How do therapists ally with adolescents in family therapy? An examination of relational control communication in early sessions. *Journal of Counseling Psychology, 59*, 339–351.

Muran, J. C., Safran, J. D., Gorman, B. S., Samstag, L. W., Eubanks-Carter, C., & Winston, A. (2009). The relationship of early alliance ruptures and their resolution to process and outcome in three time-limited psychotherapies for personality disorders. *Psychotherapy: Theory, Research, Practice, Training, 45*, 233–248.

Patterson, G. R., & Forgatch, M. S. (1985). Therapist behavior as a determinant for noncompliance: A paradox for the behavior modifier. *Journal of Consulting and Clinical Psychology, 53*, 846–851.

Pinsof, W. B. (1995). *Integrative problem-centered therapy*. New York: Basic Books.

Pinsof, W. B., & Catherall, D. R. (1986). The integrative psychotherapy alliance: Family, couple and individual therapy scales. *Journal of Marital and Family Therapy, 12*, 137–151.

Pistole, M. C. (1989). Attachment in adult romantic relationships: Style of conflict resolution and relationship satisfaction. *Journal of Social and Personal Relationships, 6*, 505–510.

Rait, D. (2000). The therapeutic alliance in couples and family therapy. *Journal of Clinical Psychology, 56*, 211–224.

Robbins, M. S., Liddle, H. A., Turner, C. W., Dakof, G. A., Alexander, J. F., & Kogan, S. M. (2006). Adolescent and parent therapeutic alliances as predictors of dropout in multidimensional family therapy. *Journal of Family Psychology, 20*, 108–116.

Robbins, M. S., Turner, C. W., Alexander, J. F., & Perez, G. A. (2003). Alliance and dropout in family therapy for adolescents with behavior problems: Individual and systemic effects. *Journal of Family Psychology, 17*, 534–544.

Safran, J. D., Crocker, P., McMain, S., & Murray, P. (1990). Therapeutic alliance rupture as a therapy event for empirical investigation. *Psychotherapy, 27*, 154–165.

Safran, J. D., & Muran, J. C. (2000). *Negotiating the therapeutic alliance: A relational treatment guide*. New York: Guilford Press.

Santisteban, D. A., Szapocznik, J., Perez-Vidal, A., Kurtines, W. M., Murray, E. J., & LaPerriere, A. (1996). Efficacy of intervention for engaging youth and families into treatment and some variables that may contribute to differential effectiveness. *Journal of Family Psychology, 10*, 35–44.

Sheehan, A. S., & Friedlander, M. L. (2015). Therapeutic alliance and retention in Brief Strategic Family Therapy: A mixed-methods study. *Journal of Marital and Family Therapy, 41*, 415–427.

Sluzki, C. E. (1992). Transformations: A blueprint for narrative changes in therapy. *Family Process, 31*, 217–230.

Smerud, P. E., & Rosenfarb, I. S. (2008). The therapeutic alliance and family psychoeducation in the treatment of schizophrenia: An exploratory prospective change process study. *Journal of Consulting and Clinical Psychology, 76*, 505–510.

Symonds, D., & Horvath, A. O. (2004). Optimizing the alliance in couple therapy. *Family Process, 43*, 443–455.

Wampold, B. E., & Imel, Z. E. (2015). *The great psychotherapy debate: The evidence for what makes psychotherapy work* (2nd ed.). New York: Routledge.

Chapter 2
Couples' Cross Complaints: "I Want… but She/He Doesn't Want to…"

An eye for an eye only ends up making the whole world blind.

—Mahatma Gandhi

Ellen Rosario was reluctantly convinced by her husband, Frank, to seek the help of a couple therapist, but privately she had already decided to attend only one session. If she did not feel markedly better about their 27-year marriage after that session, it was all over for her. In her mind, Frank was far too similar to his father—"both of them are overbearing and emotionally aloof." At age 63, Ellen felt she only had a few good years left to find a better partner. One therapy session—that's all she would give Frank. But you, the therapist, have no idea that this is her intention.

You open the first session confidently, warmly introducing yourself to the couple. Then you turn to Ellen and say, "In our brief conversation on the phone, Frank told me that you're looking for help with some marital issues that have been troubling you both for awhile. That's about all I know. Could you give me some idea of how I can be of help, from your perspective?" Your intention in starting off this way is to draw Ellen in, since Frank was the one who had called for the appointment. It's your usual practice to begin therapy this way with couples.

Ellen doesn't look at Frank. She demurs: "Oh, I don't know. The problems have been going on for a long time." Silence.

"Can you be more specific?"

"Well, I'm not happy. I don't think Frank is happy either, actually."

Since it's clear that Ellen is disinclined to say much more, you wonder how to engage her in the intake process. Knowing that agreement on therapeutic goals is one component of a strong working alliance (Bordin, 1979), you decide to summarize the little she's said to this point, hoping for an agreement: "So, I understand that there are longstanding problems in your relationship as a couple and you, Ellen, have not been satisfied with the way things have been going for a while now. So, our work together would be to help you with these problems, right? to improve your marriage?" Looking at Ellen, you smile encouragingly. She simply says, "You got it."

With a different component of the alliance, the tasks of therapy (Bordin, 1979), in mind, you then ask, "Ok, so could you fill me in on what you'd like to discuss today?"

© Springer International Publishing AG 2017
V. Escudero, M.L. Friedlander, *Therapeutic Alliances with Families*,
Focused Issues in Family Therapy, DOI 10.1007/978-3-319-59369-2_2

"Frank can tell you."

This is not going well. You figure that Ellen's deferral to her husband might be characteristic of their style—Frank, holding the power in their relationship, speaks for Ellen. You're wrong, of course, but you don't know that.

"Frank, what are you and Ellen hoping to get out of our work together?"

Ellen repositions herself in her chair so that she is turned away from Frank. She stares out the window, seemingly disinterested. Frank replies, "Like you said, we need to work on our marriage. I love my wife." He tries to catch Ellen's eye, but she refuses to look at him.

Figuring that you might be able to win Ellen over by focusing on your bond with her, you say, empathically, "Ellen, I gather this process is somewhat difficult for you. I'd like to help."

Silence.

At this point, you realize that your alliance with this couple is in trouble. Although Frank seems willing enough to have a conversation with you about the potential goals and tasks of couple therapy, Ellen clearly is not. What to try next?

The classic model of the working alliance, as defined by Bordin (1979), requires clients to negotiate the goals and tasks and be interested in creating an emotional bond with the therapist. However, as illustrated in this example, this negotiation process can fail even in the first moments of the initial session. Something else needs to happen for the therapy to get off the ground.

In this case, Ellen privately thinks that therapy will save their marriage only if Frank changes his overbearing manner, but she is too fearful to say that aloud. She is not feeling safe in the therapeutic context—one she didn't choose and doesn't trust. If you, as the therapist, do not take action to help her feel safe, there is little hope of her becoming meaningfully involved in the therapy. Even attending a second therapy appointment is unlikely.

Here is where, in our view, the classic model of the working alliance falls short when applied to conjoint couple therapy. In particular, safety is essential for effective negotiation of goals and tasks. Unlike safety in individual therapy, which is of course essential, in the couple therapy context, partners need to feel safe with each other. Although the emotional bond aspect of the therapeutic alliance is also essential, in the absence of safety, a strong connection with the therapist is not sufficient. The therapy is likely to falter, later if not sooner.

Couples like the Rosarios are not unique. Indeed, couples often seek professional help for their relationship problems when they are at the end of their rope. A major obstacle to successful couple therapy occurs when the partners disagree on the problem, with each person locating the difficulty within the other, and when their goals for treatment are dissimilar. Even if both partners were to view the problem *and* the goal similarly (say, "We don't have nearly the same kind of emotional or physical intimacy we had when we got together and we'd like help finding it again"), they may disagree about whether therapy is the optimal way to go about addressing their problems.

Unfortunately, the most challenging couple cases tend to be ones in which both partners feel unsafe in therapy. Their conflicts and insecure attachments with each other result in polarized views about the therapist or about the value of obtaining professional help in the first place.

Not only do these kinds of couples have a hard time fully engaging in the therapeutic process, but when they feel particularly unsafe, they also tend to lack a strong sense of "we-ness" about working together toward common goals. However, when the therapist is able to significantly enhance the within-couple alliance, the partners can come to see their situation similarly, and they may even begin to feel excited about working together in therapy to improve their lives. Generally, this attitude bodes well for the treatment, regardless of the therapist's preferred therapeutic approach.

Therapy with a couple is a triadic system: two partners + one therapist. Generally, the addition of a third person to an anxious dyad tends to stabilize the system (Bowen, 1978), which is what happens when couple therapy works well. However, when members of a couple are in deep conflict with one another and the therapist supports one person's position over the other's position, he can wind up destabilizing the dyad.

Clients like Ellen Rosario, who see their problems in black and white terms, often take note of the therapist's personal characteristics, particularly gender, in order to figure out whose side she's likely to take. With same-sex couples, the therapist's gender is either the same or different from the partners' gender, but with opposite-sex couples, the therapist's gender is the same as one partner's and different from the other partner's. In some cases, gender matters in couples' choice of a therapist, while in other cases gender only becomes salient as the therapy progresses.

Consider these other examples. Oscar, who was furious about Hector's reluctance to "come out," preferred a female therapist, believing that a (straight) male therapist would be less accepting of their gay lifestyle. Denyse and Jonathan, on the other hand, did not consider gender to be important in choosing a therapist to help them settle their dispute about whether or not to start a family. Early on, however, Denyse sensed that the female therapist was critical of her refusal to have children—in fact, Denyse became convinced that the therapist was making a play for Jonathan. Feeling unsafe, Denyse told her husband that the therapy was going nowhere and she would not continue.

Gender is not the only personal characteristic that affects the therapist's alliance with couples. Effective therapy with sexual, religious, or racial/ethnic minority couples requires therapists to be knowledgeable about these clients' unique concerns, self-aware, and vigilant of their own biases. Navigating a couple's culturally rooted relationship disputes requires considerable skill, particularly when there are multiple sociocultural differences between the therapist and the couple or when the partners themselves have diverse backgrounds.

Gayle, an atheist, was married to Al, whose family of origin was strongly evangelical. The religious difference seemed manageable when the couple first met but became a central focus of their difficulties when Gayle's extramarital affair with a co-worker came to light. Knowing that she had no future with her lover, Gayle agreed to begin couple therapy with Al, who desperately wanted to save their marriage.

In the second session, the couple's stark religious differences took center stage. Al explained that due to "the sanctity of marriage," absolutely nothing could make him want to end it, even Gayle's "disgusting behavior with an even more disgusting human being." Reacting to Al's condemnation of her, Gayle countered by accusing him of being a "hypocrite" who hid behind his religious beliefs: "*You* can do *whatever*, since your *god* will forgive you, but *I* will never forgive you."

Not knowing what was behind this provocative statement, the (female) therapist asked Gayle to explain. At first Al listened to his wife with undisguised hostility. When he began talking over her, the therapist interrupted, asking him to "just listen, to try and understand where Gayle is coming from." Incensed, Al turned on the therapist, yelling, "Of course, we know *you're* a Jew, and *everyone* knows Jews are okay with divorce!" Then he stomped out of the session…and out of the therapy.

In this case, Gayle's and Al's religious differences became a lightning rod for many deep-seated betrayals of trust that threatened the couple's relationship. Even though they had begun therapy with a strong shared sense of purpose—to rekindle their 15-year marriage—the within-couple alliance plummeted when Al attacked Gayle and she defended herself by hinting at a shameful secret in their past. At that point, Al's fear of what his wife might disclose in the heat of the moment threatened his safety and fueled his mistrust of the therapist. Covertly, he had already convinced himself that the female therapist would take Gayle's side against him due to her gender and what he assumed to be her religious values.

Like hidden agendas ("We'll find a therapist and *then* I'll tell him our marriage is over – the therapist can take care of him"), secrets can cripple therapeutic work. When the secret involves a betrayal of any kind, couple therapy will be rough going. The challenge is compounded when rather than directly addressing the betrayal of trust, partners cross complain about one another's personality, attitude, or past behavior. In the case of Gayle and Al, diverse religious beliefs fueled their cross complaints, and the therapist's personal characteristics wound up becoming entangled in the couple's power struggle.

How is it that lovers can become bitter enemies? While there is no clear answer to this question, couple therapists need some way to understand how such a transformation can come about in each unique case. In this chapter, we discuss the challenges of working with high-conflict couples in which one partner refuses to engage in treatment or feels unsafe in the therapeutic context, couples who define their conflicts in zero-sum (win-lose) terms, and partners whose divergent views on the problem compromise their alliance with each other and with the therapist. After a review of relevant literature, we describe and illustrate how alliance-empowering strategies can help couples who have seemingly intractable conflicts.

Unique Challenges

"I Will…But S/he Won't Come to Therapy"

Eve had a horrible trauma history. Although she frequently attended Narcotics Anonymous meetings where she spoke candidly about her background, she balked when her partner, Julia, asked her to start couple therapy. Julia, for her part, had seen therapists regularly since her adolescence and believed that conjoint therapy could save her relationship with Eve, which was deteriorating rapidly. The two women fought over every issue, small and large, but as Julia told the therapist over the phone, "We do love each other."

Eve's staunch refusal to consider therapy was rooted in her long-standing mistrust of authority figures, stemming from the severe abuse she'd endured at the hands of multiple foster parents. Learning of Eve's history in the first session with Julia, the therapist agreed to focus on improving the couple's relationship in Eve's absence. The situation was far from ideal, but in time the therapist helped Julia disengage from cross complaining, and the couple's fights decreased in intensity and frequency.

Sometimes one partner is far too mistrustful to engage in conjoint treatment. As in Eve's case, the aversion to therapy may stem from trauma. In these cases, the unwilling partner may feel certain that any therapist would blame her for the couple's problems. In other cases, one member of the couple refuses treatment, fearful that acknowledging difficulties in the relationship will invariably result in separation or divorce.

In situations like these, therapists should carefully consider whether individual therapy with the willing partner might wind up harming the couple's relationship. After all, spending an hour each week with an empathic listener is likely to heighten a person's dissatisfaction with a partner who doesn't listen, who doesn't seem to care, who resists compromise, and so on. When the client is aware of the potential pitfalls, however, is able to see her contribution to the relational conflict from her partner's point of view, and is motivated to change her own behavior, individual work may well be beneficial for the couple.

Resistance is common when divorce is imminent. For most people, divorce spells failure, and the typical polarization—one person holding onto the relationship at all costs, the other person all too ready to abandon it—often results in cross-blaming. Resistance is particularly common when one spouse, the husband, for example, is convinced that *any* therapist would support his wife's contention that he is alienating the children from her.

Even psychologically healthy individuals tend to feel helpless and defeated in the face of divorce, which can evoke a flood of feelings that exceed the person's ability to self-regulate (Baris et al., 2001). In high drama cases, such as when the sexual abuse of a child is alleged, conjoint therapy may be contraindicated, even if the resistant partner eventually agrees to be seen.

"I Feel Comfortable Here, but S/he Doesn't"

A client who feels unsafe in the therapeutic context with her partner is unlikely to engage freely in the process. As a *therapy hostage* (Friedlander, Escudero, & Heatherington, 2006a, p. 88), he may have been coerced ("You'll come or else I'll…"), or if he is initially willing, he may be highly uncomfortable when certain topics are raised. If he shuts down in the session, therapy cannot proceed without addressing the lack of safety.

Safety can also become an issue when one member of the couple believes that her personal problems are at the root of the relational conflict. Sandy, an unemployed landscape artist, knew that her obsessive-compulsive disorder had escalated to such a degree that life had become unbearable for her partner, Dale, and their three children. Reluctantly, she agreed to "go with" Dale to see a mental health professional. Sandy's comfort improved considerably after spending some time alone with the therapist, who normalized her embarrassment and compassionately pointed out Dale's apparent caring and concern for her.

*"I Want **This**, but S/he Wants **That**"*

Since much of society is organized around winners and losers (sports, politics, the justice system, and so on), it is not surprising that couples' problems often feel like a tug of war. Indeed, some polarizing issues invariably result in a "win" and a "loss"—Will we relocate for your job? Will we have another child? Will we invite my mother to move in with us? Will we force Junior into rehab?

Relationships, however, are not a zero-sum game. In fact, "winners" sometimes wind up feeling like losers. And "losers" who nurture their loss at the other's expense sometimes feel like winners.

On the other hand, partners who feel cared for, supported, and respected in their relationship are usually able to negotiate zero-sum problems to a satisfactory conclusion. Sometimes he gets his way, sometimes she does. They figure out that the "winner" in a particular conflict situation should be the person for whom the decision matters most, or they decide on a third choice of action, one that they both can live with and that neither person abhors (Wachtel, 1999).

In therapy, zero-sum problems may mask a covert quid pro quo: "Since I gave in and came to therapy with you, now you need to give in and do things my way." Often the therapist gets caught in the conflict, feeling a push to pronounce who's right and who's wrong. In the absence of significant health and safety concerns, however, choosing sides is likely to result in a seriously split alliance, possibly irretrievably so.

Stuart Hoffman and Madeline Thayer were locked in a bitter zero-sum fight over finances. He wanted to declare bankruptcy and start afresh. She insisted that they ask her parents to lend a hand. The couple's attack/defend fights had become particularly acrimonious, with cursing, name-calling, and even some minor property damage. Like other seemingly unresolvable conflicts, theirs was clearly deep-seated. However, as they began to trust the therapist to contain their hostility, hidden emotions slowly came to light. Stuart felt like a failure as a provider—going to Madeline's parents for help would make him feel less of a man. Madeline didn't see Stuart as a failure—rather, she was sure he blamed her for having purchased some "luxuries" that they clearly couldn't afford. When the therapist helped them see how they both projected their experience of self-blame onto the other, they were able to make some financial decisions that suited them both.

"I Think the Problem Is This, *but S/he Thinks the Problem Is That"*

Even when both members of a couple are equally committed to their relationship and to working out their problems in therapy, their views on the issues may be in stark contrast. Alec thinks Don drinks too much. Don thinks Alec is a workaholic. Jalil thinks Aaliyah is too close to her sister and not fully committed to him. Aaliyah thinks Jalil criticizes her because he is depressed and needs medication.

It is a rare couple that can see through these kinds of cross complaints to recognize the circularity of their problems. After all, she is focused on his problematic behavior and not her own, while he is focused only on her behavior. For the therapist, the key is to avoid taking sides but rather to help the couple see the circularity: Don drinks alone since Alec works late most nights, and Alec stays at the office to avoid watching Don drink. Jalil criticizes Aaliyah for spending more time with her sister than with him, and Aaliyah escapes to her sister's home to avoid Jalil's criticism.

The challenge of developing a new understanding of relational problems is made all the more difficult when partners argue about *how* they communicate. Don complains that Alec shuts down when he brings up problems to discuss, and Alec counters that Don becomes enraged whenever he takes too long to answer. Aaliyah complains that Jalil follows her from room to room with his demands, and he complains that she gets defensive when he tries to "reason with her." Eventually every argument ends with despair: "We just can't communicate." The impasse shows up in therapy conversations time and time again. If the therapist can't help the partners break the self-perpetuating cycle, all too often they drop out, demoralized.

Recommendations from the Literature

Not All Conflicts Are the Same

Some level of conflict is inevitable in intimate relationships. There is, however, a difference between *destructive* and *constructive conflict* (Cummings et al., 2016, pp. 125–127). Destructive conflict is emotionally intense, often nonverbal (withdrawal or "the silent treatment" on the one hand, aggression or violence, on the other hand) and can threaten the very existence of the relationship. In contrast, partners who are able to use conflict constructively are able to do so because they each have a capacity to self-regulate in response to the other's feedback (Beach, 2016). Constructive verbal conflict results in resolution or, if not, involves some degree of problem solving that is approached from an emotionally centered place of mutual respect (Cummings et al., 2016).

Since conflict tends to highlight partners' differences and each person's individuality, it is important to consider the forces that impede constructive conflict. One author (Basham, 1992) theorized that resistance to conflict resolution, and thus resistance to couple therapy, derives from sociocultural influences, including ethnicity, socioeconomic class, and religion; systemic factors like patriarchy and social class; the couple's interactional patterns, such as reactive distancing and detouring to the children; and intrapersonal factors, particularly those described by object relations theorists. In object relations terms, people who have achieved "object constancy" are best able to tolerate ambiguity and conflict in their relationships. They can see that their own point of view is subjective and accept that the other person sees the situation differently. On the other hand, people who resist conflict resolution tend to be those who project negativity onto others or who isolate themselves emotionally in order to focus on gratifying their personal needs (Basham, 1992, p. 253).

Individual Differences Matter

Results of many research studies suggest that men and women tend to experience couple therapy differently. Moreover, the gender dynamics in couple therapy are complex. Whereas a strong within-couple alliance seems to be most influential for women (Anderson & Johnson, 2010), maintaining a favorable alliance with the therapist is particularly important for men (e.g., Anker, Owen, Duncan, & Sparks, 2010; Knobloch-Fedders, Pinsof, & Mann, 2007), who are traditionally less likely to request couple therapy.

In a study of micro-processes (Thomas, Werner-Wilson, & Murphy, 2005), both members in a sample of heterosexual couples had stronger bonds with the therapist when their partners were disclosing and weaker bonds with the therapist when their partners made disparaging remarks about them. However, the men were less likely to concur with the therapist about the *goals* for treatment (e.g., to increase emotional intimacy) when their partners challenged them, whereas the women were less likely to agree with the therapist about the *tasks* of therapy (e.g., plan a "date night" during the session) when challenged by their partners.

Gender dynamics were particularly notable in a larger study with 168 married couples (Knerr & Bartle-Herring, 2010). At the beginning of therapy, husbands whose wives reported relatively more distress tended to be dissatisfied with their marriage. As treatment progressed, though, the alliance with the therapist overshadowed these individual differences. Alliance development differed for the men and women in this sample, however: When the wives had a strong bond with the therapist, their marital satisfaction improved slowly, but the husbands' satisfaction increased only when their wives' bonds with the therapist improved.

In building strong alliances, clients' gender interacts with their levels of psychological and relational functioning. Although having psychiatric symptoms does not seem to deter alliance formation (Knobloch-Fedders, Pinsof, & Mann, 2004; Mamodhoussen et al., 2005), being more distressed with one's partner and having less trust in the couple relationship seem to hinder the development of a strong alliance with the therapist (Johnson & Talitman, 1997). In one study (Knobloch-Fedders et al., 2004), sexual dissatisfaction also hindered alliance development, but only for women.

In another study (Anderson & Johnson, 2010), women's levels of personal distress increased as their husbands' alliance with the therapist increased, but women's distress decreased as the within-couple alliance increased. Anderson and Johnson explained these results in terms of split alliances: "In couples where the husband is forming an alliance with the therapist at the expense of his wife, her symptoms increase. In couples that come together to form a strong within-system alliance, her symptoms decrease" (p. 232). The authors concluded that, "a particularly dangerous scenario in therapy is one in which the therapist aligns with the male partner at the expense of the alliance with the female partner and couple's within-system alliance during the initial stage of therapy" (p. 233).

Clients who experienced distress in their family of origin seem to have a particularly difficult time developing a strong therapeutic alliance. Knobloch-Fedders et al. (2004) found that recalling negative family-of-origin experiences hindered early alliance formation for men and contributed to a split alliance for women. Differentiation of self, which develops from how well a person's family of origin functioned (Bowen, 1978; Skowron & Friedlander, 1998), seems to have important implications for progress in conjoint treatment. In Knerr and Bartle-Herring's (2010) study, for example, partners who were less psychologically differentiated and had more stress began therapy with significantly greater marital dissatisfaction. Being emotionally cutoff, one aspect of self-differentiation, was the most detrimental contributor to dissatisfaction for both male and female partners.

Conflict and the Within-Couple Alliance

Across the clinical literature, the key to success in treating distressed couples involves building and maintaining a strong within-couple alliance or, in SOFTA terms, a *shared sense of purpose* (similar views of the problems, common goals for treatment, and valuing time spent together in therapy). Many authors describe the need to transform couples' cross complaints into mutually acceptable goals, such as regaining intimacy (e.g., Johnson, Makinen, & Millikin, 2001; Karam, Sprenkle, & Davis, 2015) or learning to co-parent effectively (e.g., Baris et al., 2001).

In the research literature as well, a strong within-couple alliance has been shown to predict improvement (e.g., Anderson & Johnson, 2010; Knobloch-Fedders et al., 2007) as well as clients' (Heatherington & Friedlander, 1990) and therapists' session evaluations (Friedlander et al., 2006). In one recent study (Biesen & Doss, 2013), for example, couples who agreed on the nature of their relationship problems before beginning therapy tended to remain in treatment for the recommended number of sessions and made more clinically significant gains than couples whose initial views on their problems were dissimilar. Notably, another study found when the goal was to reduce problems between the partners rather than to manage their psychological symptoms, starting therapy with a strong within-couple alliance predicted success more so than either partner's individual alliance with the therapist (Anderson & Johnson, 2010).

Establishing and maintaining a strong within-couple alliance is challenging, however. As in family work, this aspect of alliance tends to fluctuate over time (Escudero, Friedlander, Varela, & Abascal, 2008), and sharing a sense of purpose depends on the degree to which clients feel safe in the conjoint therapeutic context (cf. Friedlander et al., 2008). In recent case studies using the SOFTA-o with Spanish (Mateu, Vilaregut, Artigas, & Escudero, 2014) and Italian (Zaffarano, 2015) couples, both SAFETY WITHIN THE THERAPEUTIC SYSTEM and SHARED SENSE OF PURPOSE were highly variable. In Zaffarano's analysis of three sessions with four high-conflict heterosexual couples, all of whom dropped out of treatment prematurely, SAFETY was the most variable alliance dimension, particularly among the husbands, most of whom demonstrated problematic SAFETY in the first session. Whereas a negative SHARED SENSE OF PURPOSE was observed in three of the four couples, one of whom evidenced problematic ratings in every session, this dimension improved in the three other couples as therapy progressed. Of note, the fluctuations in these two aspects of alliance differed from the consistently positive ENGAGEMENT and EMOTIONAL CONNECTION observed over time in all four couples.

An analysis of the content of the four dropout cases supported the SOFTA-o analyses (Zaffarano, 2015). In the couple that had a consistently poor SHARED SENSE OF PURPOSE, for example, the cross complaints precluded the development of a relational perspective on the problem. Specifically, the wife complained of her husband's gambling, which he denied. Instead, he complained that his wife was not giving him enough "space." Based on the qualitative analyses and the SOFTA-o results, Zaffarano concluded that the premature termination of these couples was primarily due to the high conflict and lack of trust between the partners.

Alliance-Empowering Strategies

Managing Cross Complaints

Safety first. If members of the couple agree on the need for therapy but locate the problems in each other, it's likely that they will engage in cross complaining which, when intense, can escalate into cross attacking. Ground rules are essential to prevent irreparable harm.[1] That is, the therapist must make it clear as soon as hostilities mount that name-calling, yelling, and physical outbursts will not be tolerated; rather, therapy is "the place to learn how to fight fairly." When it's put this way, couples will usually agree that despite their years together, they never learned to resolve their disagreements constructively, i.e., through problem solving.

Managing safety also involves attending to each partner's expressions of vulnerability and protecting the more vulnerable partner from acrimonious blame and hostility. If the emotional heat becomes unbearable, one partner may get up and leave the office. This reaction signals that safety is sorely compromised. Generally speaking, it's unwise to coax the escaping client to return to the session, since such extreme discomfort needs to be respected and high-conflict partners need to give one another the space to calm down before reengaging.

Safety also involves teaching couples that people have varying needs for closeness or distance, especially in the face of conflict. Elena and Carlos Guzmán had different appetites for lovemaking, which were reflected in how they argued about this problem. Carlos blamed Elena for leaving the room when he got loud. Elena blamed Carlos for not comforting her when she sobbed during their fights. Elena felt supported when the therapist explained to Carlos that a "cooling-off period" was acceptable, even desirable, so that Elena could "re-center" before returning to the argument. Carlos felt supported when the therapist helped him explain to Elena that his way of re-centering made it difficult for him to comfort her when emotions ran high. Both members of the couple were relieved when the therapist explained that neither partner had the corner on Truth: When Carlos brought up problems in their sex life, his *intention* was not to "hurt" Elena, but the *effect* of his doing so did hurt her. In other words, just because Elena felt hurt didn't mean that Carlos's intention was to hurt her.

By empathizing with each partner's pain, a therapist can create emotional connections with both members of the couple. Then, by pointing out their common experience of feeling hurt, misunderstood, and unloved, the therapist begins to formulate a shared sense of purpose around improving the couple's relationship. And, by refusing either partner's subtle or not-so-subtle attempt to align with her, the therapist demonstrates that her role is not to take sides in the fight but rather to strengthen the partners' bonds with each other.

Some conflicts are so intense that the partners need to be restrained from interacting with one another in the session. To maximize safety in her emotion-focused approach to couples work, Johnson (e.g., 2004) typically directs her comments about attachment needs and fear of abandonment to each partner separately. In this way each partner hears the other's deepest feelings without being put on the spot to respond.

Therapy sessions like these tend to be quite emotional. When the session ends, the therapist can direct the couple to refrain from discussing the same issues for the

---

[1] A careful assessment of a history of intimate partner violence is necessary before undertaking conjoint therapy, which is contraindicated in these cases. The discussions in this chapter only reflect conjoint therapy in which violence is not a concern.

remainder of the day or, when emotions are running particularly high, until the next therapy appointment.

When conflicts center around the children, couples often request family therapy. If, however, the partners begin cross complaining about one another's parenting[2] in front of the children, the therapist should work with the couple alone, at least at first. Doing so protects the children and sends the message that as parents, they need to avoid using the children as pawns in their fight.

When separation or divorce is unavoidable, each partner should be seen individually to create a strong bond with the therapist. Hopefully, a strong individual alliance will help the therapist foster a within-couple alliance focused on the children's needs. Unfortunately, not all clients can set aside their complaints with their partner to engage in problem solving around co-parenting. To do so requires each parent to forego the gratification of personal needs (like revenge or monetary gain) for the good of the children. When only one partner can put the children first, conjoint couple therapy may be unworkable.

Managing Zero-Sum Conflicts

Not surprisingly, when there is a zero-sum conflict, one member of the couple may actively resist engaging in therapy. It is important to recognize, however, that resistance is a systemic dynamic, not an individual trait. That is, while resistance may be located within one member of the couple, it actually reflects both partners' ambivalence about therapy and/or their fear of change. Janice mostly wanted to leave Dave but a part of her wanted to hold on. For his part, Dave was fed up with Janice but was very afraid to end their 10-year relationship. Finally, he acceded to her demand that they consult a therapist. At first the couple's polarization intensified: The more Janice voiced her determination to leave, the more Dave pleaded with her to stay. Once the therapist helped them recognize their shared ambivalence, they were able to make a less emotionally charged decision about their future.

Illustrating the successful resolution of resistance, Basham (1992) described the process of working with Mary Lou and Paul Jensen. As explained to the therapist, the couple sought help due to "intense arguments" over Mary Lou's infidelity with a family friend; their goal was to decide whether to separate and eventually divorce or to reconcile (p. 257). At the outset, the therapist recognized that the partners' sociocultural and religious backgrounds made Paul, in particular, "averse to therapy" (p. 257).

To reduce resistance and enhance engagement, the therapist began by explaining the purpose, processes, and potential outcomes of couple therapy. Early on, the objective was to create an individual bond with each client. Safety was of concern for both partners: Paul, who was on active duty in the Navy, worried about confiden-

---

[2] See Chap. 4 for a discussion of the challenges of working with one parent when the other parent is absent or not involved with the children.

tiality, and Mary Lou asked the therapist not to tell Paul a secret about her extra-marital affair. Addressing these issues, the therapist assured the couple of confidentiality and contracted with them about the policies (e.g., not keeping secrets) and length of therapy.

The therapist began fostering the couple's shared sense of purpose by exploring their views on marriage, family, and power dynamics in relationships. Early discussions revealed that both partners' family backgrounds, although different (Paul was raised in a Scandinavian farming community and Mary Lou's Irish Catholic family worked in the coal mines), stigmatized professional help seeking.

Shared purpose was also addressed when the therapist explained that the specific goals for treatment needed to be determined by the partners themselves. Helping them do so, the therapist pointed out their mutual feelings of hurt, mistrust, and anger, "review[ed] the strengths and problem areas in the marriage" (Basham, 1992, p. 258), and emphasized "empowerment and enhanced self-differentiation for each partner" (p. 260). A sailing metaphor was introduced to describe the therapist's role: "to guide the couple through various impasses to meet their destination, much as a navigator might assist a sailing crew with their journey" (p. 258).

Undoubtedly, the therapist's consistent focus on the relationship was instrumental in helping the couple to heal. During treatment the partners created a "fidelity agreement," which they then solidified in a "renewal ritual" that symbolized a renewed commitment to their marriage (p. 259).

Case Example: The Singh-Whalens

Camille lamented, "I gave up *everything* for you – my religion, my *family!*" Joel, furious, threw back at her, "And what did I do for *you?!*" (negative SAFETY[3]). Then, turning to the therapist, he said, "Do you see how she twists everything?"

On the surface, Joel (35) and Camille (33) Singh-Whalen led a privileged lifestyle. They were solidly middle class and well educated, and both of them had achieved some important milestones in their respective professions. Nonetheless, they were miserable with each other, emotionally cutoff from their respective families of origin and struggling to raise a hyperactive 6-year-old with little support from others.

Refusing Joel's bid to align with him (negative SHARED PURPOSE[4]), the therapist pointed out that both he and Camille were hurting "with the way things stand between you now" (SHARED PURPOSE[5]). Quick to interrupt, Camille lashed out at the therapist sarcastically, "Do you think you're really prepared for this fight?" (negative EMOTIONAL CONNECTION[6]).

---

[3] Client responds defensively to another family member.

[4] Family members try to align with the therapist against each other.

[5] Therapist draws attention to clients' shared feelings.

[6] Client comments on the therapist's inadequacy.

The Singh-Whalens argued about virtually everything. In their first session, Joel blamed Camille for being "a workaholic"—she was "never home, never available for the family." Defensive, Camille reacted: "I converted [to Catholicism] for *you*, and what did it get me? My parents won't talk to me, and yours are barely civil to me! What do I have besides my work?" (negative SAFETY[7] and negative SHARED PURPOSE[8]).

Surprised at their bitterness toward one another, the therapist asked to see each partner alone before contracting for conjoint treatment, an approach that enhances safety and emotional connection. In his individual session, Joel tearfully revealed the source of the problems from his perspective: Camille had no sexual interest in him and wouldn't even allow him to touch her with affection (SAFETY[9]). In her individual session, Camille explained that while she loved Joel, she felt that she'd lost her "self" in their relationship along with her religion and her family. In both of these sessions the therapist worked to create a bond with each partner (EMOTIONAL CONNECTION[10]) that he hoped would foster a within-couple alliance in the subsequent conjoint session.

With both partners present, the therapist explained his role (ENGAGEMENT[11])—not to take sides but rather to "help you step outside of the deep rut you're both in, to stop blaming each other and instead find the kind of love and commitment you once had, which led you, Camille, to convert to Catholicism over the protests of your parents and you, Joel, to take her side against your own parents. This won't be easy – you'll need to open up to each other in a way you haven't in a long time" (SHARED PURPOSE[12] and SAFETY[13]). Leaning forward (ENGAGEMENT[14]), Joel murmured, "I only want the best for us both." Camille looked at the floor (negative CONNECTION[15]), stoically silent.

Focusing his efforts on SAFETY, the therapist proposed four ground rules for their work together (SAFETY[16]): (1) not talking over one another; (2) discussing only one problem at a time; (3) focusing on observable behavior rather than on motives, attitudes, or personality; and (4) not characterizing each other's behavior using the terms "always" and "never" (e.g., "You never listen to me"; "You always treat me badly"). In response, Joel suggested that he and Camille commit to these rules "even at home" (ENGAGEMENT[17]). Smiling for the first time, Camille teased him, "If you really think we can do this, then maybe you'll finally agree to let me

---

[7] Client responds defensively to another family member.

[8] Family members blame each other.

[9] Client shows vulnerability (e.g., discusses painful feelings, cries).

[10] Therapist expresses empathy for the clients' struggle.

[11] Therapist explains how therapy works.

[12] Therapist draws attention to clients' shared experiences and feelings.

[13] Therapist acknowledges that therapy involves taking risks.

[14] Client leans forward.

[15] Client avoids eye contact with the therapist.

[16] Therapist provides structure and guidelines for safety.

[17] Client describes a plan for improving the situation.

buy the car I want!" (SAFETY[18]). "Only if you let me drive it from time to time!" Joel quipped with a smile (SHARED PURPOSE[19]).

Encouraged by this shift in tone, the therapist pointed out the partners' common experience of feeling rejected by the other "in the ways that hurt most" (SHARED PURPOSE[20]). The remainder of the session was devoted to exploring, separately with each partner, "how you fell in love." Uncharacteristically, Camille began crying (SAFETY[21]) when Joel mentioned his admiration for her professional achievements and her "spunk in standing up to her sexist boss."

Paying attention to Camille's vulnerability in the moment, the therapist got up, gently turned Joel to face his wife and motioned for him to take her two hands in his (SHARED PURPOSE[22]): "Joel, tell her how much you miss her" (SAFETY[23]). Joel did just that (ENGAGEMENT[24]), and Camille began sobbing in earnest. To give them privacy, the therapist said, "I'll be back," and stepped out of the office for a few minutes.

The therapist realized that as encouraging as this intimate moment had been, Camille and Joel were likely to revert to cross complaining. For this reason, he ended the session by proposing a "homework assignment" and asking if they would be willing to commit to trying it in the coming week (ENGAGEMENT[25]). The task was to keep a writing pad on the table next to their bed; each person should write a brief note to the other every day, starting with the affirmation "I appreciate you for...." Smiling, Joel remarked, "It seems like we do need something like this to stay positive" (ENGAGEMENT[26]), to which the therapist replied, "I'm impressed by both of you – you seem willing to do the hard work to get back on track. I'm hopeful that we can do this together" (ENGAGEMENT[27]).

Of course, the mutual blaming did not end quickly, but the couple kept their appointments and, from time to time, spontaneously mentioned that "things seem a little better at home" (ENGAGEMENT[28]). Each partner saw progress in the other that mattered: Joel was encouraged by Camille's occasional affectionate touch. Camille was encouraged by Joel's genuine interest in what she was doing at work. The therapist was encouraged when Camille told him, "Well, we started to get into it [a fight] last Sunday, but then we looked at each other and stopped. We remem-

---

[18] Client varies her emotional tone during the session.

[19] Family members share a lighthearted moment with each other.

[20] Therapist draws attention to clients' shared experiences and feelings.

[21] Client shows vulnerability (e.g., discusses painful feelings, cries).

[22] Therapist encourages clients to show caring, concern, or support for each other.

[23] Therapist helps clients talk truthfully and nondefensively with each other.

[24] Client complies with therapist's request for an enactment.

[25] Therapist asks clients whether they are willing to do a specific homework assignment.

[26] Client expresses optimism.

[27] Therapist expresses optimism.

[28] Client indicates that a positive change has taken place.

bered the ground rules you set when we started here (ENGAGEMENT[29]) and so we decided to wait till we came today to talk about it" (SAFETY[30]).

As the therapy progressed, the couple's conflicts slowly eased. In Session 8, Camille began the session by saying that they'd agreed it was time to work on "solving the Parents Problem" (ENGAGEMENT[31]). Joel explained that now that their son was 6 years old, they'd decided that it was "time to bring down the walls with his grandparents – on both sides." Recognizing that developing a common goal outside the therapy office signaled an improving within-couple alliance, the therapist asked for an explanation of their intentions. Although he'd surmised that Camille's conversion to Joel's religion over the protest of both families might be at the heart of the couple's difficulties, the therapist took a step back to observe how well the partners were approaching this problem together. Camille put it eloquently: "It's time we stopped using our parents to destroy each other."

The plan was not altogether successful. Camille's parents were unforgiving, but Joel's parents warmed considerably toward her when she told them how important she thought it was to raise their son in Catholicism. More notable than the couple's project to restore bonds with their parents, Joel and Camille demonstrated that they'd learned to trust and respect one another in a way that was altogether new for them.

Naturally, the couple's other problems did not magically disappear. When they decided to end the therapy, Joel still wanted more sexual contact than Camille was comfortable with, and Camille sometimes found it hard to assert herself with Joel. On the whole, though, this very challenging case was remarkably successful.

Final Thoughts

Although most people expect the outcome of couple therapy to be positive, they tend to have higher expectations for their own engagement in the process than for that of their partner (Friedlander, Muetzelfeld, Re, & Colvin, 2016). Nonetheless, clients expect their partners to participate freely in the therapeutic process, and they expect their therapists to be supportive and provide an alternative perspective on the relational problems they bring to treatment (Tambling, Wong, & Anderson, 2014).

We began this chapter with the question of how is it that lovers can become enemies. Of course every couple is unique, and this question has no answer. As therapists, we just need to muddle through. Although high-conflict couples rarely turn their enmity into romantic bliss, they can make meaningful progress. The key for the therapist is to maintain a consistent focus on safety and the within-couple alliance in order to leverage the hard work of relational transformation.

---

[29] Client mentions the therapeutic process.

[30] Client implies that therapy is a safe place.

[31] Client introduces a problem for discussion.

References

Anderson, S. R., & Johnson, L. N. (2010). A dyadic analysis of the between and within system alliance on distress. *Family Process, 49*, 220–235.

Anker, M. G., Owen, J., Duncan, B. L., & Sparks, J. A. (2010). The alliance in couple therapy: Partner influence, early change, and alliance patterns in a naturalistic sample. *Journal of Consulting and Clinical Psychology, 78*, 635–645.

Baris, M. A., Coates, C. A., Duvall, B. B., Garrity, C. B., Johnson, E. T., & LaCrosse, E. R. (2001). *Working with high-conflict families of divorce: A guide for professionals*. Northvale, NJ: Jason Aronson.

Basham, K. (1992). Resistance and couple therapy. *Smith College Studies in Social Work, 62*, 245–264.

Beach, S. R. H. (2016). Expanding the study of dyadic conflict: The potential role of self-evaluation maintenance processes. In A. Booth, A. C. Crouter, M. L. Clements, & T. Boone-Holliday (Eds.), *Couples in conflict* (pp. 83–94). New York: Routledge.

Biesen, J. N., & Doss, B. D. (2013). Couples' agreement on presenting problems predicts engagement and outcomes in problem-focused couple therapy. *Journal of Family Psychology, 27*, 658–663.

Bordin, E. S. (1979). The generalizability of the psychoanalytic concept of the working alliance. *Psychotherapy, 16*, 252–260.

Bowen, M. (1978). *Family therapy in clinical practice*. New York, NY: Jason Aronson.

Cummings, E. M., Goeke-Morey, M. C., & Papp, L. M. (2016). Couple conflict, children, and families: It's not just you and me, babe. In In A. Booth, A. C. Crouter, M. L. Clements, & T. Boone-Holliday (Eds.), *Couples in conflict* (pp. 117–147). New York: Routledge.

Escudero, V., Friedlander, M. L., Varela, N., & Abascal, A. (2008). Observing the therapeutic alliance in family therapy: Associations with participants' perceptions and therapeutic outcomes. *Journal of Family Therapy, 30*, 194–204.

Friedlander, M. L., Escudero, V., & Heatherington, L. (2006). *Therapeutic alliances with couples and families: An empirically-informed guide to practice*. Washington, DC: American Psychological Association.

Friedlander, M. L., Escudero, V., Horvath, A. S., Heatherington, L., Cabero, A., & Martens, M. P. (2006). System for observing family therapy alliances: A tool for research and practice. *Journal of Counseling Psychology, 53*, 214–225.

Friedlander, M. L., Lambert, J. E., & Muñiz de la Peña, C. (2008). A step toward disentangling the alliance/improvement cycle in family therapy. *Journal of Counseling Psychology, 55*, 118–124.

Friedlander, M. L., Muetzelfeld, H., Re, S., & Colvin, K. F. (2016, August). *Introducing the expectations for couple therapy scale: Initial development and validation*. Poster presented at the annual convention, American Psychological Association, Denver, CO.

Heatherington, L., & Friedlander, M. L. (1990). Couple and family psychotherapy alliance scales: Empirical considerations. *Journal of Marital and Family Therapy, 16*, 299–306.

Johnson, S. M. (2004). *The practice of emotionally-focused couple therapy: Creating connection* (2nd ed.). New York: Brunner-Routledge.

Johnson, S. M., & Talitman, E. (1997). Predictors of success in emotionally focused marital therapy. *Journal of Marital and Family Therapy, 23*, 135–152.

Johnson, S. M., Makinen, J. A., & Millikin, J. W. (2001). Attachment injuries in couple relationships: A new perspective on impasses in couples therapy. *Journal of Marital and Family Therapy, 27*, 145–155.

Karam, E. A., Sprenkle, D. H., & Davis, S. D. (2015). Targeting threats to the therapeutic alliance: A primer for marriage and family therapy training. *Journal of Marital and Family Therapy, 41*, 389–400.

Knerr, M., & Bartle-Herring, S. (2010). Differentiation, perceived stress, and therapeutic alliance as key factors in the early stage of couple therapy. *Journal of Family Therapy, 32*, 94–118.

Knobloch-Fedders, L. M., Pinsof, W. B., & Mann, B. J. (2007). Therapeutic alliance and treatment progress in couple therapy. *Journal of Marital and Family Therapy, 33*, 245–257.

Knobloch-Fedders, L. M., Pinsof, W. M., & Mann, B. J. (2004). The formation of the therapeutic alliance in couple therapy. *Family Process, 43*, 425–442.

Mamodhoussen, S., Wright, J., Tremblay, N., & Poitras-Wright, H. (2005). Impact of marital and psychological distress on therapeutic alliance in couples undergoing couple therapy. *Journal of Marital and Family Therapy, 31*, 159–169.

Mateu, C., Vilaregut, A., Artigas, L., & Escudero, V. (2014). Construcciòn de la alianza terapéutica en la terapia de pareja: Estudio de un caso con dificultades de manejo terapéutico. *Anuario de Psicologìa/The UB Journal of Psychology, 44*, 95–115.

Skowron, E. A., & Friedlander, M. L. (1998). The differentiation of self inventory: Development and initial validation. *Journal of Counseling Psychology, 45*, 235–246.

Tambling, R. B., Wong, A. G., & Anderson, S. R. (2014). Expectations about couple therapy: A qualitative investigation. *American Journal of Family Therapy, 42*, 29–41.

Thomas, S. E. G., Werner-Wilson, R. J., & Murphy, M. J. (2005). Influence of therapist and client behaviors on therapeutic alliance. *Contemporary Family Therapy, 27*, 19–35.

Wachtel, E. (1999). *We love each other, but…*. New York: Golden Books.

Zaffarano, I. (2015). *Clinica di coppia e dropout: un'analisi di processo dell'alleanza terapeutica mediante il sistema di codifica e-SOFTA. (Couples therapy and dropout: A process analysis of the therapeutic alliance with e-SOFTA.)* Unpublished master's thesis, Università Cattolica del Sacro Cuore di Milano, Italy.

Chapter 3
Engaging Reluctant Adolescents and Their Parents

Be yourself; everyone else is already taken.

Oscar Wilde

No clinical term describes the kind of family in which the adolescent is "a problem" and the parent(s) are "lost" or "frustrated." As family therapists, however, we all recognize this type of family. The adolescent feels accused of multiple faults that, from his point of view, are simply his "way of being." Somewhere along the way, his sense of identity shifted to become confused and highly negative. His parents also struggle with their own negative sense of identity, as "ineffective" or "bad" parents.

In short, this is a family system stuck in a specific life cycle transition, one that is particularly challenging for therapeutic work. Usually each of the two subsystems, adolescent(s) and parent(s), considers that it is the other (subsystem) that needs to "admit to" wrongdoing and thus be willing to change. Both subsystems suffer because they believe that their well-intentioned efforts and their subjective experiences—indeed, everything they have tried to that point—are not recognized or appreciated by the other subsystem.

What underlies the failure to transition from a family with young children to a family with adolescents? (Note that the transition refers to changes made in the *whole* family, not just the teenager(s)!) In general, several essential factors contribute to the family's difficulty. With respect to the adolescent, causal factors have to do with her personal characteristics, the kind and extent of her risk behaviors, and her overall psychobiological maturation. Not surprisingly, causal factors also lie within the parental subsystem: the parents' ability to recognize and understand the process of change in the family from a dynamic or systemic perspective, their ability to adapt to rapid changes in their child(ren), and the extent of interference in this process due to difficulties in the parents' relations with each other. Sometimes the transition to a family with adolescents reveals latent difficulties in the parents as a couple or uncovers conflicts and rigid patterns in the family as a system that were easily postponed (or camouflaged) when the children were younger. In a sense, the whole process of attachment in raising a child from birth can be severely tested during early adolescence. To sum it up, the transition to a family with adolescents tests the whole family, both individually and relationally. And for many families this transition is the first serious challenge they face.

© Springer International Publishing AG 2017   55
V. Escudero, M.L. Friedlander, *Therapeutic Alliances with Families*,
Focused Issues in Family Therapy, DOI 10.1007/978-3-319-59369-2_3

A key aspect in this transition period has to do with the adolescent's growing need for autonomy, balanced by her need for a continued sense of belonging (Eyrich-Garg, 2008; Santrock, 2015). This developmental process, simple to understand, is the source of management difficulties for the kinds of families we have been describing. The adolescent has a clear normative task: His developmental process has reached a point where he has to demonstrate his independence from parents or other adult caretakers. Simultaneously, he needs to show himself and other family members that his emotional security is no longer tied to the parents. It becomes ever more urgent for him to create a private world of peer relationships and develop some degree of emotional security within those relationships.

Parents are inevitably affected by this change in their child—they need to modify their disciplinary practices and their oversight to work *with* him in renegotiating the family rules and norms. For many parents, it comes as a surprise that as their parental role with their children changes, they also need to renegotiate their couple relationship. Not uncommonly, they also need to shift their relations with extended family and/or people outside the family. Although many parents understand the need to renegotiate these relationships, it may be shocking for them to realize that their personal emotional security may be affected by these changes.

In other words, it is no longer only the parents who set the tone for attachment. Rather, the attachment bonds in adolescence become more reciprocal or bidirectional (Diamond, Russon, & Levy, 2016). That is, as the child moves away emotionally, the parents need to respect his distance yet also remain a secure base in times of turmoil in his life.

So, imagine a therapeutic scenario in which the transition to adolescence (with all of the optimally co-occurring changes in family bonds) is not working. Everyone in the family is experiencing a high level of frustration—indeed, in a sense the family is breaking apart. Coming into treatment, the teenager initially experiences therapy as a punishment or negative judgment. She feels trapped—therapy is something that belongs to the world of adults, *aka* her parents. Her initial reaction is most likely defensive, avoidant, or even hostile to any context in which she is expected to let down her guard. Simultaneously, the parents are protecting themselves from their own frustration (and their own insecurity, not always recognized) by rigidly interpreting the family's problems as entirely due to the "bad" attitude or behavior of their daughter. Any attempt by the therapist to explore a new, broader, and more flexible framework in which to view the family's difficulties (including recognition of the parents' lack of effectiveness) is likely to be seen as blaming. The result, not surprisingly, is defensiveness, avoidance, and sometimes even hostility on the part of the parents.

In this chapter, we describe the kinds of challenges that arise during the transition to adolescence and ways in which the therapeutic alliance can be leveraged to create a safe space to renegotiate familial bonds. In contrast to the solo parenting issues discussed in Chap. 4, the focus in this chapter is on the kinds of adolescent behavior that challenge parents and therapist alike.

Unique Challenges

"Clearly, He Is the Problem"

Obviously, starting conjoint therapy when you feel like a defendant in a courtroom would be distressing for any of us, in individual as well as conjoint family therapy. Unfortunately, when parents identify their teenager as the sole "motive" for seeking therapy, he is likely to feel a need to defend himself as if he were facing criminal charges from a prosecutor.

Even in modern Western society, adolescents are unlikely to view family therapy as a context for solving problems that a parent defines as solely their own or as a result of their "bad behavior." For children and adolescents, therapy belongs to the world of adults—in fact, it usually can only be initiated by adults.

One understandable consequence of the fairly common identification of the adolescent as "the family problem" is that it may be extremely difficult for him to trust the therapeutic context. Notably, his mistrust and lack of safety make it hard for him to let down his guard enough to be fully understood. As a result, the family therapist needs to overcome this initial hurdle by making it clear, from the outset, that "as a group, *we*" are searching for a broader, more systemic understanding of the problem, one that includes the entire family and does not place guilt on any one individual. Moreover, the therapist needs to convince the adolescent that she is interested in him and that she wants to relate to him only "as a person," not as "the family problem."

"No, No … I Don't Have Any Problems"

A contradiction that has a strong impact during the initial stage of therapy occurs when the client—any client, not just an adolescent—claims that he has no problems whatsoever. This contradiction may seem strange, but when parents identify an adolescent as "the problem," denial is natural.

The therapist should not interpret the adolescent's defensive position literally, but rather as a challenge that requires the creation of a strong therapeutic alliance. The key is to doing so involves interpreting her position of staunch denial relationally, not only by listening to the "notes" but also to the "melody" in her communication.

So how should therapists approach a teenager's "I don't have a problem" position (Madsen, 2007)? From a relational perspective on communication (Rogers & Escudero, 2004), in order to create a strong alliance with the adolescent (indeed, with the whole family system as a unit), the most immediate answer to this question is what we should NOT do. That is, we should NOT accept at face value the adolescent's statement that he doesn't know or doesn't feel, we should NOT view his rejection of the therapy as indicative of psychopathology, and we should NOT see the adolescent's apparent boycott of the therapy as a total rejection of his parents' efforts.

Rather, we should attempt to discover the relational meaning behind the adolescent's negative stance on the problem: Is it rebellion against what she sees as a blaming definition of the problem (and/or the solution)? Is it a difficulty in understanding the consequences of her behavior? Is it avoidance due to deep mistrust of any attempt to help her (possibly due to a characteristically avoidant attachment style or because of previous negative experiences with "helpers")? Is it a deep sense of helplessness and/or a lack of self-efficacy for facing or addressing difficulties?

Understandably, the therapist's first challenge is to begin to understand what is keeping the adolescent in a position of denying the problem and rejecting the offer of therapy. Ultimately, adopting an attitude of curiosity is most likely to create the kind of emotional connection with the adolescent in which she starts to feel understood.

"If You Really Want to Help, Why Are You Forcing Therapy on Me?"

One of the most fascinating challenges for building a therapeutic alliance with an adolescent is to help her see therapy as a context in which she can feel cared for. For many adolescents, the tendency is to interpret the therapeutic context as one of correction and coercion (Raviv, Raviv, Vago-Gefen, & Fink, 2009; Shirk & Karver, 2003). In part, she is right. Her message to her parents is something like this: "If you say you want to help me, why did you bring me to a place where I'm seen as The Problem? Why did we start off talking about everything I do wrong or about everything that is not right in my life?"

The challenge is to transform the adolescent's view so that she sees therapy as a place of caring and collaboration, not only with the therapist but also—and especially—with her parents. One way to do so is by surprising the adolescent by behaving in a way that contradicts her negative expectations about what therapy entails. The "surprise" is only effective if the adolescent does not become frightened by the novelty and her parents do not wind up feeling misunderstood, challenged, or disqualified by the therapist.

Consider Nathaniel, an adolescent who came to the initial session with a highly negative attitude. All he had heard at home was that therapy was the parents' last resort before reporting his aggressive and disobedient behavior to a juvenile court: "If you don't accept help from a therapist, if you don't change, you won't leave us any way out … we simply will not continue to put up with your lifestyle and your lack of respect."

In Nathaniel the therapist saw an irritated adolescent who was locked in a closed off, defensive position. His mother sat at a distance, scrutinizing Nathaniel before anyone else, even the therapist, had said a single word. Without consulting the therapist, his father excused himself from the therapy "to avoid fighting with Nathaniel."

Nathaniel reacted with surprise and incredulity when the therapist said, "First, it'd be good to get to know each other a little…I don't exactly know how to do it… but, Nathaniel, I'd like you to start us off by introducing me to your mother, and then to your father, even though he couldn't make it here today. What would you like to say as an introduction?" This is just a small example of how, at the outset of therapy, the therapist can begin to break down an adolescent's defensive position.

"We Have Already Done Everything Possible, So Why Should We Go to Therapy?"

It is understandable that many parents feel they have already done everything possible to solve the problems caused by the adolescent's attitude or behavior. Indeed, it is common to consult with parents who have already made many futile attempts to address their children's problems. They amply describe the many sacrifices they have made. They appear psychologically and physically worn out, ready to hand their children over to a professional.

Not surprisingly, when problems with their children have become complicated and prolonged over time, parents tend to feel deeply frustrated. Along with this frustration is a negative sense of identity: "We are bad parents, we have failed." The challenge is to engage them in therapy, not as quasi co-therapists to "change" their children, but rather as clients who, just like their teenagers, are experiencing a strong sense of frustration and lack of control.

In the most difficult cases, it is not simply a matter of helping parents improve their parenting skills—rather, it is a matter of emotional recovery. The therapist's objective needs to regenerate the parents' hopefulness, their motivation, and their positive sense of identity. Logically, the first step involves understanding and accepting their discouragement and skepticism about what they can contribute to the therapy.

Often the parents' feeling that they have already tried "everything" is reflected in their urgent need to describe in great detail all the avenues they have pursued to date. While they believe it is essential to tell the therapist about their anguish over the situation with their children, they are generally oblivious to the fact that providing specific details about the adolescent's lack of respect or a previous fight at home is not particularly helpful, particularly when the teenager is present in the room. Rather, the therapist needs to help the parents come to see that they, too, need help and guidance. However, the parents' cooperation tends to be difficult to obtain if the therapist is not first able to make them feel that he understands their sense of lack of control and failure.

The empathic process cannot be overlooked. It must be among the first goals of the therapy for the therapist to *accept* the parents' position of discouragement, fatigue, and helplessness. Acceptance of their sense of negative feelings is essential for planting the seed of mutual collaboration that is at the heart of the therapeutic alliance.

"It's Just What Kids Do Nowadays"

In our experience working with adolescents and their families, we have witnessed a wide range of risk awareness on the part of parents and teens. Often the therapeutic alliance with these families is influenced by extreme intrafamilial differences in perceptions of what is "normal" adolescent behavior versus behavior that carries significant risk. Clearly this divergence is due in part to rapid changes in the social mores for millennials brought about by the Internet and consequent safety threats.

Increasingly, therapists find themselves stuck in the middle of divergent perceptions within a family about what should be expected of adolescents—that is, behaviors that should be encouraged or discouraged. This challenge to a therapist's alliance with the family as a group has become ever more pressing in recent years due to the many social factors affecting family life. Not only are there microcultural factors (the idiosyncratic characteristics of each family as they relate to the wider social system), but also there are macro-cultural or sociological factors at play. Among others, these factors include intergenerational conflicts over "appropriate" behavior; differing, potentially conflictual acculturation levels between parents and adolescents in immigrant families; and a generational gap in the value and use of technology and social networking.

From a purely clinical point of view, perhaps the most essential strategy for building a strong alliance involves staying centered (rather than emotionally reactive) when a family escalates a cycle of minimization/maximization. This cycle refers to a dynamic in which one subsystem or family member minimizes the teen's risk behavior, while another subsystem or family member maximizes or dramatizes its risk. As an example, the more mother frets about her daughter's quasi-addictive use of social media, the more father minimizes the concern and vice versa.

Raúl's mother appeared in the first session, dramatically expressing her alarm and heartbreak when she discovered her 17-year-old son's stash of marijuana. The display of anguish was so extreme that the therapist had great difficulty structuring the conversation to obtain a sense of the family and the circumstances that had precipitated the urgent request for therapy. Nonverbally, Raúl showed disdain for his mother's exaggerated claims, almost mocking her when he sarcastically pointed out that she did "not understand" the effects of marijuana and how smoking was "integrated" in the social life of adolescents.

Raúl's father remained silent and showed no sign of his position in the conflict. When at last he spoke, his request was clear and direct: "Please tell us if it is normal for a teenager to smoke three or four joints in a weekend? What are the health risks, and what are the legal consequences?"

Obviously this question can be reasonably answered but, taking sides at this point, in an initial therapy session, runs the risk of alienating one or more family members due to their intense conflict over the issue. In this particular case, the therapist was able to redirect the conversation with an intervention that fortunately caught Raúl's attention and reduced the urgency of his parents: "First, can I ask some questions?... I'd like to ask each of you some questions to help me understand how you're feeling as individuals and how you're experiencing this problem. That is, I want to know what worries each of you personally and how you see the concerns of the other two of you. Does this seem like a good way for us to get started here?"

Rebellion Can Trap an Adolescent

Some risky behaviors clearly spell "rebellion" in the context of parent-child conflict. To illustrate, consider the abrupt change in Ruth who, until her parents separated when she was 15, maintained excellent grades in school and was a "model kid." After the separation, she began having almost daily fights with her mother, the custodial parent. Ruth's grades dropped precipitously and her behavior at home became erratic. In response, her mother adopted a strong, confrontational stance that was clearly ineffective. Ruth reacted by demonstrating even less "good sense" and ever more risky and rebellious behavior.

Finally, Ruth absconded from her mother's home in the middle of the night, intending to live with her father. However, when she arrived at his apartment, he ignored and rejected her, wanting nothing to do with her difficulties—at least that was Ruth's interpretation of her father's response.

One of Ruth's provocative behaviors, the one that produced the most intense level of despair on her mother's part, was Ruth's friendship with a group of girls who were committing various petty crimes and "engaging in criminal mischief." Having been caught shoplifting, Ruth was referred for therapy by the juvenile justice system.

Ruth's criminal activities had not only exacerbated the ongoing conflicts with her mother but also added to her father's justification for his increased distancing. Paradoxically, however, Ruth's rebellion turned out to be the most effective "weapon" in dissolving the mother-daughter conflict. A while after being completely rejected by her father, Ruth's relationship with her mother improved. The key to this momentous change was the therapist's reframing of their relational problems as due to the shared pain they were both experiencing due to the marital separation. Ruth's shoplifting was framed as "collateral damage" during a time that she was distanced from both parents and had turned to her peer group for emotional support.

From this point on, the therapeutic focus was on helping Ruth cope with the serious negative educational and judicial consequences of her criminal activities.

Despite the repair in her relationship with her mother, Ruth was unfortunately trapped by rebellious, criminal behavior that had no antisocial motivation.

In our clinical experience, the occasional consumption of an illegal drug often reflects adolescent protest or rebellion. While the drug use may begin as a rebellious challenge to the authority of the parents or other caregivers, it can result in more serious and long-lasting consequences, even after the relational bonds within the family have been strengthened and the family conflict has been resolved. In this situation, the challenge for the therapist requires a careful balancing of alliances. To do so, one strategy involves providing a systemic perspective on the family's conflict, framing the adolescent's risky behaviors as relationally motivated but without losing sight of the huge risk posed by those behaviors.

Recommendations from the Literature

Engagement Is Key

In the past decade or so, researchers have paid close attention to processes that optimize therapeutic work with adolescents. This attention is reasonable not only because several mental disorders have a typical onset in adolescence (Kessler et al., 2007), but also because adolescents without diagnosed disorders are nonetheless likely to encounter extra stress during this life transition period (Niwa et al., 2016). A dramatic indicator of the impact of psychological stressors on adolescents is reflected in the suicide rate; in 2013 the U.S. Center for Disease Control reported that among students in grades 9 to 12, 8% had attempted suicide one or more times in the previous 12 month period.

Rapid creation of the therapeutic alliance, optimally in the first session, is particularly important when working with teenagers. For those who are reluctant to participate in therapy, engagement is the first objective, particularly in a conjoint family context (e.g., Higham, Friedlander, Escudero, & Diamond, 2012). Engagement is essential to form an alliance with a resistant adolescent for two reasons: (1) active involvement in the therapeutic process is necessary for any client to have a meaningful experience of the therapy (Boggs et al., 2004; Frankel & Levitt, 2009), and (2) for adolescents in particular, active involvement in the therapy promotes a sense of autonomy (Eyrich-Garg, 2008).

Indeed, research suggests that the therapist's ability to rapidly develop an alliance with the adolescent is strongly predictive of outcome and is a key predictor of retention in treatment (Boggs et al., 2004; Thompson, Bender, Lantry, & Flynn, 2007). Karver, Shirk, Handelsman, and Fields (2008), for example, reported that regardless of therapeutic approach, alliance formation during the initial phase of treatment was associated with the adolescent's level of involvement in the process.

A Different Kind of Therapeutic Relationship

A review of the research literature on the therapeutic alliance with adolescents challenges the assumption that the process of alliance building is identical to that process in working with adult clients. Some authors emphasize the importance of creativity in approaching adolescents (Bennett, Le, Lindahl, Wharton, & Weng Mak, 2017; Utley & Garza, 2011) due to the fact that teens are transitioning from children to adults and traditional "talk" therapy may seem alien. For this reason, creative interventions that combine talk with "play" are promising for facilitating teenagers' verbal and nonverbal expressions of thoughts and feelings.

Creativity, as defined by Veach and Gladding (2007, cited in Bennett et al., 2017), refers to the capacity to create a product that is original or unexpected and useful for the task at hand. In our experience, creative interventions can be particularly effective to reduce an adolescent's experience of the therapy as blaming and threatening.

In an empirically based case study (Heatherington, Escudero, & Friedlander, in press), for example, the therapist asked siblings who were estranged from one another to work together to create a slide show of "happy" photographs from their childhood. In this creative intervention, the therapist gave brother and sister a face-saving way to become engaged with each other and—by extension—with the therapy.

Factors that Matter

Literature on creating an alliance with adolescents suggests many factors to take into consideration. Jones (1980), for example, highlighted three factors: power (help the adolescent see himself as making a difference in the therapeutic relationship), competence (stimulate the adolescent's awareness of his talents, skills, or abilities), and significance (highlight the adolescent's sense of belonging). We suggest that in conjoint therapy, these factors should be promoted in the parents' relationship with the adolescent as well as in the therapeutic relationship.

Highly relevant for the alliance building process with adolescents is attachment theory (cf. Feder & Diamond, 2016). In the same way that the adolescent develops relationships with others based on her attachment history, the way that she approaches the therapeutic relationship will be in part be determined by her attachment style. An adolescent's difficulties with emotion regulation and her expectations for new relationships, observable in the context of therapy, are relevant factors for optimizing the alliance. In other words, understanding the teen's typical attachment style and how her parents are reacting to that style can help the therapist select appropriate strategies and interventions to enhance engagement. Just as with adult clients in individual therapy (cf. Daly & Mallinckrodt, 2009), family therapists need to carefully calibrate their emotional distance with any adolescent whose presentation suggests an anxious-avoidant attachment style.

The process of engaging a reluctant adolescent in productive therapeutic work is especially difficult when the teenager was not consulted by his parents in their decision to seek professional help or when the therapy was mandated by some other authority figure, such as a school official or probation officer (Shelef, Diamond, Diamond, & Liddle, 2005; Sotero, Major, Escudero, & Relvas, 2016). In these involuntary situations, it is critically important for the therapist to bring the adolescent's concerns and personal goals forward into the treatment process (Diamond, Liddle, Hogue, & Dakof, 1999; Friedlander, Escudero, & Heatherington, 2006).

Autonomy is another factor to consider in developing an alliance with adolescents. As they begin to seek more independence, adolescents typically confront their parents and, by extension, any adult in an authoritative role, including and especially a therapist (Diamond, Diamond, & Liddle, 2000). For this reason, effective therapeutic interventions with reluctant adolescents involve promoting their voice in the therapeutic process (Diamond et al., 1999; Hogue, Dauber, Stambaugh, Cecero, & Liddle, 2006). In fact, a review of literature on psychotherapy with adolescents (Bolton Oetzel & Scherer, 2003) concluded that recognition of a teenager's developing sense of autonomy has critical implications for alliance formation. Adolescents whose sense of personal autonomy is enhanced in therapy tend to report greater satisfaction with treatment.

Split Alliances

Not surprisingly, differing levels of alliances between individual family members and the therapist, *split alliances* (e.g., Heatherington & Friedlander, 1990; Pinsof & Catherall, 1986) occur frequently in work with adolescents and their parents and, when severe, can profoundly interfere with the therapeutic process (Muñiz de la Peña, Friedlander, & Escudero, 2009). As discussed earlier, although parents tend to have a relatively stronger bond with the therapist than do their adolescent children (Diamond et al., 2000; Friedlander, Escudero, & Heatherington, 2006), this is not always the case (Muñiz de la Peña et al., 2009). Failure to form a solid alliance can occur with any family member who is resistant to the process of change, when the therapist provides insufficient support (Diamond et al., 2000; Higham et al., 2012) or when family members feel unsafe with each other and do not share a common sense of purpose about the problems, goals, and value of treatment (Friedlander et al., 2006).

Toward an Empirical Process Model of Engaging Reluctant Adolescents

As summarized in Chap. 1, we conducted an exploratory but practically informative study (Higham et al., 2012), which was a first step in building a conceptual model for successfully engaging reticent adolescents in family therapy. The research, based on the SOFTA model of the alliance, indicated that acceptance, respect, and validation for the adolescent's perspective were core aspects that contributed to enhancing the therapeutic alliance. Specifically, we qualitatively analyzed sessions in which a resistant adolescent either did or did not shift from negative to positive engagement in the therapeutic process. Two successful and two unsuccessful engagement events were selected from an archival data set of sessions previously rated using the SOFTA-o.

Results indicated that the presence of one parent element (support) and five therapist elements (structuring therapeutic conversations, fostering autonomy, building systemic awareness, rolling with resistance, and understanding the adolescent's subjective experience) appeared critical for successfully facilitating the adolescents' engagement in the session. Table 3.1 presents operational definitions for the five critical elements, including a list of the behavioral indicators that we considered to be the most effective therapeutic interventions in the positive engagement sessions.

An earlier study by Diamond et al. (1999) that compared initially poor adolescent alliances that improved over time with alliances that did not improve reached similar conclusions. Results showed that attending to the adolescent's experience, orienting her to the collaborative nature of therapy, helping her formulate personally meaningful goals, and behaving like her ally were associated with an improvement in the alliance. Similarly, in a study of high-risk teens participating in home-based family therapy (Thompson et al., 2007), the adolescents reported that the therapist's openness, impartiality, activity, and authenticity contributed to the development of a favorable therapeutic relationship.

We used a quantitative methodology in another study that analyzed observable therapist-adolescent interactions in conjoint family sessions (Muñiz de la Peña, Friedlander, Escudero, & Heatherington, 2012). Specifically, using sequential analysis, we examined associations between the alliance and therapist-adolescent communication patterns in ten Spanish cases of brief conjoint family therapy. Early sessions with strong versus problematic alliances, as rated by observers, were selected for coding of relational control communication patterns (Rogers & Escudero, 2004).

No differences were found in the frequencies of different kinds of social exchanges, but competitive responding by the therapists (reflecting an interpersonal struggle for control) was significantly more likely to occur in the problematic alliance sessions than in the strong alliance sessions (Muñiz de la Peña et al., 2012). When the adolescent's alliance with the therapist remained positive from Session 1 to Session 3, there was an observable decrease in the likelihood of competitive responding. On the other hand, when the alliance quality deteriorated over the same period of time, the therapists were increasingly more likely to respond to the adolescents' domineering communications in a competitive manner.

Taken together, results of the relevant alliance studies underscore the need to avoid domineeringness with teens in conjoint family treatment. Rather, the therapist should strive to validate and demonstrate acceptance and respect for the adolescent's unique perspective on her own and the family's situation.

Table 3.1 Model for Shifting Adolescent Engagement (from Higham et al., 2012, p. 37)

Element	Description	Behavioral indicators
Structuring therapeutic conversation (STC)	Therapist attempts to structure the conversation to facilitate engagement or elaboration on a specific topic	• Using off-topic discussions to build rapport • Eliciting parent/adolescent interactions using enactments • Switching the focus of the conversation between the parent and the adolescent • Taking the focus off the adolescent (after multiple questions with limited response) • Bringing the adolescent's attention/focus back to the topic at hand
Fostering autonomy (FA)	Therapist distinguishes between the parent's thoughts or feelings and what the adolescent feels/thinks, pointing out that the adolescent is able to make some decisions independently	• Prompting honest responses and differing opinions • Validating the adolescent's feelings/thoughts • Creating safety for the adolescent to express self openly • Inquiring about a feeling/thought that might be difficult for the adolescent to voice
Building awareness of systemic issues (BASI)	Therapist draws attention to the discussion topic as an issue that is relevant to the entire family rather than solely the parent or the adolescent	• Eliciting perspectives from other family members on a specific topic (to better understand the problem) • Validating the family's experience • Asking the parent to fill in the gaps • Referring to a family goal • Focusing on a problem that is relevant and of interest to all family members
Rolling with resistance (RWR)	Therapist responds to adolescent disengagement in a positive manner	• Asking multiple questions (despite limited input from the adolescent) • Reframing disengagement (i.e., as a way of coping with difficult situations) • Maintaining a calm demeanor
Understanding the adolescent's subjective experiences (UASE)	Therapist attempts to elicit clarification or elaboration to better understand the adolescent's unique perspective	• Giving examples/options for responding • Clarifying what the adolescent is feeling/thinking • Expanding on the adolescent's reasoning • Labeling and verifying feelings • Asking leading open-ended questions • Making an effort to probe for a deeper response from adolescent
Parental support	Parent provides encouragement	• Encouraging the adolescent to respond honestly • Participating in enactments

Alliance-Empowering Strategies

Roll with Initial Resistance

Therapeutic work on adolescents' initial resistance to the therapeutic process needs to avoid an escalation of defensive, reluctant, or hostile positioning. To avoid an amplification of resistance, the therapist must make a concerted effort to understand and accept the position of the adolescent. Obviously, accepting a negative or resistant position about the need or the value of therapy by the adolescent (or by the parents) is not equivalent to agreeing with that position. Rather, acceptance simply involves understanding that there may have been many previous experiences with "helpers" that justify the teenager's feelings of mistrust.

When an adolescent verbalizes that she "doesn't have a problem" and/or that "all the problems are because my parents don't understand me," the therapist needs to avoid the natural temptation to "probe" around to "prove" to her that she "really" does have a problem worthy of psychotherapy. This attitude is only likely to increase her defensive posturing, reflected in a problematic valence in the SAFETY dimension of the alliance.

Rather, it is essential to attend to the adolescent's expressions of insecurity that are likely to underlie his resistance to the therapy. Usually nonverbal indicators of a lack of safety are particularly informative. Expressions of emotion should also be closely attended to. For example, is he furious? (If so, the therapist could demonstrate an interest in the reasons for his anger.) Is he scared? (If so, the therapist can try to discover the circumstances underlying his fear and protect him to the extent possible.) Or is he trying hard to hide his sadness? (If so, the therapist can demonstrate empathy and interest in everything that contributes to his suffering).

When there is a high level of conflict, intrusion, or blaming in the adolescent's interaction with his parents, the therapist can offer protection by inviting each subsystem to speak with him alone. In so doing, the therapist needs to empathize with the difficulty of each perspective without implying that this perspective is the only "correct" one.

Unfortunately, at times therapists find themselves in the middle of a blatant contradiction: Despite having requested or accepted a referral for family therapy, the parents explain that they "can't do anything more," and therefore the therapy "should focus on changing the adolescent." It seems logical to try reasoning with the parents in order to show them that as part of the family system, they need to "own" their contribution to the child's problem. This approach is likely to backfire, however. In especially difficult cases, creating a strong therapeutic alliance with the parents requires a softer approach to help them feel understood, safe, and empowered in the therapeutic process. In particular, the therapist should avoid increasing the parents' pressure to resolve the problems with their adolescent son or daughter. We have found it to be more effective to focus on enhancing the parents' emotional bond with the therapist. Generally, parents will feel deeply understood if the therapist is willing to hear all that they have endured, all the sacrifices they have made, all the strategies they have tried, and all they have suffered before any alternatives are recommended.

At this point two logical questions arise. First: "Isn't our role as therapists to change the parents' negative attitudes?" From a position of family empowerment, our answer is "No, our role is to build a context of therapeutic support in which clients can begin overcoming their reluctance and despair." To create this supportive context, the optimal strategy is to focus on SAFETY, which is arguably the best avenue to ENGAGEMENT and EMOTIONAL CONNECTION with all clients, parents, as well as adolescents (Friedlander et al., 2006).

Second: "Isn't our role to bring about change in the family system?" Also from a position of family empowerment, our answer is "No, our objective is not to *produce* change but rather to *empower* change by building SAFETY so that everyone in the therapeutic environment feels emotionally understood."

These alliance-informed empowerment strategies offer the optimal opportunity to facilitate the family's own change initiatives, particularly for trying out behaviors that shift the child-parent relations. A specific intervention to move forward toward this goal is to reframe the family's disengagement. By focusing on every family member's experience of despair over the difficult situation they find themselves in, the therapist can interpret the disengagement as a natural reaction to the difficulties, even as evidence of the parents' well-intentioned attempts to cope with and overcome these difficulties.

Foster Autonomy and Individuation

Creating safety is essential to help adolescents reflect on their own ideas and experiences and then be able to express them openly and respectfully to their parents. The therapist should make it clear that she distinguishes between the parents' thoughts or feelings and what the teenager feels or thinks, all the while emphasizing that adolescents are capable of making some decisions independently. It may be helpful to remind the parents of a 15-year-old, for example, that "she's only three years away from adulthood. She needs practice in independent decision making, doesn't she?"

This strategy can be carried out using various other interventions. These include conversations during which the therapist underscores points in common and differences; circular questioning to explore how each family member interprets the interactions of the others ("How did you feel, watching your parents argue with each other about whether or not you should work after school?"); conversations in which one family member is asked to take the role of silent observer; and requesting everyone's permission to hold individual therapy sessions with various family members. In short, promoting and protecting the adolescent's autonomy is one strategy that simultaneously enhances the alliance with the adolescent and also empowers the family as a system to value negotiation and commitment to change.

Validate the Adolescent's Subjective Experience

The various alliance-related studies reviewed earlier in this chapter have one aspect in common: the conclusion that it is critically important to validate the adolescent's subjective experience. This strategy is related to two SOFTA dimensions in particular, EMOTIONAL CONNECTION and SHARED PURPOSE.

First, validation is crucial for creating a bond with teenagers in order to help them feel deeply understood on an emotional level. One caveat, however, is essential. Validation is not equivalent to complicity with the adolescents' beliefs or actions. Rather, the purpose of validation is to help her clarify her thoughts and feelings, particularly in relation to the family's difficulties, and then to help her find a language that can increase other family members' understanding of her personal experience.

It cannot be overemphasized that validation facilitates a teenager's belief that the therapist recognizes her as a valid and interesting source of opinions about the family dynamics, and that, as a person, she is not the problem, but rather she has a unique perspective on the family, one that is solidly based in her subjective experience. While the validation process is an essential building block of the alliance with teenagers, it must be accomplished cautiously so that neither the adolescent nor the parent(s) confuse the therapist's validation of the teenager's experience with agreement about the validity of her ideas or behavior. As an example, a therapist can demonstrate an understanding of the adolescent's rage over a particular family situation or event that she experienced as abandonment, but without implying that she is justified in her verbal attack on her mother.

Second, validation of an adolescent's subjective experience tends to increase the entire family's SHARED SENSE OF PURPOSE. Since, as noted above, a strong SHARED PURPOSE is the key to building an expanded alliance with each family member, this essential alliance-empowering strategy has systemic consequences. After all, parents usually want the therapist to like their child just as they usually want the child to like the therapist.

The results of therapeutic interventions focused on the subjective experience of the adolescent are observable when "family members validate each other's point of view," one of the behavioral indicators in the SHARED PURPOSE dimension in the SOFTA-o. In fact, the SOFTA-o includes several strategies that therapists can use to enhance this dimension of the alliance, including *therapist encourages clients to ask each other for their perspective, therapist praises clients for respecting each other's point of view, therapist emphasizes commonalities among clients' perspectives on the problem or solution,* and *therapist draws attention to clients' shared values, experiences, needs, or feelings.*

With all of these interventions, the therapist's objective is to help the adolescent express his subjective experiences (both thoughts and feelings) and then to connect these experiences with those of other family members. In the earlier example with Ruth, by encouraging and then validating her expression of pain over her father's abandonment, the therapist tied Ruth's felt experience to that of her mother, who clearly also felt abandoned. No doubt this enhancement of the family's SHARED PURPOSE was critical for resolving the intense mother-daughter conflict.

Reframe the Problem Systemically

As mentioned above, development of systemic awareness emerged as a salient element in our study of fostering adolescent engagement in the therapeutic process (Higham et al., 2012). In fact, a defining characteristic of the systemic family approach is a consideration of how problems are maintained interpersonally, i.e., circular causality, rather than how, in whom, and why they originated (Rohrbaugh, 2014).

Consequently, effective therapeutic intervention requires a redefinition of the presenting concern so that all participants in the therapy understand that their difficulties are being maintained by recursive patterns that they co-created. *Reframing* is one technique featured in the literature to obtain a transformation of a blaming problem definition (Friedlander, Heatherington, & Marrs, 2000; Robbins, Alexander, Newell, & Turner, 1996). From the perspective of the therapeutic alliance, the beginning of therapy is usually characterized by the challenges we described thus far: Parents are attributing all the problems to the adolescent, who maintains an attitude of rejection, extreme defensiveness, or avoidance, so that frustration and conflict invade the emotional climate. By "reframing the problem," the therapist prompts a change in the family's perspective—replacing guilt with responsibility and commitment. In short, reframing permits the reconciliation of very different views on the problems and solutions based on whatever can be identified as common in the experiences of family members.

In the SOFTA-o, specific contributions to SHARED PURPOSE dimension provide a practical guide for reframing. For example, a therapist can counteract family members' negative behavioral indicators of SHARED PURPOSE (e.g., *family members blame each other, family members devalue each other's opinions or perspective,* and *family members try to align with the therapist against each other*) by, for example, *encouraging clients to compromise with each other, encouraging clients to ask each other for their perspective,* and *emphasizing commonalities among clients' perspectives on the problem or solution.*

Empower the Parental System: Three Layers of the Onion

As laid out in the first chapter of this book, we consider the four SOFTA dimensions of the therapeutic alliance to be a road map for understanding what is thought, felt, and observed when family alliances are strong, regardless of the therapist's theoretical approach and regardless of the kind of difficulty experienced by the family. In Chap. 7 we provide a practical formulation for empowering any family through enhancement of the therapeutic alliance. In the kinds of challenging cases described in this chapter, we believe it is highly important to assess and then address the role played by the parental subsystem in maintaining the problems that are the focus of the therapy.

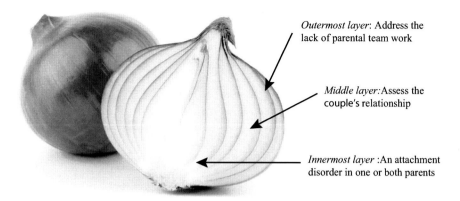

Outermost layer: Address the lack of parental team work

Middle layer: Assess the couple's relationship

Innermost layer :An attachment disorder in one or both parents

Fig. 3.1 Empowering the Parental Subsystem: "Three Layers of the Onion"

Empowering the parental subsystem through the therapeutic alliance is certainly one way to help adolescents demonstrate their ability to be independent and safe without destroying family bonds in the process. To construct a strong alliance with each family member and with the family as a system, the therapist must consider various factors that influence the parents' (or other caregivers') lack of effectiveness. Methods for developing and then maintaining the alliance depend on the therapist's recognition of these factors and the patterns of difficulty that are being maintained in the parental subsystem.

Figure 3.1 represents a simple schematic, configured from our clinical experience, that represents three distinct levels of difficulty in the parental subsystem. We use the metaphor "layers of an onion" to point out that the three layers represent somewhat different levels of depth in relation to parental difficulties. Like an onion, when the difficulty lies deep within the subsystem, the outer layers are affected.

Outermost Layer: Address the Lack of Parental Teamwork Difficulties in the parental subsystem are often associated with ineffective or inappropriate management of changes taking place during the family's transition periods. Usually parents have not adjusted priorities and strategies to the changes that are occurring as their children approach adolescence. Other factors may also result in parental ineffectiveness, including stressful work circumstances, the need to devote extra attention to younger children or to their own aging parents, and adjustments in the life of the couple due to retirement or illness.

Understandably, most parents try to use the same disciplinary strategies with their adolescents that were effective in earlier years. It is even more understandable that parents want to retain the same kind of parental relationship and family routines that worked well when their children were younger. However, when all of the parents' strategies, routines, rules, and disciplinary styles stop working and wind up becoming a source of conflict, therapeutic help may become necessary.

When the behavioral and relational factors between adolescent and parent(s) are the primary source of conflict, the therapeutic strategy should be to empower the parental subsystem. Once a strong alliance with both parents is in place, therapists can easily effect change in transitional adjustment problems by focusing on two specific aspects of co-parenting:

- *Consensus* between the parents on how to manage the adolescent's continued need for parental control versus growing need for independence. For example, parents need to agree on routines (e.g., time allotted for homework, for screen-play, etc.), on the appropriateness of the adolescent's peer groups and activities, including sexual activity, and on restrictions around engaging in risk behaviors.
- *Coordination* between the parents on how to carry out the agreed-upon rules and norms, disciplinary strategies, and so on. That is, mutual agreement and support are needed for parents to decide, in a timely manner, whether the adolescent's infraction of a particular rule should involve a punishment or restriction.

Interventions around this simple scheme, which colloquially we call *C & C* (consensus and coordination), require that parents have a sense of SAFETY in discussing these issues with the therapist. In fact, parental SAFETY is critical for working toward a SHARED SENSE OF PURPOSE that, in turn, has been shown to facilitate therapeutic progress (Friedlander, Lambert, & Muñiz de la Peña, 2008). Two requirements of any *C & C intervention* are to minimize (1) the parents' feelings of frustration and (2) any mutual recrimination between them about past failures. It is also essential not to flood the parents with suggestions, which could overwhelm their motivation or capacity to change.

When these parenting issues are being addressed, parents often want to assure the therapist that they are "very much in agreement" on the major disciplinary issues with their adolescent son or daughter. In minutes, however, therapists often discover no such consensus or coordination. A meaningful exploration of the lack of C & C is possible only in the context of a strong SHARED SENSE OF PURPOSE, that is, when the parents see the problems and goals similarly and are unified in working together in therapy to improve their parenting skills. For example, a father realized that he had subtly disqualified the mother's reprimand of the son, who had slipped out of the house to join his friends at a concert, by commenting, "I've always loved that band."

The first step is for the parents, with the therapist's help, to determine their general level of consensus since in its absence, good parental coordination or teamwork is unlikely. However, while strengthening parental consensus around fundamental issues, such as those regarding parent-child conflict or risky behaviors, is necessary, consensus is not sufficient. Even when parents agree on rules and norms, there can be serious lapses in the execution of discipline or unequal levels of attention paid to carrying out a disciplinary action.

For example, the Duval parents had a clear rule about how to respond when Jerome violated his curfew on weeknights. Although they agreed to adhere strictly to their rule around curfews and the consequences for coming in late, the mother ignored Jerome's violation of the rule because that night she was exceptionally tired and also because Jerome was at a party with friends – she wanted him to be more social. Aware that his mother was not concerned about his rule breaking, Jerome felt justified in yelling at his father when he tried to enforce the agreed-upon consequence for violating the curfew.

Middle Layer: Assess the Couple's Relationship   Adolescence has a tendency to reveal inconsistencies between the parents. This is to be expected, particularly when the teenager is requesting many changes in her relations with her parents, or when she is insisting on having more autonomy to try out new behavior, or when she is actively resisting her parents' rules and routines. These kinds of demands pose a challenge for parents, as we have just explained, in terms of their skills in the areas of consensus and coordination.

On the other hand, parental empowerment often requires therapeutic attention at a deeper level when the couple's relationship is in crisis or when it has endured a strain or break for a prolonged period of time. To the extent that this emotional rupture is influencing—or is influenced by—the adolescent's behavior, it may necessitate therapeutic intervention apart from the conjoint sessions with the adolescent.

Undeniably, many separated and divorced couples are able to effectively agree on and coordinate their parental responsibilities, even while living apart and even when stepparents are involved. Yet in the process of building a working alliance with the parental subsystem, we often find that what is initially defined as an "adolescent problem" is intricately linked with an unresolved dispute, conflict, or crisis in the parents' relationship as a couple.

Uncovering this dynamic, while important, often poses a major challenge to the therapeutic alliance, because in most cases the parents want the therapist to focus on the adolescent and not on their private difficulties. This preference is absolutely legitimate, except when the couple's conflicts are determined to have a negative effect on the adolescent's developmental needs. When the couple is in crisis, it is unlikely that the adolescents in the family are unaffected.

The negative influence on the child can be direct, for example, when parents unduly focus on or even exaggerate the child's problems to avoid their own relational distress, a process called *triangulation* (e.g., Bowen, 1978). Triangulation is often unintentional but can nonetheless be harmful when, for example, a mother disqualifies, confronts, or undermines the father's influence with the adolescent. Even when the parents hide their conflicts from the children, parental C & C are likely to be negatively affected by problems in their relations with one another.

In our experience with adolescents and their families, it often occurs that the adolescent discloses her parents' relationship problems—in an individual therapy session or, less often, with the parents present—before the parents have acknowledged these problems to the therapist or even to themselves. In fact, it is not uncommon for parents to believe that their children had no clue about the crisis in their relationship.

Reciprocity is not inevitable. That is, the couple's and the adolescent's problems do not invariably affect one another. However, uncovering the reciprocity when it does exist is crucial for understanding and eventually helping the family navigate its mutually reinforcing problems.

Innermost Layer: An Attachment Disorder in One or Both Parents Michael was a 14-year-old boy diagnosed with oppositional defiant disorder who had previously been seen in individual psychotherapy for a year with no improvement. His individual therapist recommended conjoint family therapy, to which his mother, Aimee, accepted. She was eager to try any new treatment in hopes of improving her conflicts with Michael, which in recent days had come alarmingly close to violence.

For the past 3 years, Michael had been living with Aimee and her partner, Elaine. Aimee had left Michael's father, Corey, due to the many violent conflicts to which Michael had been exposed.

At the start of family therapy, Michael had no relationship with his father. Explaining the lack of contact, Aimee said, "Michael hates his father and Corey hasn't shown any interest in his son either, no interest whatsoever."

Prior to marrying Corey, Aimee had had a tumultuous relationship when she was very young, which ended with the birth of Grace, now 21. Aimee had no contact with Grace, who lived in a distant city with her paternal grandparents. The distance between them was not the only factor in their estrangement, however. Since her teen years, Grace and Aimee had had a very poor relationship. Apparently, neither was interested in renewing ties with the other.

This is an example of a case in which the therapist needed to navigate the "three layers of the onion." In a first phase, in addition to some individual sessions with Michael, the therapist focused on alliance-empowering strategies to improve the levels of consensus and coordination (C & C) between Aimee and Elaine. The reason for this approach was based on the previous therapist's recommendation to strengthen the parental subsystem as a way to address Michael's acting out.

Unfortunately, the couple sessions resulted in a rupture to the therapeutic alliance along the SHARED PURPOSE dimension, which became evident when Aimee blamed Elaine for continually attacking her and simultaneously complained that she was not being supported or protected by the (male) therapist. In addressing the alliance rupture, the therapist found a way to gently communicate to the couple that their romantic relationship seemed fragile and fraught with conflicts that often directly involved Michael.

As the therapy progressed, the therapist felt thwarted in his attempts to build an alliance around repairing the couple relationship as a way to address Michael's oppositional behavior. Intuiting the many attachment difficulties that Aimee had experienced in her life based on her relationship history, the therapist recognized the basis for the many negative indicators of SAFETY in the couple sessions. These indicators included Aimee's reluctance to make eye contact with Elaine and her angry, defensive posture in the couple sessions. At one point she stormed out of the office in tears.

As a result, the therapist held a series of individual sessions with Aimee that focused on generating more safety and enhancing their emotional bond. Feeling more connected to the therapist as a result of these private sessions, Aimee disclosed her complicated family history, which was strongly affected by her father's chronic alcoholism and a sexual assault that occurred during her adolescence.

By working toward and eventually achieving an excellent therapeutic alliance in the individual work with Aimee, the therapist was able to help her become aware of her limitations in parenting as well as her difficulties maintaining a successful intimate relationship. Specifically, Aimee came to understand that her anxious/avoidant attachment style with romantic partners (and with her two children) was likely due to the trauma she suffered as a child and adolescent. Eventually, Michael's oppositional disorder was better addressed with the family therapist's knowledge of and attention to Aimee's personal limitations.

This example illustrates the complex challenges that therapists face in working systemically with adolescents and disheartened parents. In brief, difficulties in the parental subsystem, or in the individual parent(s), are often connected with difficulties in the childhood and/or adolescence of one or both parents. As in Michael's case, an intergenerational pattern of emotional difficulties is not uncommon in adolescents with oppositional or violent tendencies.

Case Example: What's on Marta's Smartphone?

Marta (14) Guzmán spent the 20 first minutes of her family's initial therapy session in stubborn silence, gazing distractedly out the window and sitting in the chair furthest from the couch where her parents were sitting. Even though the therapist had directed comments and questions to all three family members and had specifically asked Marta for her thoughts on some of her parents' answers, the teen worked hard to maintain her silence (negative EMOTIONAL CONNECTION[1]) and demonstrate a lack of interest in what was being said about her (negative ENGAGEMENT[2]). Her meaning was clear: Participating in therapy was neither her decision nor her intention.

Marta's parents agreed on the reasons that prompted their request for therapy (SHARED PURPOSE[3]): Marta's anxious and excessive use of her smartphone to continuously chat and monitor her various social networks. The parents' consensus and coordination seemed almost perfect. In minute detail they each described how Marta was always attached to her cell phone, so much so that it invariably interfered with the family's activities (particularly meals) and—more importantly—with her studies. The parents also described Marta's highly aggressive response to their attempts to regulate her phone time. They had proposed a plan that would allow her to use the phone for a few hours in the evening but to turn it off an hour before bedtime. As a consequence of refusing to comply, they threatened to monitor Marta's text messages, which only served to enrage her further.

Respecting Marta's apparent desire to say nothing, the therapist made a simple proposal to the parents, one that really caught the adolescent's attention:

---

[1] Client refuses or is reluctant to respond to the therapist.

[2] Client shows indifference about the tasks or process of therapy.

[3] Family members validate each other's point of view.

Therapist: I'd like to suggest that you (parents) try to imagine what is happening in Marta's life "inside" her smartphone. Would you be willing to give it a try? (ENGAGEMENT[4])

Father: You mean what Marta does on her phone?

Therapist: I mean try to figure out, or simply imagine, what kinds of experiences, interactions with others, whatever gives Marta pleasure when she uses her phone.

Mother: Well, I always feel like we are being invaded when she's on the phone, like we've lost all our privacy in our own home.

Therapist: Because of Marta's cell phone? How is that possible?

Mother: Because I know that when we discuss anything at home, she turns around to tell her friends and then makes comments on whatever we're saying or doing. It's as if we have 40 or 50 people in our house at all times. She's just destroying our privacy, our family life.

This comment made Marta squirm in her chair (negative SAFETY[5]). She seemed about to make a retort but decided instead to sit back, brimming with frustration.

Therapist (to Mother)*:* What you just said is very interesting. I think Marta's having a reaction (looking at Marta)…but you say that you "know" that she's discussing your conversations at home on her phone with her friends … Do you KNOW that for a fact, or is this simply your FEAR?

Mother: Well, I'm not sure … Once I checked her phone after I'd punished her by not letting her go to a party. She'd gotten all kinds of texts from her friends about how to make me drop the punishment.

Therapist (to Father)*:* I see that everything on Marta's smartphone makes your wife quite nervous …she feels that whatever is on the phone is interfering with your life… In fact, it seems she finds the instantaneous intrusion of Marta's friends on a daily basis to be very threatening for the family as a whole…. How do you see it? (SHARED PURPOSE[6])

Father: I never thought of it like that. I just think that Marta's life is very exciting—with all her friends, many fun conversations, much social time… I don't know…but it's all through her phone. And the problem is that she doesn't know how to manage it all.

Mother (to Father)*:* Are you saying that our family life is not at all interesting or fun?

---

[4] Therapist asks client(s) whether they are willing to do a specific in-session task.

[5] Client expresses anxiety nonverbally.

[6] Therapist draws attention to clients' shared values, experiences, needs, or feelings.

Surprisingly given the parents' previous apparent accord on the problem, this last comment suggested some frustration, even anguish. The father, apparently deeply affected by his wife's question and tone of voice, did not respond (negative SAFETY[7]). Simultaneously, Marta's expression changed from defensive resistance to sadness. A tear ran down her cheek (SAFETY[8]).

Noting all of these reactions, the therapist proposed that they divide the remaining time in the session so that she could speak privately with Marta and, later on, with her parents (SAFETY[9]). Just as the therapist expected, the three family members seemed to consider this plan with some relief—the stress in the room was becoming unbearable.

Alone with the therapist, Marta had a remarkable change of attitude. She maintained eye contact, and she leaned forward when answering questions (ENGAGEMENT[10]), with no hesitation or reluctance. Starting off, the therapist's objective was to empathize with Marta in terms of how unpleasant it must have been to hear her parents describe her as "addicted" to her phone.

Therapist: I realize that it must be quite unpleasant for you, hearing all your parents had to say about how they see your anxious and obsessive use of the phone—just as we're getting started in our work together. But what do *you* think about what your parents had to say about what's "inside your smartphone?" (EMOTIONAL CONNECTION[11]).

Marta: Thanks. The truth is that it's very hard for me to talk to them. I'm not surprised by what they said. I think my mother is very unhappy and she harasses me about everything I do and what I don't do. Really, I don't know why. I have good grades. It's like she thinks I'm betraying her or abandoning her or something.

Therapist: But in fact, it seems like when you're home you put all your attention on your social life, which is on your phone, right? ... So maybe there's also a bit of *you* abandoning *her*?

Marta: Yes...maybe....The tone between my parents has been very strange the past year. I don't know why, but I try to escape them and hide in my phone. I'm always looking to escape—on my phone. My sister is gone, she's away at college, so I'm by myself with them at home.

Therapist: Do you feel lonely, too?

Marta: Yes, and I think both my parents are very isolated... or they're very busy with work. My mother is always complaining about her loneliness.

---

[7] Client refuses or is reluctant to respond when directly addressed by another family member.

[8] Client shows vulnerability (e.g., cries); client varies her emotional tone.

[9] Therapist asks one client (or a subgroup of clients) to leave the room in order to see one client alone for a portion of the session.

[10] Client leans forward.

[11] Therapist expresses empathy for the client's struggle and normalizes a client's emotional vulnerability.

Evident in this short segment of dialogue, this conversation was a turning point for Marta's ENGAGEMENT in the therapy. She realized that her parents' complaints about her "smartphone addiction" were in some way tied to a sense of loneliness that pervaded the entire family—something Marta had not previously recognized. In response to Marta's positive shift in ENGAGEMENT, the therapist inquired about her social life, her expectations for her future, her leisure interests, etc. and pointed out some activities that they (she and Marta) had in common (EMOTIONAL CONNECTION[12]).

Subsequently, in her time alone with the parents, the therapist asked the mother to expand on her comments about intrusiveness and a lack of privacy caused by Marta's social networking on her phone. While these questions had at their aim to show that the therapist was taking the parents' concerns seriously, her other objective was to find some common ground between the parents. Specifically, she asked them what united them as a family before Marta became a teenager (SHARED PURPOSE[13]). In response, both parents described a family that had been very cohesive and emotionally connected, with a high level of mutual trust. Notably, the mother spoke with a somewhat melancholy tone when describing her image of their earlier family life.

Therapist (to Mother): What is it that you had then as a family that you miss these days? It seems like you need something more from Marta….

Mother: At this stage in our life, my husband works a lot…and our communication…it's just not like it was before. I understand that our oldest daughter is not at home anymore, but I can't stand the fact that Marta is "physically" at home but she's not really "there"—she's not at all communicative with us. We're left alone…Well, this is just what I feel.

Therapist: Could it be that this feeling is actually undermining your effectiveness as parents…in terms of setting limits and handling how you both, and Marta, live together as a family? Maybe this feeling of loneliness is also confusing for Marta?

Father: Well, our relationship is downright bad, not only with Marta. But we want help for her. She has to stop being addicted to her phone, which is causing all her disobedience and lack of respect.

Mother: Yes I agree, but when we're not doing well….when I'm not well with you (turning to Father), I wind up blaming Marta. The truth is we never have a pleasant conversation,

---

[12] Therapist expresses interest in the client apart from the therapeutic discussion at hand; therapist remarks on how his/her experiences are similar to the client's.

[13] Therapist draws attention to clients' shared values, experiences, needs, or feelings.

| | a place where she might want to communicate with us. This is our reality. |
| *Therapist:* | This must be a very harsh reality for you right now. I'd like to help all of you with that—I think you can turn it around (EMOTIONAL CONNECTION[14]). |

In this initial session, the therapist was able to identify a latent conflict within the family, especially within the couple's relationship, that the parents had originally defined as solely Marta's misuse of her smartphone. This reductionist definition of the family stress had pushed Marta into a defensive position that led her to refuse to participate in the therapy. The therapist's approach was alliance empowering by focusing first on SAFETY and then by deliberately working to foster a strong EMOTIONAL CONNECTION, first with the adolescent and then with her parents.

More specifically, the context of SAFETY, primarily developed by having time alone with the therapist, allowed Marta the space to acknowledge her overuse of her phone, but not in a negative or pathological way. Rather, Marta had the space to fully explain what she felt was going on in the family and how it was affecting her, finally recognizing "the emotional escape" she was engaging in by staying on her phone at all hours. Simultaneously, the parents found the courage to begin addressing how their sense of helplessness as parents was tied to a previously unacknowledged crisis in their relations as a couple.

Final Thoughts

Adolescence is merely one transition in the life cycle, a transition that most people face and succeed at without undue trouble. Yet adolescence is also a transition that can complicate relations within an entire family. When complications arise, particularly when an adolescent rejects the offer of therapeutic help, the family can find itself in a precarious position.

As we have described in this chapter, addressing the adolescent's disengagement requires deliberate attention to building and maintaining strong therapeutic alliances with each family member and with the family as a whole. Central to this alliance building process is empowerment through the creation of safety and emotional connections, despite the apparent contradiction of asking for yet rejecting help with comments like "I don't have a problem," "The problem is my parents," or "We've already done everything possible as parents, so obviously the problem is our son."

---

[14] Therapist expresses empathy for the clients' struggle; therapist expresses confidence, trust, or belief in the clients.

References

Bennett, E. D., Le, K., Lindahl, K., Wharton, S., & Weng Mak, T. (2017). Five out of the box techniques for encouraging teenagers to engage in counseling. *Vistas, 2017*: http://www.counseling.org/knowledge-center/vistas

Boggs, S. R., Eyberg, S. M., Edwards, D. L., Rayfield, A., Jacobs, J., Bagner, D., et al. (2004). Outcomes of parent-child interaction therapy: A comparison of treatment completers and study dropouts one to three years later. *Child and Family Behavior Therapy, 26*, 11–22.

Bolton Oetzel, K. B., & Scherer, D. G. (2003). Therapeutic engagement with adolescents in psychotherapy. *Psychotherapy: Theory, Research, Practice, and Training, 40*, 215–225.

Bowen, M. (1978). *Family therapy in clinical practice*. New York, NY: Jason Aronson.

Daly, K. D., & Mallinckrodt, B. (2009). Experienced therapists' approach to psychotherapy for adults with attachment avoidance or attachment anxiety. *Journal of Counseling Psychology, 56*, 549–563.

Diamond, G., Russon, J., & Levy, S. (2016). Attachment-Based Family Therapy: A review of the empirical support. *Family Process, 55*, 595–610.

Diamond, G. M., Diamond, G. S., & Liddle, H. A. (2000). The therapist–parent alliance in family-based therapy for adolescents. *JCLP/In Session: Psychotherapy in Practice, 56*, 1037–1050.

Diamond, G. M., Liddle, H. A., Hogue, A., & Dakof, G. A. (1999). Alliance building interventions with adolescents in family therapy: A process study. *Psychotherapy, 36*, 355–368.

Eyrich-Garg, K. M. (2008). Strategies for engaging adolescent girls at an emergency shelter in a therapeutic relationship: Recommendations from the girls themselves. *Journal of Social Work Practice, 22*, 375–388.

Feder, M. M., & Diamond, G. M. (2016). Parent-therapist alliance and parent attachment promoting behaviour in attachment-based family therapy for suicidal and depressed adolescents. *Journal of Family Therapy, 38*, 82–101.

Frankel, Z., & Levitt, H. (2009). Clients' experiences of disengaged moments in psychotherapy: A grounded theory analysis. *Journal of Contemporary Psychotherapy, 39*, 171–186.

Friedlander, M. L., Escudero, V., & Heatherington, L. (2006). *Therapeutic alliances with couples and families: An empirically-informed guide to practice*. Washington, DC: American Psychological Association.

Friedlander, M. L., Heatherington, L., & Marrs, A. (2000). Responding to blame in family therapy: A narrative/constructionist perspective. *American Journal of Family Therapy, 28*, 133–146.

Friedlander, M. L., Lambert, J. E., & Muñiz de la Peña, C. (2008). A step toward disentangling the alliance/improvement cycle in family therapy. *Journal of Counseling Psychology, 55*, 118–124.

Heatherington, L., Escudero, V., & Friedlander, M. L. (in press). Where systems theory and alliance meet: Relationship and technique in family therapy. In O. Tishby & H. Wiseman (Eds.), *Developing the therapeutic relationship: Integrating case studies, research and practice*. Washington, DC: American Psychological Association.

Heatherington, L., & Friedlander, M. L. (1990). Couple and family psychotherapy alliance scales: Empirical considerations. *Journal of Marital and Family Therapy, 16*, 299–306.

Higham, J., Friedlander, M. L., Escudero, V., & Diamond, G. M. (2012). Engaging reluctant adolescents in family therapy: An exploratory study of in-session processes. *Journal of Family Therapy, 34*, 24–52.

Hogue, A., Dauber, S., Stambaugh, L. F., Cecero, J. J., & Liddle, H. A. (2006). Early therapeutic alliance and treatment outcome in individual and family therapy for adolescent behavior problems. *Journal of Consulting and Clinical Psychology, 74*, 121–129.

https://www.cdc.gov/violenceprevention/pdf/suicide-datasheet-a.pdf.

Jones, V. F. (1980). *Adolescents with behavior problems: Strategies for teaching, counseling, and parent involvement*. Boston: Allyn & Bacon.

Karver, M., Shirk, S., Handelsman, J. B., & Fields, S. (2008). Relationship process in youth psychotherapy: Measuring alliance, alliance-building behaviors, and client involvement. *Journal of Emotional and Behavioral Disorders, 16*, 15–28.

Kessler, R. C., Amminger, G. P., Aguilar-Gaxiola, S., Alonso, J., Lee, S., & Ustun, T. B. (2007). Age of onset of mental disorders: A review of recent literature. *Current Opinion in Psychiatry, 20*, 359–364.

Madsen, W. C. (2007). *Collaborative therapy with multi-stressed families*. New York: Guilford Press.

Muñiz de la Peña, C., Friedlander, M. L., & Escudero, V. (2009). Frequency, severity, and evolution of split family alliances: How observable are they? *Psychotherapy Research, 19*, 133–142.

Muñiz de la Peña, C., Friedlander, M. L., Escudero, V., & Heatherington, L. (2012). How do therapists ally with adolescents in family therapy? An examination of relational control communication in early sessions. *Journal of Counseling Psychology, 59*, 339–351.

Niwa, M., Lee, R. S., Tanaka, T., Okada, K., Kano, S. I., & Sawa, A. (2016). A critical period of vulnerability to adolescent stress: Epigenetic mediators in mesocortical dopaminergic neurons. *Human Molecular Genetics, 25*, 1370–1381.

Pinsof, W. B., & Catherall, D. R. (1986). The integrative psychotherapy alliance: Family, couple and individual therapy scales. *Journal of Marital and Family Therapy, 12*, 137–151.

Raviv, A., Raviv, A., Vago-Gefen, I., & Fink, A. S. (2009). The personal service gap: Factors affecting adolescents' willingness to seek help. *Journal of Adolescence, 32*, 483–499.

Robbins, M. S., Alexander, J. F., Newell, R. M., & Turner, C. W. (1996). The immediate effect of reframing on client attitude in family therapy. *Journal of Family Psychology, 10*, 28–34.

Rogers, L. E., & Escudero, V. (2004). *Relational communication: An interactional perspective to the study of process and form*. London: Lawrence Erlbaum Associates.

Rohrbaugh, M. J. (2014). Old wine in new bottles: Decanting systemic family process research in the era of evidence-based practice. *Family Process, 53*, 434–444.

Santrock, J. W. (2015). *Life-span development* (15th ed.). New York: McGraw-Hill Education.

Shelef, K., Diamond, G. M., Diamond, G. S., & Liddle, H. A. (2005). Adolescent and parent alliance and treatment outcome in multidimensional family therapy. *Journal of Consulting and Clinical Psychology, 73*, 689–698.

Shirk, S. R., & Karver, M. (2003). Prediction of treatment outcome from relationship variables in child and adolescent therapy: A meta-analytic review. *Journal of Consulting and Clinical Psychology, 71*, 452–464.

Sotero, L., Major, S., Escudero, V., & Relvas, A. P. (2016). The therapeutic alliance with involuntary clients: How does it work? *Journal of Family Therapy, 38*, 36–58.

Thompson, S., Bender, K., Lantry, J., & Flynn, P. (2007). Treatment engagement: Building therapeutic alliance in home-based treatment with adolescents and their families. *Contemporary Family Therapy, 29*, 39–55.

Utley, A., & Garza, Y. (2011). The therapeutic use of journaling with adolescents. *Journal of Creativity in Mental Health, 6*, 29–41.

Veach, L. J., & Gladding, S. T. (2007). Using creative group techniques in high schools. *Journal for Specialists in Group Work, 32*, 71–81.

Chapter 4
Parenting in Isolation, Without or With a Partner

There are no problems, only opportunities for growth.

—Jewish Proverb

When Andrea Lockhart began therapy with her sons Gabe (17) and Jonathan (14), the boys were reacting angrily to the loss of their father, who had recently left the family for a woman not much older than Gabe. In an early individual session with the therapist, Andrea disclosed that she felt "let out of jail" since her husband left. He had "fought every effort I made to discipline my sons," apparently preferring his many hobbies—which, Andrea now realized, included infidelity—over his children. "Good riddance!" she exclaimed.

At first Andrea was elated that she now had "full control" of the children. Her errant husband had made it clear that he was starting his life over and had no intention of remaining in contact with Gabe and Jonathan. Although there were financial battles still to be fought, Andrea was certain that her life as a single parent would be infinitely easier. She could raise her boys "by my own standards," no longer needing to cope with their "obstructionist" father who, in her mind, had blocked all of her attempts at discipline, "almost *ruining* my sons." (Note the phrasing: "my" sons.)

After a few months of family therapy, Andrea came to understand the reality of solo parenting. She no longer had an "obstructionist" partner to contend with, but the burden of raising two very angry teenagers alone had settled heavily on her shoulders.

As described in this chapter, the challenge of what we call *parenting in isolation* comes with unique challenges to the family and—consequently—to the therapeutic alliance. Whether the other parent is actively "obstructionist," covertly disparaging (e.g., McHale, 2004), or absent psychologically (Buehler & Pasley, 2000) or in reality, the family therapist must tread cautiously. Like a three-legged stool, the triadic therapeutic system (parent-child(ren)-therapist) can tip over without a great deal of pressure from the outside.

© Springer International Publishing AG 2017
V. Escudero, M.L. Friedlander, *Therapeutic Alliances with Families,*
Focused Issues in Family Therapy, DOI 10.1007/978-3-319-59369-2_4

Unique Challenges

With the changing mores at the end of the twentieth century, more people—mostly, but not only, women—are choosing to become a parent without a partner. These one-family systems come about through solo birthing as well as through adoption. Nowadays many single women who decide to give birth to a child do so by choice, having actively sought out a male donor, who is sometimes a friend or acquaintance. These women's life stories and those of their children differ from the life stories of people who become families through adoption, but solo parenting by either means generally has fewer challenges than solo parenting that results from a parent's death or separation from the family. When separation or death results in a child being raised in a one-parent household, the degree of challenge depends not only on the reason for the parent's absence but also on the child's age, the memory of the absent parent, and the extent to which the remaining parent also experiences a sense of loss or abandonment.

In both circumstances—solo parenting by choice or through loss—the primary issue for the children is attachment. When children grow up never having known or remembering one of their parents, there can be wide variability in how deeply the absence is experienced. A girl adopted by a single adult who keenly feels the absence of a second parent longs for her birth family. A boy whose mother gave birth to him in the absence of a partner has vivid fantasies about his "ghost father." A teenager whose parents separated early in his life feels to blame for his father's absence regardless of his mother's explanation for the divorce.

Circumstances are altogether different when two parents are in the home but one is either uninvolved in parenting or, as Andrea Lockhart saw it, actively "obstructing" the efforts of the other parent. Sometimes the differences in parenting style are due to personality—some people are competitive and others are cooperative in parenting (McHale, 2004) as in other endeavors. Sometimes parenting differences may have less to do with personality and more to do with systemic forces. One or both parents may be attempting to replicate family-of-origin experiences or deliberately trying to avoid repeating those experiences with their children (cf. Bowen, 1978). Alternatively (or additionally), the parents may be reacting to one another in a circular fashion so that eventually their parenting styles become highly polarized: She becomes more lenient with the children in response to his being overbearing, and he becomes more overbearing in response to her leniency.

Sometimes polarized parenting becomes de facto solo parenting when the point of contention is not how to raise the children in general but rather has to do with meeting the needs of a particular child. Perhaps nowhere is parental polarization more apparent than when a child has a minority identity—for example, as gay or transgender, as a student of color in an all-white neighborhood, or as requiring special needs due to a physical disability, a developmental delay, or an emotional, learning, or behavioral disorder. When both parents are united in advocating for their child with people (a teacher) or systems outside the family (a school district), differences in parenting style are less problematic than when parents disagree with one another about how to help their child: Should they medicate the child or not? Should they pay for private schooling or not? Should they support the child's gender nonconformity or not? And so on.

Often the parent who is in favor of special treatment for the child is the one who reaches out for professional help. The other parent may refuse to become involved in the therapy or may attend sessions only under duress. It is also commonplace for the problem child to refuse to engage in the therapy, fearing that doing so could alienate the less involved parent.

In separated/divorced and remarried families, co-parenting effectiveness varies depending on the psychological functioning of each parent (and stepparent) as well as the children's reactivity to the new family configuration. Challenges arise when a child who had never witnessed his parents arguing is blindsided by their decision to separate. Covert disparaging of one parent by another (McHale, 2004) is particularly damaging to everyone involved. Additional challenges arise if a new romantic partner comes into the child's life shortly after the parents separate, particularly if this person is believed to have caused the breakup of the family. Even when the custodial parent waits a long while before bringing a new partner into the home, co-parenting can be difficult if this individual interacts with the children as a peer rather than as another adult whom the children are expected to respect.

When there has been violence in the home, the children are often relieved by the parents' decision to separate yet nonetheless feel an acute sense of loss. Not surprisingly, co-parenting is seriously compromised when one parent accuses the other parent of abusing the children, particularly when sexual abuse is alleged. If abuse is suspected but not proven, a family court may require that visits with the children by the noncustodial parent be supervised by a social service agency. When domestic abuse results in a parent being incarcerated, the challenge is extreme if the children blame the custodial parent for initiating the criminal charges. (See Chap. 5 for a discussion of the challenges in working with cases of child maltreatment.)

When one parent is absent—in reality or in level of involvement with the children—there is a strong pull for the therapist to think, feel, and behave like the absentee parent (Rober, 2012). After all, emotional connection is a crucial element of all therapeutic relationships. When a lonely, desperate parent turns to a therapist for help, it is natural to resonate with that need for attachment—to a fault. Therein lies the unique challenge of working with these kinds of families.

Recommendations from the Literature

One-Parent Families

Salvador Minuchin, creator of the structural approach to family therapy (e.g., Minuchin, 1974; Minuchin & Fishman, 1981), began his career working with overburdened single parents who were raising their children in poverty. Added to the demands of being the sole economic provider for the family is the reality of carrying the full responsibility for bringing up the children. In these circumstances, it is not surprising when the oldest child in the family becomes parentified, a systemic dynamic that may relieve the single parent's burden but in most cases is detrimental to the child's personal development and well-being (Earley & Cushway, 2002). When, in order to relieve pressure on the child, the therapist steps in to fill the void, the short-term relief may be counteracted by the parent's dependency on the therapist and consequent failure to develop a sense of personal agency (Rober, 2012).

Single parents tend to seek therapy either to help their children cope with the loss of the other parent or to obtain help when one or more of the children is experiencing significant problems. When the therapeutic focus is the absent parent, it is not as challenging to build and sustain the alliance as it is when a single parent and child are in conflict with one another (Friedlander, Escudero, & Heatherington, 2006; Friedlander, Lambert, Escudero, & Cragun, 2008). When the parent is strongly convinced that all the problems lie solely within the child, she tends to resist acknowledging the interpersonal aspects of the problem (Coulehan et al., 1998), particularly when her own stressors are exacerbating the child's difficulties (Escudero et al., 2012).

Several studies have notable considerations for practice in a single parenting context. In a qualitative study of problematic within-system alliances (Lambert et al., 2012), one case involved a mother and her two children who began therapy shortly after the father's death. The adolescent son, pressured by the therapist to explain his resistance, finally disclosed that his sole reason for attending the sessions was to support his mother in her grief. Unfortunately, the therapist missed an opportunity to strengthen the family's SHARED SENSE OF PURPOSE by drawing attention to the boy's concern and attachment for his mother. In another qualitative study (Friedlander, Heatherington, Johnson, & Skowron, 1994), one case involved an adolescent boy whose behavior was a particular source of concern for his mother. The son's ENGAGEMENT in the session markedly improved after he acknowledged a fear that his mother would remarry, a disclosure that followed the therapist's focus on the relational impasse between mother and son.

How do skilled family therapists manage problematic alliances like these? Recall the case study with Rosa and Ms. M described in Chap. 1 (Escudero et al., 2012). In that case, a severe alliance rupture was apparent. First, the therapist attended to SAFETY by asking Ms. M to leave the room briefly in order to check on his connection with the adolescent daughter, Rosa. When she returned, the therapist used many CONNECTION and SHARED PURPOSE interventions to help Ms. M. acknowledge that her "stress" was negatively affecting Rosa's functioning as well as the mother-daughter relationship. In another case (Friedlander et al., 2008), an African-American teenage boy and his single father were constantly arguing about the boy's externalizing behavior and noncompliance. In one session, the therapist encouraged the father to tell his son about his own experience of racism, which was similar to what the boy was going through in his predominantly white high school. By encouraging a more compassionate father-son dialogue focused on their similar experiences (SHARED PURPOSE), the therapist intervened in a way that was visibly meaningful for the teenager.

Notably, research suggests that the quality of a client's alliance with the therapist differs for parents and children (Friedlander, Escudero, Heatherington, & Diamond, 2011). In a sample of mostly one-parent families headed by mothers, for example, the adolescents' alliances (on the SOFTA-s) were positively associated with their perceptions of a session's depth or value, but the parents tended to see their children's high alliance sessions as less valuable, perhaps out of a concern that the therapist was too caught up in the teenager's perspective (Friedlander, Kivlighan, & Shaffer, 2012). Indeed, the prevalence of split (e.g., Muñiz de la Peña, Friedlander, & Escudero, 2009) or unbalanced parent-child alliances (e.g., Robbins et al., 2006) underscores the delicate balancing act that is needed to keep both parents and children engaged in the therapy so as to prevent dropout and facilitate meaningful systemic change.

Two-Parent Families

Compared with the substantial literature on co-parenting with divorced and remarried couples, little has been written about parenting in isolation, that is, when two parents live in the home but only one parent is actively involved with the children. Although numerous studies attest to the negative effects of parental noninvolvement on children's school achievement, there seems to be wide variability in the effects on children when only one parent is meaningfully engaged in the children's lives. In fact, one study found no association between child adjustment, as rated by the mother, and the father's psychological presence in the home as rated by the child (Buehler & Pasley, 2000).

In couple therapy, parenting often takes a back seat to other issues when working therapeutically with high-conflict couples, despite the well-established relationship between parental conflict and child adjustment. Notably, the effects on children are most pronounced when the conflicts center on the children's behavior and when the couple's arguments are intense, frequent, violent, and unresolved (Beach, 2016). When the conflict is related to depression in one of the parents, children tend to suffer even more (Cummings, Goeke-Morey, & Papp, 2016).

The literature on therapy with high-conflict, divorced families consistently points to the importance of creating a SHARED SENSE OF PURPOSE, or within-couple alliance, by putting the children's welfare above the individual interests of the parents (e.g., Bernstein, 2007; Blow & Daniel, 2002). As Bernstein put it, divorced parents need to work together to restructure a new, extended family by reducing "accusatory suffering" and "self-defeating spite" in order to build "good fences" and "good bridges" (p. 67).

Alliance research with high-conflict couples underscores the importance of creating SAFETY and motivating the parents to overcome their relational stalemate. For instance, in a qualitative study comparing families that were or were not able to move from disengagement with each other to engagement in a specific session (Friedlander et al., 1994), the therapists in two of the successful cases enhanced SAFETY by excusing the children from the room while they focused on the couples' motivation for co-parenting despite their differences.

More recently, in a case study with a high-conflict couple (Blow et al., 2009), the therapist's focus on the couple's shared concern for their daughter was seen as instrumental. Speaking with the couple about their parenting conflicts, the therapist reframed their adversarial positions, a SHARED PURPOSE intervention: "You may have different solutions, but you both want the same thing for your child" (p. 362).

In yet another case study (Friedlander, Lee, Shaffer, & Cabrera, 2014), an estranged couple sought therapy with their adolescent daughter after the mother had left the family "temporarily" to live with another man. Although the father earnestly wanted his wife to return to the family, even taking responsibility for having chronically neglected her, she adamantly refused to focus on the couple relationship in the therapy. Rather, the only problem which both parents agreed to discuss was their daughter's intense anger. Focusing on this concern (to build a SHARED SENSE OF PURPOSE), the therapist used many EMOTIONAL CONNECTION interventions to convey empathy for each parent's individual struggle with the ambiguous situation. Simultaneously, the therapist helped the daughter voice her feelings about the breakup of the family and her belief that the boyfriend had "stolen" her mother. Throughout the process, the therapist helped each family member speak authentically to the others and created SAFETY by removing the daughter from discussions of her parents' relationship. Notably, the therapist remained neutral about the mother's behavior and the couple's incompatible goals for their marriage, instead enhancing the parents' SHARED SENSE OF PURPOSE by pointing out similarities in their attachment needs and concerns for their daughter's welfare.

After the mother-daughter relationship had notably improved, the family sessions ended, and the couple continued working with the therapist to discuss the future of their marriage. Their decision to do so may have been prompted by the relational improvements the couple experienced in the family therapy context. That is, it seemed that the parents came to trust the therapist to help them resolve their ambiguous marital situation without blame. In the end, the couple therapy resulted in the spouses' reconciliation (Friedlander et al., 2014).

Alliance Empowering Strategies

The various theory-based approaches to family therapy focus on challenging emotional and behavior disorders in children and adolescents, such as drug abuse (Brief Strategic Family Therapy; Szapocznik & Williams, 2000; and Multidimensional Family Therapy; Liddle, 2010), conduct disorders and delinquency (Functional Family Therapy; Sexton, 2011), major depression (Attachment Based Family Therapy; Diamond, Diamond, & Levy, 2014), and anorexia nervosa (the Maudsley family approach; Rhodes, 2013). A similar goal underlies all of these manualized treatments: Parents need to work collaboratively to set limits yet be emotionally available to their children. Although single parents tend to be over-represented in the target populations of these varied approaches, the treatment manuals vary in the extent to which they attend to issues of family structure.

Moreover, evidence-based approaches vary in the degree to which the therapeutic alliance is a specific focus of treatment versus a "given" that enhances the therapy's general effectiveness. That is, although a strong alliance, or "joining" with the family (Szapocznik & Williams, 2000) is seen as a necessary component in these therapies (e.g., Diamond et al., 2014), typically less attention is paid to the specific solo parenting challenges we have been describing in this chapter. Rather, there seems to be the assumption that these approaches will "work" regardless of differences in family structure and degree of parental involvement. Since the therapeutic alliance is a factor common across therapies, the alliance-empowering strategies described below, which differ somewhat for one- and two-parent families, can be used with any of the many evidence-based approaches to family treatment.

Flying Solo: Families with a Physically Absent Parent

As discussed earlier, therapy with one-parent families differs depending on whether the issue at hand concerns problems with the child(ren) or focuses on reactions to a parent's absence. These families also differ based on their referral status as voluntary or mandated. More often than not, single parents who are having significant difficulties tend to be referred by the school, social services, or the criminal justice system, whereas parents who want to help their children grieve the loss of the other parent tend to be self-referred. In these and other self-referred cases, the children's behavior problems don't rise to the level of a *disorder* but rather reflect relational conflicts with the single parent, due either to developmental changes in the child or to problems adjusting to the new family configuration.

In all cases of solo parenting, as in virtually all conjoint therapy, SAFETY is the first concern. Sometimes the parent is so relieved to find an empathic listener in the therapist that she discloses disparaging information about the absent parent that is not appropriate and is highly disturbing for the children to overhear. The therapist can circumvent this problem by seeing the parent alone in the first session to set a boundary around appropriate topics for discussion when the children are present. Interviewing the parent alone also promotes ENGAGEMENT and EMOTIONAL CONNECTION, which may forestall a split alliance when the children join the therapeutic system in a later session. For similar reasons, it may be beneficial to interview the children individually or as a sibling group, depending on their age and capacity to benefit from an individual session.

As an example, in her first session alone with the therapist, Carmen Fernández revealed that her husband, Hector, had been incarcerated for the past 6 months after having beaten her regularly in front of their four children. Carmen blamed herself for Hector's violence, seeing deference to her husband even in the face of abuse as upholding the Latino value *marianismo* (cf. Edelson, Hokoda, & Ramos-Lira, 2007). Now that Hector was gone, the oldest child, Pedro (13), was intensely angry at his mother, and the three younger children were acting out.

In exploring Carmen's experience further, the therapist learned that despite her marianismo values, she decided to initiate criminal proceedings against her husband. Doing so, however, challenged another marianismo value, a mother's spiritual duty to keep the family together. Her personal conflict about this decision was being enacted in daily fights with her son Pedro.

Based on the family's history and Carmen's emotional isolation, the male therapist was aware that his gender might complicate his relationship with the family. For this reason, he chose to focus first on repairing the mother-son relationship, which had been sorely strained since the father's absence. To enhance SAFETY, the therapist saw Pedro alone for a session to listen to his anger toward his mother and, in doing so, create a strong EMOTIONAL CONNECTION with him and secure his ENGAGEMENT in the therapy. The next few sessions were held with Carmen and Pedro together, focused on the SHARED PURPOSE of repairing their relationship. The younger children were invited to participate in the therapy only after mother and son had the opportunity to freely and fully discuss their feelings about the father's violence and subsequent incarceration.

By handling the case in this way, the therapist avoided the pitfall of stepping into the shoes of the absentee father (cf. Rober, 2012), which would have undermined Carmen's parental authority with her children and encourage her to become unduly dependent on the therapist. Whereas attending to his EMOTIONAL CONNECTION with both mother and son in their individual sessions was essential, the therapist used more influential alliance strategies, first to assess and ensure SAFETY and then to use SHARED SENSE OF PURPOSE interventions to foster a more authentic, trusting relationship between mother and son and empower Carmen as the new head of household.

Also Flying Solo: Families with a Psychologically Absent Parent

In Jason Stuart's first therapy session, he began by describing the back story. He loved his wife, Mary Alice, but when they married, she was adamant that she didn't want children. Originally on board with this decision, Jason eventually started to feel a strong pull toward fatherhood. The couple finally agreed to have one child, with Jason having "full responsibility" for the child's care so that Mary Alice could be free to pursue her dream career in advertising. Now, however, their 19-year-old son, Todd, was addicted to heroin, living on the streets. It was only a matter of time before he was arrested—he'd stolen money not only from his parents but also from his former employer. Mary Alice, not one to mince words, had told Jason that Todd was "*your* problem, pure and simple."

Like most parents, Mary Alice loved her son. Unlike most psychologically absent parents, however, she had intentionally and decisively removed herself from child-rearing even before the boy was born. More often, a parent's psychological absence comes about as the other parent gradually assumes more and more of the childcare responsibilities, until the less involved parent has little or no say over the children's upbringing. Sometimes this parent, finding the home situation barely tolerable, loses himself in work, in alcohol, in golf, or in a new romantic partner. Often the marriage ends, but just as often the couple's relationship limps along, lifeless.

In these kinds of families, the need for psychological help becomes apparent when a crisis arises, usually due to a child's internalizing or externalizing behavior. Not surprisingly, usually only the involved parent comes to the first appointment, making some excuse for the other parent's inability to attend the session: "She's too busy at work" or "He'll go along with whatever I decide to do" or "He would only make it worse, since he never backs me up with the children."

Regardless of the kind of justification, the therapist's initial objective is to try to involve the (psychologically) absent parent in the therapy—ideally, when the first appointment is made by phone. Sometimes the referring parent promises to "try" to involve the absent parent, but "trying" doesn't facilitate success.

When the more involved parent—the mother, for example—comes alone to the first session, usually excusing the other parent's failure to attend, the therapist should accept the excuse at face value (so as not to doom the therapy from its beginning). To make an EMOTIONAL CONNECTION, the therapist can hear her complaints, empathize with her struggle to "do it all alone," and ENGAGE her in the initial goal of involving the absent parent "just to support you during this difficult time in your child's life." Even if the solo parent is unconsciously invested in keeping the other parent well away from "her" children, confronting this investment early on is unlikely to be successful. Rather, a more workable strategy involves helping her see that sharing the burden of responsibility with the psychologically absent parent "even a little bit" would likely be to her advantage.

This conversation should not take place in front of the children, however, since drawing attention to the absent parent's lack of emotional involvement can be incredibly hurtful. Indeed, the children may decide to resist the therapy so as not to further alienate the uninvolved parent. To maximize SAFETY, the children should be excused from the end of the session when the therapist proposes the objective of engaging the uninvolved parent in the treatment plan.

Often, the absent parent will agree to one session as a "consultant" to the therapist. By using ENGAGEMENT and CONNECTION interventions and asking him to provide an "important understanding" of the problem child "from your own perspective," the therapist can often set the groundwork for a SHARED SENSE OF PURPOSE—not with the goal of improving the couple's relationship but rather "to work together to help your child get back on track." The therapeutic outcome is likely to be most favorable if a strong within-couple alliance helps the absent parent become more meaningfully involved in the child's life, not only in terms of discipline but, more importantly, in terms of emotional attachment and responsiveness.

When, however, the psychologically absent parent refuses to attend even one session (usually claiming work responsibilities), other steps can be taken to achieve some measure of involvement. The therapist can call or write the absent parent, using CONNECTION strategies to empower him to take a more active role with the children. A home visit is often helpful, since reluctant parents tend to experience more SAFETY at home than in a therapist's office. And SAFETY is the key to ENGAGEMENT.

If all of these attempts fail, the only alternative may be to engage the uninvolved parent in absentia, that is, by guiding the solo parent to encourage the other parent to take a meaningful role in the child's life. If the solo parent comes to see that the one-sided parenting dynamic is contributing to the children's difficulties, she may well be receptive to the idea of actively facilitating her partner's involvement with the children. As is the case for any behavior change, the therapist should direct the solo parent to refrain from blame and accusations in favor of encouraging, supporting, and suggesting readily achievable small behavior changes (e.g., "you could take him out for ice cream").

Family systems therapists (e.g., Bowen, 1978; Minuchin, 1974) put forward the paradoxical notion that an intense focus on a problem child actually stabilizes the family by allowing the parents to avoid confronting serious problems in their relationship—problems that could lead the relationship to deteriorate further. For this reason, therapists working with these kinds of challenging cases need to be vigilant of their alliances with each individual, even the ones who refuse to attend the therapy. (These non-clients usually hear about the therapy process from the participating family members and, depending on their power in the family, can either support or diminish the therapist's influence.) Working with different family constellations at various times can often prevent seriously split alliances and maintain a focus on the family's SHARED SENSE OF PURPOSE, namely, for the family "to get back on track."

While a worthwhile objective is to rebalance the parenting responsibilities, this goal may be too far out of reach for some families. Rather, the prime objective is to help the problem child (to reduce her behavior problems, face her fears, recover from substance abuse, and so on) through a joint parenting effort. Even if the less involved parent reverts to psychological absence when the crisis is past, the family now has a blueprint for collaborative parenting if and when another serious problem arises.

Case Example: The Wong Family

Mei-Lin Wong (age 39) sounded panicked when she called for an initial appointment. She'd been referred by her son's pediatrician, who had insisted that she "consult a therapist." Her son Han (13), who had Down's syndrome, had been sent home from school after groping another boy's testicles in the cafeteria. On the phone, Mei-Lin indicated that she had to see the therapist alone since her husband, Jiang, was away on business for 2 weeks and she couldn't wait that long to be seen.

The therapist offered Mei-Lin an appointment, making it clear that she expected Jiang to join the therapy at a future date. In the first session, Mei-Lin explained that she and Jiang had come to the USA from China as graduate students 17 years previously. Like Jiang, she worked full-time in the corporate world, but Mei-Lin had sole responsibility for Han's care and schooling. She explained that when Han was born, Jiang was distraught to discover that their newborn son had Down's syndrome. In fact, no one in Jiang's company even knew he had a child, and Mei-Lin suspected that Jiang had told his parents that Han died at birth.

For many years, Mei-Lin had had no contact with her in-laws because she refused to go along with Jiang's plan to return to China in order to build his parents a new home. The traditional Chinese arrangement, in which the daughter-in-law cares for her aged in-laws, in no way appealed to Mei-Lin, who much preferred the western way of life.

Mei-Lin's sister, a 24-year-old medical student, lived nearby and helped Mei-Lin out with childcare. Jiang had little to do with his son, and Mei-Lin never pushed him to do so, respecting the rigid gender roles in Asian family life (Kim, Atkinson, & Umemoto, 2001). Han was a happy, loving child whose joy in living more than made up for Mei-Lin's stale marriage. She explained to the therapist that she and Jiang had made a bargain when Han was born: He wouldn't insist that she return to China, and she wouldn't insist that he be involved in their child's care. After all, she said, "In the old Chinese way, fathers leave all the parenting to the mothers."

In her first session alone with Mei-Lin, the therapist quickly discovered that this overburdened mother was eager to tell her story (ENGAGEMENT[1]) and felt comfortable doing so (SAFETY[2]). The session was characterized by the therapist's use of EMOTIONAL CONNECTION,[3] as she empathized with Mei-Lin's sense of isolation and mentioned that like Mei-Lin, she too was a "working mother." Sensing that Mei-Lin was touched by this similarity, the therapist set the stage for facilitating a within-couple alliance by floating the suggestion that one goal for their conjoint work might be to "encourage Jiang to take a more active role in joint parenting." Mei-Lin, clearly skeptical about Jiang's willingness to become involved with Han, nonetheless agreed with this objective (ENGAGEMENT[4]).

The therapist, aware that Asian clients tend to prefer a directive approach and defer to therapists as authority figures (Kim et al., 2001), called Jiang and invited him to the next appointment alone, "just to consult about Han's difficulties." In point of fact, the individual session was held so that the therapist could make a CONNECTION with Jiang in order to enhance his willingness to attend future conjoint sessions with Mei-Lin.

Knowing that Jiang was reluctant to attend the session, the therapist began by discussing the confidentiality of the "consultation," assuring him that his employer

---

[1] Client introduces a problem for discussion and leans forward.

[2] Client varies his/her emotional tone during the session.

[3] Therapist expresses empathy for the client's struggle and remarks on how her values or experiences are similar to the client's.

[4] Client indicates agreement with the therapist's goals.

would not be informed about the appointment and acknowledging that "it's hard to discuss very private matters with someone outside the family" (SAFETY[5]). As the session progressed, Jiang appeared to be more comfortable, eventually making eye contact with the therapist and responding to questions with less reluctance (suggesting greater SAFETY). Discussing the presenting problem, Jiang made it clear that he saw his son as an "embarrassment" and that Han's "homosexual inclination" was one more source of shame. Jiang further explained that the boy's "inclination" was no doubt "acceptable to his mother" because she "wanted nothing more than to be an American feminist."

Perhaps emboldened by the therapist's willingness to hear him out, Jiang also aired his feelings toward Mei-Lin, who "doesn't behave like a good wife." Careful not to imply that the marriage would be the focus of their conjoint work, the therapist normalized the couple's difficulties (CONNECTION), by saying that in her experience, "having a special needs child tends to put a strain on most couples."

As the individual session wound down, the therapist firmly asserted that Mei-Lin needed Jiang's help, "as father to son, to keep Han from acting on his sexual impulses inappropriately." The therapist knew that since Jiang saw his son's behavior as shameful, this was the only goal that was likely to motivate him to become more involved in parenting.

The therapist ended the session by handing Jiang photocopies of three psychology articles on how to teach developmentally delayed adolescents about sexuality: "Please tell me what you think about these articles when we meet with your wife next week. I'm looking forward to hearing your thoughts on the articles." Jiang agreed to do so (ENGAGEMENT[6]), as this request spoke to his strengths and did not require him to interact with his son.

The first couple session was devoted to enhancing SAFETY and SHARED SENSE OF PURPOSE. Mei-Lin seemed surprised that her husband was more ENGAGED and relaxed (SAFETY) than she had anticipated, especially when he spontaneously described the value of the reading he'd done at the therapist's suggestion (ENGAGEMENT[7]). Perhaps encouraged by Jiang's attitude, Mei-Lin took a risk (SAFETY[8]) by asking him if he blamed her for Han's disability.

This sensitive issue was one that the couple had never before discussed. Jiang was silent, looking uncomfortable (negative SAFETY[9] and SHARED PURPOSE[10]). To reduce the tension and promote CONNECTION,[11] the therapist interjected that Mei-Lin's worry was a common one for mothers of disabled children and praised

---

[5] Therapist provides structure and guidelines for safety and confidentiality; therapist acknowledges that therapy involves taking risks or discussing private matters.

[6] Client agrees to do homework assignments.

[7] Client indicates having done homework or seeing it as useful.

[8] Client directly asks another family member for feedback about his/her behavior.

[9] Client expresses anxiety nonverbally.

[10] Family members avoid eye contact with each other.

[11] Therapist reassures or normalizes a client's emotional vulnerability.

her for being "brave enough" to ask Jiang what he really thought (SAFETY[12] and ENGAGEMENT[13]). Taking this cue, Jiang directed his next remark to the therapist, saying that no, he didn't blame his wife. When Mei-Lin teared up, the therapist suggested that Jiang hand her a tissue (the tissue box was closer to him; SHARED PURPOSE[14]), which he did (ENGAGEMENT[15]). In doing so, Jiang made a tangible (but not intimate) overture to his wife in her distress.

In the remainder of the session, the therapist made several SHARED PURPOSE[16] interventions, for example, commenting that both parents were "embarrassed" about their son's sexual behavior at school and upset about how Han's teacher had handled the situation. As the session ended, Jiang spontaneously suggested that he wanted to talk with Han "as father to son" about his sexual urges (ENGAGEMENT[17]). When the therapist enthusiastically supported this "plan," Mei-Lin looked skeptical but remained silent. The therapist suggested that, for her part, Mei-Lin search for an online support group for parents of teens with Down's syndrome, which she agreed to do (ENGAGEMENT[18]).

Jiang was "too busy at work" to come to the next two appointments. Mei-Lin used this time alone with the therapist to air her frustration with Jiang, who apparently had not followed through on his plan to speak with Han. Reframing, the therapist empathized with Mei-Lin's "disappointment" (CONNECTION[19]) but encouraged her to be patient, pointing out that Jiang was more engaged in their joint session than Mei-Lin had originally anticipated.

During the second couple session, Jiang told the therapist that 2 weeks previously he'd "done my homework" (ENGAGEMENT[20]) by talking with Han about "how boys should and shouldn't behave when they have certain feelings." The therapist complimented Jiang (ENGAGEMENT[21]) on having followed through with his plan. However, before Jiang could respond, Mei-Lin angrily asked him, "So why didn't you tell me you'd talked to him? I had no idea!"

Here was a therapeutic land mine. Mei-Lin's outburst revealed the depth of the couple's relational problem, but allowing the conversation to move in that direction would diminish Jiang as both father and husband. Rather, relying on her strong bond with Mei-Lin, the therapist stepped in to reduce blame (SAFETY[22]) by asking her to recall the primary therapy goal: "Mei-Lin, I'm sure Jiang now realizes you'd have liked him to tell you about his talk with Han, but I also know that you've been

---

[12] Therapist helps clients to talk truthfully and not defensively with each other.

[13] Therapist praises client motivation for engagement or change.

[14] Therapist encourages clients to show caring, concern, and support for each other.

[15] Client complies with the therapist's request for an enactment.

[16] Therapist draws attention to clients' shared feelings.

[17] Client describes a plan for improving the situation.

[18] Client agrees to do homework assignment.

[19] Therapist expresses empathy for the client's struggle.

[20] Client indicates having done the homework or seeing it as useful.

[21] Therapist notes that a positive change has taken place.

[22] Therapist actively protests one-family member from another (e.g., blame).

wanting Jiang to help you out with this delicate problem by talking to Han as only a father can." Mei-Lin, quieter now, responded simply, "I guess so."

Although clearly peeved as Jiang continued to ignore her, Mei-Lin regained her composure. Noting this change, the therapist directed Jiang to ask Mei-Lin what she thought about his having spoken with Han (SHARED PURPOSE[23]). He did so, albeit reluctantly (ENGAGEMENT[24]). Seeing Jiang's discomfort but aware that he was in fact making an effort, Mei-Lin said, "I'm glad you talked with him…I am. He really needs you."

At this point, sensing that Mei-Lin might follow up by blaming Jiang for his typical lack of involvement with Han, the therapist intervened quickly: "You two are working together now as parents (ENGAGEMENT[25]). Each of you has something very valuable and unique to offer your son (SHARED PURPOSE[26]). I feel confident that you'll get through this difficult period of his life" (ENGAGEMENT[27]).

In the termination session, Mei-Lin and Jiang were visibly more relaxed with one another, even laughing together (SHARED PURPOSE[28]) as they told the therapist about something Han had done that amused them both. While the marital problems—deep seated, culturally bound, and of long duration—were not addressed in this therapy, Jiang and Mei-Lin were able to make some important joint decisions about their son's future.

As the session closed, Jiang expressed gratitude to the therapist for her "guidance." She acknowledged the remark with a smile and pointed out that she was "delighted to see you two working together to be the best possible parents for Han."

Final Thoughts

As challenging as it is to work with isolated parents—those who have a partner in the home as well as those whose partners are really absent—the attachments between parent and child(ren) tend to be very strong. When parents can acknowledge the benefits of solo parenting (not having to negotiate decisions around parenting with anyone else) as well as the costs (having to shoulder the full burden of those decisions), they are more likely to seek and accept support from others. The ultimate therapeutic goal is to mobilize the solo parent's resources to obtain the needed support from people and systems other than the therapist. After all, family therapy is meant to be a stopgap measure, not a lifetime sentence.

---

[23] Therapist encourages clients to ask each other for their perspective.

[24] Client complies with therapist's request for an enactment.

[25] Therapist notes that a positive change has taken place.

[26] Therapist draws attention to clients' shared values, experiences, needs, or feelings.

[27] Therapist expresses optimism.

[28] Family members share a lighthearted moment with each other.

References

Beach, S. R. H. (2016). Expanding the study of dyadic conflict: The potential role of self-evaluation maintenance processes. In A. Booth, A. C. Crouter, M. L. Clements, & T. Boone-Holliday (Eds.), *Couples in conflict* (pp. 83–94). New York: Routledge.

Bernstein, A. C. (2007). Re-visioning, restructuring, and reconciliation: Clinical practice with complex postdivorce families. *Family Process, 46*, 67–78.

Blow, A. J., Morrison, N. C., Tamaren, K., Wright, K., Schaafsma, M., & Nadaud, A. (2009). Change processes in couple therapy: An intensive case analysis of one couple using a common factors lens. *Journal of Marital and Family Therapy, 35*, 350–368.

Blow, K., & Daniel, G. (2002). Frozen narratives? Post-divorce processes and contact disputes. *Journal of Family Therapy, 24*, 85–103.

Bowen, M. (1978). *Family therapy in clinical practice*. New York: Jason Aronson.

Buehler, C., & Pasley, K. (2000). Family boundary ambiguity, marital status, and child adjustment. *The Journal of Early Adolescence, 20*, 281–309.

Coulehan, R., Friedlander, M. L., & Heatherington, L. (1998). Transforming narratives: A change event in constructivist family therapy. *Family Process, 37*, 17–33.

Cummings, E. M., Goeke-Morey, M. C., & Papp, L. M. (2016). Couple conflict, children, and families: It's not just you and me, babe. In I. A. Booth, A. C. Crouter, M. L. Clements, & T. Boone-Holliday (Eds.), *Couples in conflict* (pp. 117–147). New York: Routledge.

Diamond, G. S., Diamond, G. M., & Levy, S. A. (2014). *Attachment Based Family Therapy for depressed adolescents*. Washington, DC: American Psychological Association.

Earley, L., & Cushway, D. (2002). The parentified child. *Clinical Child Psychology and Psychiatry, 7*, 163–178.

Edelson, M. G., Hokoda, A., & Ramos-Lira, L. (2007). Differences in effects of domestic violence between Latina and non-Latina women. *Journal of Family Violence, 22*, 1–10.

Escudero, V., Boogmans, E., Loots, G., & Friedlander, M.L. (2012). Alliance rupture and repair in conjoint family therapy: An exploratory study. *Psychotherapy, 49*, 26–37.

Friedlander, M. L., Escudero, V., & Heatherington, L. (2006). *Therapeutic alliances with couples and families: An empirically-informed guide to practice*. Washington, DC: American Psychological Association.

Friedlander, M. L., Escudero, V., Heatherington, L., & Diamond, G. M. (2011). Alliance in couple and family therapy. *Psychotherapy, 48*, 25–33.

Friedlander, M. L., Heatherington, L., Johnson, B., & Skowron, E. A. (1994). "Sustaining engagement": A change event in family therapy. *Journal of Counseling Psychology, 41*, 438–448.

Friedlander, M. L., Kivlighan, D. M., & Shaffer, K. (2012). Exploring actor-partner interdependence in family therapy: Whose view (parent or adolescent) best predicts treatment progress? *Journal of Counseling Psychology, 59*, 168–175.

Friedlander, M. L., Lambert, J. E., Escudero, V., & Cragun, C. (2008). How do therapists enhance family alliances? Sequential analyses of therapist → client behavior in two contrasting cases. *Psychotherapy: Theory, Research, Practice, Training, 45*, 75–87.

Friedlander, M. L., Lee, H. H., Shaffer, K. S., & Cabrera, P. (2014). Negotiating therapeutic alliances with a family at impasse: An evidence-based case study. *Psychotherapy, 51*, 41–52.

Kim, B. S., Atkinson, D. R., & Umemoto, D. (2001). Asian cultural values and the counseling process: Current knowledge and directions for future research. *The Counseling Psychologist, 29*, 570–603.

Lambert, J. E., Skinner, A., & Friedlander, M. L. (2012). Problematic within-family alliances in conjoint family therapy: A close look at five cases. *Journal of Marital and Family Therapy, 38*, 417–428.

Liddle, H. (2010). Multidimensional Family Therapy: A science-based treatment system. *Australia and New Zealand Journal of Family Therapy, 31*, 133–148.

McHale, J. P. (2004). Overt and covert parenting processes in the family. *Family Process, 36*, 183–201.

Minuchin, S. (1974). *Families and family therapy*. Cambridge, MA: Harvard University Press.

Minuchin, S., & Fishman, C. (1981). *Techniques of family therapy*. Cambridge, MA: Harvard University Press.

Muñiz de la Peña, C., Friedlander, M. L., & Escudero, V. (2009). Frequency, severity, and evolution of split family alliances: How observable are they? *Psychotherapy Research, 19*, 133–142.

Rhodes, P. (2013). The Maudsley model of family therapy for children and adolescents with anorexia nervosa: Theory, clinical practice, and empirical support. *Australian and New Zealand Journal of Family Therapy, 24*, 191–198.

Robbins, M. S., Liddle, H. A., Turner, C. W., Dakof, G. A., Alexander, J. F., & Kogan, S. M. (2006). Adolescent and parent therapeutic alliances as predictors of dropout in Multidimensional Family Therapy. *Journal of Family Psychology, 20*, 108–116.

Rober, P. (2012). The single-parent family and the family therapist: About invitations and positioning. *The Australian and New Zealand Journal of Family Therapy, 31*, 221–231.

Sexton, T. L. (2011). *Functional Family Therapy: An evidence-based treatment model for working with troubled adolescents*. New York: Routledge.

Szapocznik, J., & Williams, R. A. (2000). Brief Strategic Family Therapy: Twenty-five years of interplay among theory, research and practice in adolescent behavior problems and drug abuse. *Clinical Child and Family Psychology Review, 3*, 117–134.

Chapter 5
Child Maltreatment: Creating Therapeutic Alliances with Survivors of Relational Trauma

The mind replays what the heart can't delete.

—Bob Marley

A major challenge to the therapeutic relationship occurs when a child who experienced maltreatment at the hands of a caregiver has virtually no trust in adults. In cases of abuse, abandonment, and severe neglect, the mere offer of psychotherapy—or any other type of help or care—is enough to elicit the child's fear, shame, and even terror.

In this chapter, we discuss alliance empowerment strategies for working with families who experienced relational trauma (Sheinberg & True, 2008). Specifically, we describe strategies for creating a therapeutic environment conducive to the healing process. In our experience, safety and a strong personal bond with the therapist are essential for helping especially fearful children accept care, affection, and protection from the non-abusive parent or other caregivers (extended family member, foster, or adoptive parent).

Undoubtedly, therapists feel a strong responsibility to help people, especially children, when their physical and emotional security has been fractured or violated. Family therapists tend to be quite aware of the complexity involved in working with children who were attacked or sexually abused by family members or who witnessed violence against their parents. Often enough, therapists also see children whose families suffered other kinds of trauma, such as a high-conflict divorce, the sudden death of a parent (e.g., by accident or suicide), severe social isolation, alcoholism, or other substance dependence.

In the following discussion of child maltreatment, we refer to all of these circumstances, despite their obvious differences. We also refer to what Van der Kolk (2005) described as *developmental trauma disorder*, i.e., a child's prolonged exposure to interpersonal trauma, including abandonment and betrayal as well as witnessing intimate partner violence. The term *disorder* refers to the fact that chronic exposure to trauma has predictable effects on many aspects of a child's functioning.

In a general sense, when we speak of *psychological trauma*, we are referring to (a) exposure to a dangerous or potentially dangerous event that posed a real threat to life or to a person's psychological integrity or (b) exposure to the serious harm or

© Springer International Publishing AG 2017
V. Escudero, M.L. Friedlander, *Therapeutic Alliances with Families*,
Focused Issues in Family Therapy, DOI 10.1007/978-3-319-59369-2_5

possible death of someone close with whom the person identifies. We consider the response to be *traumatic* when the event or situation generated fear and an inability to exercise control. In the case of minor children, traumatic responses tend to be expressed behaviorally by extreme disorganization, explosiveness, and/or oscillations between evasiveness and aggression. Other common reactions include confusion, disorientation, and dissociation (Van der Kolk, 2005, 2014).

In all kinds of traumatic situations, family therapists encounter similar difficulties establishing a strong therapeutic relationship with the youth, as well as with the caregivers involved in the child's support network. Common to these cases are the cognitive, emotional, and physical effects of trauma on the individual survivor and a loss of confidence in relating to others. The latter effect can be varied. Some survivors develop a reactive attachment disorder. Others only lose trust in the abusive caregivers. Still others lose trust in anyone who offers them affection or intimacy.

Obviously as a context of care, psychotherapy is likely to provoke attachment fears in maltreated children. For family therapists, it is even more challenging to conduct conjoint sessions with the child survivor and her protective (or potentially protective) caregiver.

How can a favorable alliance develop in these types of cases? The answer is simple to understand but difficult to carry out. A poor alliance can exacerbate the child's traumatic response, particularly when social services and the judicial process are involved or when forensic psychological evaluations are mandatory. On the other hand, a positive alliance is curative in itself. A strong emotional bond can provide the traumatized child with a corrective emotional experience (Castonguay & Hill, 2011), a kind of bridge between the child's bond with the therapist and her bond with the non-abusive caregiver.

Undoubtedly, therapists working with these kinds of families feel a huge responsibility. If the therapy is not carefully managed, the child's suffering can greatly increase.

Unique Challenges

The Therapist Is Threatening to Love (aka *Take Care of) Me*

Effective therapy with maltreated children does not require a recall and description of the abusive experiences. Rather, being allied with the child involves creating a caring, supportive relationship and nurturing his collaboration in healing.

For children, collaboration requires trusting an adult whose job is to help. Trust is not a commodity for maltreated children, however. For this reason, we cannot lose sight of the potential for harm due to the emotionally charged nature of psychotherapy.

Simply experiencing a therapeutic relationship of caring concern can remind traumatized children of their vulnerability, which then generates a negative emotional response. Therapists need to be prepared to face this apparently contradictory situation, as it is not uncommon for maltreated children to react defensively to the offer of therapeutic support or to the therapist as a person. In extreme cases, simply showing up for therapy can heighten a child's fear responses.

The Vicious Cycle of Emotion Management Difficulties and Negative Identity

Figure 5.1 schematically represents the cyclical emotional processes that a child who has suffered relational trauma needs to manage, beginning with intense anxiety about the adverse experiences and resulting in a negative sense of personal identity. By *manage*, we mean identifying various feelings and expressing them to others—a necessary first step in the recovery process. For children, the ability to manage emotions depends on the availability and safety of caregivers who can detect, recognize, and respond appropriately to volatile affective states.

Anger and Fear In working individually or in conjoint family sessions with maltreated children, it is easy to detect two emotion management difficulties provoked by the context of therapy: anger and fear. The natural response to any threatening

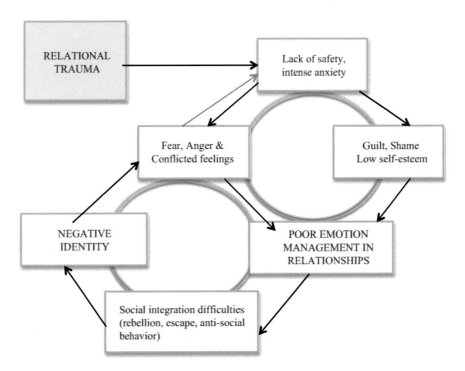

Fig. 5.1 The vicious cycle of emotion management difficulties in relational trauma

situation is to defend against intense fear with hostility or rage. Children generally express their anger with aggressiveness, sometimes in explosive reactions to caregivers. At other times children display a plaintive or manipulative attitude, or they become highly demanding and critical of others.

Fear prompts a desire to escape, to find any way possible to relieve the intense anxiety aroused by the threatening situation. From a psychobiological point of view (Van der Kolk, 2014), a fear response to relational trauma serves a basic survival function: People want to escape when they feel highly unsafe. Although a client's evasiveness is more palatable for the therapist than aggressiveness, particularly when it takes the form of superficial or pseudo-collaboration, it is important to understand that the child is trying to postpone or transform the anguish that he feels incapable of managing.

Consequently, in building alliances with traumatized children, therapists need to recognize hostility, rejection, avoidance, and defensiveness as adaptive. In the context of relational trauma in particular, anger and fear are fully understandable when personal relationships that should have been caring and affectionate were instead disappointing, frustrating, and threatening.

Guilt, Self-Blame, and Shame Paradoxically, children who experienced unsafe relationships with adults or traumatic experiences of abandonment, neglect, and abuse often blame themselves for these experiences. In the case of sexual abuse, children can interpret their natural bodily responses to physical manipulation or penetration as having desired the abuse, even having caused it. Self-blame is reinforced when the perpetrator accuses the child of having "wanted it." Moreover, by blaming herself for the abuse, the child reasons that somehow she can win her parents' love and protection.

In the therapeutic relationship, guilt and shame can block the personal connection that is so important for healing. Therapists find it painful to witness guilt in children who survived severe maltreatment at the hands of their parent(s). After all, the child was not valued, protected, or treated with care and respect in the parental relationship, which society identifies as a loving one. The logic behind these children's self-blame and low self-esteem seems to be, "If I'm not getting the attention and affection I need, there must be other things that are more important for my parents, so this means I'm not valuable at all" (Escudero, 2013).

Conflicted Feelings It seems paradoxical that for some maltreated children, the intense need to be loved causes them to be highly protective of their narcissistic, abusive parents. In therapy, it is not unusual to see maltreated children who staunchly justify the excesses and unpredictable behavior of their parents, even when the neglect or abuse resulted in severe suffering.

These conflicted feelings can be particularly challenging when the therapist is trying to build a strong personal relationship with the child. The challenge is especially poignant when the child admits to being very hurt, even providing details about the parents' abusive actions, yet still behaves in a protective manner toward them.

Countertransference is common among therapists working with maltreated children who actively protect an abusive parent. Solid training and supervision are needed to understand the very natural feelings of being frustrated with a seriously maltreated child who refuses to hold his parents accountable. Essentially, therapists need to understand that the child's contradictory behavior is due to a lack of safety at home.

Here, then, is how the *vicious cycle of emotion management* takes hold. Fear and anxiety expressed as anger or avoidance, overlaid by feelings of guilt, self-blame, and shame, bode poorly for the child's ability to establish and manage close relationships with others. The therapeutic relationship is no exception. Unable to let herself be comforted, the child sees the therapeutic context as just one more place where she is a failure, and this sense of failure reinforces and amplifies her guilt, frustration, and self-blame. With the heightening of conflicted feelings, the child increases her self-protective stance against any personal relationship suggestive of attachment, care, and concern.

Essentially, then, the challenge for the therapist is to avoid engaging in this vicious emotional cycle. Rather, what is required is to provide the child with enough safety, caring, and respect to create a "virtuous cycle" of attachment.

Negative Identity Emotional safety, or secure attachment, is the platform that allows children to build a cohesive identity or positive sense of self. Undoubtedly, adolescence is the most critical period in the life cycle for this process to take hold. However, when an adolescent's emotional safety has been compromised in a traumatic way within the family, identity development also tends to break down.

As discussed in Chap. 3, emotional safety at home is crucial for a teenager's developing sense of identity. Adolescence is a time of transition, when peer relationships tend to become more important than parental relationships. For the first time, adolescents look outside the home to meet their needs for belonging, sharing, and loyalty. As they age, their identity is continually shaped and reshaped by how peers see and respond to them. Experiencing romantic feelings for the first time is another natural part of this life stage. Inevitably, romance and sexual activity come with a price—insecurity abounds, along with privacy concerns and acute self-consciousness.

When difficulties managing emotions begin interfering with an adolescent's social relationships, it is understandable—even adaptive—for him to search for peers who share the same fears and conflicts. Unfortunately, this search can result in marginality, rebellion, or social isolation. Moreover, the adolescent's difficulties in establishing meaningful peer relationships can carry over into other areas of functioning.

Often the problems first arise in school. Since completing an education is the main developmental task of adolescents, school failure and behavior problems in the classroom are not uncommon for traumatized teens. Further complications arise when school administrators contact judicial officials about an adolescent's risk behaviors, particularly antisocial acts and illicit drug use.

When a traumatized adolescent is referred for therapy, it is generally because some adult is "complaining" about her behavior. Not surprisingly, she adopts a defensive position. Acting out her negative identity, she may present as "bad," oppositional, or unafraid of risk—the person others fear. Defying authority and social norms, she may present as having no need for any adult, particularly not a therapist. Or she may present as vulnerable, victimized, weak, and helpless. Behavior indicative of uncaring, distancing, isolation, or disengagement are also common. Unlike younger children, adolescents risk developing an entrenched negative identity when they respond poorly to the offer of professional help.

In short, it is particularly challenging to work with adolescents whose reaction to relational trauma is to engage in highly problematic behavior. However, in the context of a life history marked by abandonment or abuse, behavior that seems highly dysfunctional is actually adaptive. In other words, the seemingly problematic behavior reflects the adolescent's whole way of being, his identity so to speak—all he can do or all he knows what to do—to express who he is in the world.

Sadly, a negative identity tends to generate more problems and fails to help the adolescent manage her peer relationships. In this way, the vicious cycle of negative identity is perpetuated.

To address the cycle, therapists can talk with the adolescent about the "character" she has created for herself. Showing appreciation for that character, even acknowledging all the character's shortcomings and the negative interpretations made by other people, can prompt a more authentic therapeutic encounter.

The Challenge of Betrayal and Abandonment

One of the most poignant consequences of relational trauma (Sheimberg & True, 2008) is the sense of betrayal felt by minors whose most important adult figures hurt or left them due to addiction, incarceration, or dramatic conflict. When working with these children, it is crucial to understand how feelings of betrayal or abandonment tend to affect the therapeutic relationship.

How can therapists show these children that they are trustworthy? More to the point, can therapists ever be seen as trustworthy when they are required to report on the mandated treatment to outside agencies or other professionals? In the context of a referral from child protective services, it is difficult for the therapeutic relationship to avoid being threatened by third-party reporting procedures, forensic evaluations and judgments, or other kinds of judicial controls, such as when supervised visits with a child in residential care are allowed only after the parent has "successfully" completed psychotherapy.

Accountability and loyalty are essential for building a strong therapeutic alliance with these kinds of families. Young children, as well as adolescents (and sometimes their caregivers), often start off by testing the therapist. Obviously, it is neither constructive nor pleasant for the therapist to be faced with a loyalty test, but it is understandable. Clients need to be certain that the therapist will not re-traumatize them with more betrayal or abandonment.

Family Role Confusion

Role confusion is a primary characteristic of families that suffered relational trauma, especially families that are experiencing other ongoing adversities in their lives. In the family literature (e.g., Johnston, 1990), the term *role reversal* is used to describe frightened or inconsistent parents who use their children as caretakers. Such role reversals often occur in divorce or when the parents have a chronic addiction or mental health disorder. The parent with a disorganized attachment style can produce serious emotional damage in the child who tries in vain to be close.

In many cases, confusion of family roles results from a transgenerational transmission of trauma. In other words, parents who suffered relational trauma in their own family of origin tend to be emotionally insecure, unstable, or narcissistic (Miller, 1981). Due to their social isolation and inhibition in personal relationships, these parents behave in such a helpless or incompetent way that their children feel obliged to take on a caregiver role.

In therapeutic relationships with these kinds of families, we often find that the children are unable to accept help for themselves. Sometimes these children see themselves as their parent's therapist. Not surprisingly, this kind of over-functioning is not adaptive for the child—or for the parent.

Role Confusion with Other Professionals

Sometimes confusion about family roles is reflected in a family's confusion about the roles of various professionals in their lives. When child abuse or neglect is involved, the therapeutic system tends to be broader and thus more complex than merely family + psychotherapist. Families tend to feel confused and frustrated when multiple professional "helpers" have a stake in the outcome of the therapy, which is typical in cases of maltreatment or severe neglect. Perversely, adults as well as children tend to experience the same lack of control and structure in the professional system as they do in the family system.

Not surprisingly, a complex system of helpers can threaten the safety of the therapeutic context for vulnerable families. One source of difficulty is confusion over the function of different professionals (probation officers, judges, child protective workers, etc.). It is understandably difficult for families to sort out the authoritative control exercised by representatives of the social system versus the caring support offered by the therapist. Unfortunately, the natural wariness and passive compliance that these families tend to exhibit with the authorities can wind up "contaminating" their relationships with therapists.

In cases of severe neglect, many therapy sessions are usually needed before a family feels safe with the therapist. Despite clear and specific explanations about what can and cannot be done in therapy (e.g., return children to the parental home) and about the family's rights in the mandated therapy context, confusion often prevails. In successful cases, however, family members begin to trust that the therapist is working in their best interest within the limits imposed by the authorities.

The Obstructive Non-Offending Parent or Caregiver

Up to this point, we have been focusing on the experience of a child who suffered abuse or maltreatment at the hands of a parent figure. While it is challenging to create safety and trust with these children, it is often no less challenging to create a strong alliance with the non-offending parent or caregiver. In fact, many of the same challenges we find in working with maltreated children (conflicted feelings, role confusion, and the like) also take hold in our attempts to engage the adult who remains in the child's life. Obstruction is particularly likely when the non-offending parent minimizes or denies the extent or seriousness of the offending parent's abuse or is threatened by the child's trust in the therapist.

To address this kind of obstruction therapeutically, it helps to understand the non-offending parent's personal history. In many cases, the mother who accompanies her child to therapy has suffered her own adversity or trauma. Often she was victimized in the same way as her child. All too typical are mothers who, like their daughters, endured sexual abuse at the hands of male relatives. In other cases, the non-offending parent had an alcoholic mother or father who was full of rage, unpredictable, and violent. Imagine the courage it takes for a mother to recognize that her children have suffered the same excesses from their father, the man she married, as she did from her own father.

Perhaps the greatest obstruction in conjoint therapy with a traumatized child and her non-abusive parent is the "big wall" between them. Often the emotional barrier is huge and seemingly unsurmountable. Communication is distorted, if it exists at all, in the therapy as well as at home.

Of course, the quality of the parent-child relationship differs depending on the situation. Consider, for example, a child whose mother was also victimized by the violent father versus a child whose parents failed to protect him from his older brother's abuse. Emotional neglect is altogether different. A child can be re-traumatized by a foster parent or family caregiver (aunt, grandparent) who is too caught up in her own personal struggles to attend to the vulnerable child in her care.

Despite the specific circumstances in each case of relational trauma, therapists tend to encounter the same big wall—the challenge of (re-)establishing communication between the traumatized child and her non-offending parent or caregiver. Only by facilitating meaningful communication can the parent figure be counted on to help in the child's healing process.

This difficulty is not merely an inconvenience for the therapy. Rather, communication barriers usually reflect the deep emotional suffering and isolation felt by both child and parent. For this reason, "breaking down the wall" slowly and carefully is a therapeutic goal in itself.

Denial and Dissociation

In Chaps. 3 and 4, we discussed challenges that arise when a client begins therapy by stating, "I don't have a problem," "The problem is my child," "I will ... but s/he won't come to therapy," and so on. What all of these situations have in common is the client's difficulty recognizing a problem or situation that requires professional help. In therapy with survivors of relational trauma, however, denial is more entrenched due to the very nature of the client's emotional difficulties. For this reason, the key to building a therapeutic relationship with traumatized clients lies in understanding the psychological processes of denial and dissociation.

Denial and dissociation were first identified by psychoanalysts as unconscious *defense mechanisms* that protect people from recognizing traumatic experiences. These defenses can seriously distort a person's mental representation of events and his ability to interpret those events.

Denial can persist even when a person is made aware of what took place by others who participated in or witnessed the traumatic event. Thus it is understandable that when being asked to recognize the extent of maltreatment and the accompanying thoughts and feelings, parents as well as children are likely to engage in denial. When the trauma was experienced at home, denial can have a particularly strong negative influence on the client's willingness to engage in therapy. After all, to accept that a relational experience was "traumatic" is to accept the fact that one's family was abusive. Even when a client accepts professional assistance and sees the therapist as a safe and concerned person, denial can block progress and cause ruptures to the alliance.

Dissociation is essentially a distortion of denial. It is common for clients who experienced relational trauma to recognize that the abuse or other maltreatment occurred but nonetheless to be completely out of touch with the feelings accompanying these experiences. Dissociation is less likely when a specific, recent event has occurred, such as a parent's suicide or discovery of the sexual molestation of a child, but is more likely when the traumatic experience is continuous or repeated and secretive. In cases like these, dissociation is a survival mechanism, with the unfortunate effect that the therapeutic relationship is seen as extremely threatening.

In conjoint family work, denial and dissociation can take many forms. Sometimes family members deny that anything abusive happened, or they deny the event's extreme nature or its consequences. Alternately, denial may be the result of alcohol or chemical dependence, making it difficult a person to recognize a situation for what it is. Denial may also be due to guilt, which is understandable when parents are pressured to acknowledge that their children's suffering was caused by their own actions or neglect.

Therapists are often surprised to find that dissociation causes the perceptions, thoughts, and feelings associated with trauma to become completely cut off from awareness. When this occurs, a child might interact with her parents in a natural way, as if no abuse had ever occurred. Dissociation may become evident, however, when the child is faced with a stressor that unconsciously reminds her of the original trauma, such as when a girl whose father "lovingly" molested her is touched on the shoulder by the therapist in parting. Her overreaction to this gesture was triggered by the original, dissociated molestation experience.

The therapeutic process is even more hampered by dissociation when a traumatized child enters treatment in good spirits and talks with ease about himself. This response to therapy does not indicate that the child is meaningfully engaged in treatment. All too often the opposite is the case. When therapy threatens a dissociative defense, the child is likely to refuse to come for future appointments.

Recommendations from the Literature

Family Reattachment

Although there has been no published research specifically on how to build alliances with maltreated children and their families, one empirically supported approach, Attachment-Based Family Therapy (ABFT; Diamond, Diamond, & Levy, 2014), relies heavily on creating strong alliances with family members. ABFT was developed to treat depressed and suicidal adolescents whose parents are neglectful, abusive, or emotionally unavailable due to relationship conflict, divorce, or other significant life stressors.

Specifically, the first ABFT family session is used to reframe the adolescent's depression as due to the lack of a consistent parental figure to whom she can turn for support and help with her depression. Subsequently, the therapist sees the adolescent alone for one or more sessions to explore the ruptured parent-child bond. In private sessions, the parent is coached on how to listen to the adolescent's complaints without defensiveness or judgment. Finally, during the *reattachment* phase of ABFT, adolescent and parent are brought together for conjoint sessions, during which the adolescent is helped to express her sense of isolation and feelings of rejection or betrayal by the parent(s). Ideally, the parent responds to this disclosure with patience, acceptance, and empathy. With the therapist's help, a stronger within-family bond is the desired outcome, which is the first step toward recovery.

Success with the ABFT strategy of separating parent and child for individual work relies heavily on the creation of safety, trust, and strong personal bonds with each subsystem. Essentially, the parent-child reattachment phase is a strengthening of the within-family alliance or, in SOFTA terms, a Shared Sense of Purpose within the Family. In the context of a strong SHARED PURPOSE, the therapist can help family members work together to help the adolescent manage her turbulent emotions and get her life back on track.

Focus on Family Resilience

It is all too easy to lose sight of the fact that neglect and abuse often occur in families that have multiple problems, are highly stressed, and have few resources or social supports. Walsh (2017) wrote that in "resilience-oriented practice" (p. 313), therapists need to focus maltreating families on possibilities rather than on problems. Possibilities offer options, whereas fault finding can backfire, as shown in this case vignette:

> Crystal, age 14, was referred for therapy following her second attempt to run away from home. The therapist learned that she had been sexually abused by her grandfather when she was younger and just recently by her mother's boyfriend, Rick. Her mother had ended that relationship after the incident, but Crystal angrily blamed her for not having protected her. The therapist, intending to be supportive, joined in faulting the mother, only to find that after the session Crystal took a handful of pills in a suicide attempt. (Walsh, 2017, p. 313)

The Concept of "Both-And"

According to Sheinberg (1992), it is critically important for therapists to help children and other family members explore and acknowledge their multiple, often contradictory feelings without being obliged to privilege one feeling over the other. In the book *Relational Trauma of Incest*, Sheinberg and Fraenkel (2001) described the "both-and" strategy as a therapeutic alternative to "either-or" dichotomous thinking, which does not adequately reflect the complex feelings experienced by victims of abuse and neglect.

Unfortunately, before entering treatment, abused children and their parents are typically pressured by forensic evaluators to narrate a story of good and evil. Of course, this pressure reflects the officials' well-meaning attempt to help the abused child, her siblings, and custodial parent take a united position against the offender. However, in order to create safety and a strong bond with a traumatized child, therapists need to approach the family in a different, more complex fashion. While it is absolutely necessary to take a clear, strong position against the maltreatment, therapists nevertheless need to accept the fact that family members who have suffered relational trauma often express conflicting thoughts and emotions about the experience, even denial, particularly early on in the therapy process.

As an example, consider the case of 14-year-old Subrina, who had an infant son as a result of being raped by her uncle. Social services placed Subrina in residential care when her parents abandoned her for denouncing the uncle (even though he confessed to the crime and DNA evidence proved that he had fathered the baby).

Subrina began therapy shortly after her uncle's incarceration. She experienced a tremendous sense of loss, which she felt whenever happy memories of her childhood came to mind or when she found herself missing her parents and siblings. At the same time, she clearly knew that it was her uncle's actions, not her own, that made her lose her close-knit family. Subrina had no doubt that what he had done to her was "bad." She worried that her uncle might have also molested her cousins. Alternately she felt terror and betrayal, as well as hurt, sadness, guilt, shame, and rage.

Subrina was helped in therapy by being validated for her "both-and" feelings. Through the therapist's unconditional acceptance and validation, Subrina worked through this confusing and turbulent phase of her life, eventually coming to a different, more positive view of herself and her new reality. Amazingly, she faced up to the challenge of being a mother, which meant forfeiting a normal adolescence due to the great harm inflicted on her by her own family.

Sharing Control

The treatment model developed by Sheinberg and colleagues (Sheinberg & Fraenkel, 2001; Sheimberg & True, 2008; Sheinberg, True, & Fraenkel, 1994) contains several recommendations for aligning with traumatized families. Two techniques in this model, the *decision dialogue* and *talking about talking*, are particularly congruent with the SOFTA's "Safety first" (Friedlander, Escudero, & Heatherington, 2006) recommendation and alliance empowerment through Emotional Connection.

Simply put, the decision dialogue refers to a private conversation between therapist and child during which they decide together (1) what should and should not be shared with family members and (2) whether the child or therapist should be the one to make the agreed-upon disclosures. The second point is important since many abused children cannot even imagine telling their parents about the trauma experience or the extent of their suffering. By empowering the child to decide how and what she wants to communicate to her parents, the therapist is essentially sharing control of the treatment.

Decision dialogues also involve exploring the child's fears about the disclosure process. Central to this process is the therapist's guarantee that she will not take action or make recommendations to the family without the child's prior agreement and preparation. Sharing control in this way is likely to be a novel and welcome experience for any child or adolescent who was subjected to abuse or neglect by adults.

These dialogues should take place recursively, that is, the child's concerns are communicated to the parents, whose response informs future conversations with the child and others, as needed (Sheimberg & True, 2008). Having private sessions with a child is indicated whenever he is reluctant to participate in conjoint family sessions due to feeling intimidated or ashamed, as indicated by a reluctance or refusal to make eye contact, or by highly protective behavior toward the parents. All of these behaviors are SOFTA indicators of a lack of Safety, which in any context might prompt an individual session with a child.

The other strategy, *talking about talking*, occurs in conjoint family sessions when the therapist identifies a need to have individual sessions with the child.

Talking about talking goes beyond identifying this need; rather, it is a collective decision with the family about the importance of private sessions and when and how they should proceed. Essentially, the talking about talking strategy is designed to strengthen the family's Shared Sense of Purpose.

In short, sharing control with the child and the family system is a critical aspect of the healing process in cases of relational trauma. Throughout, the therapist should emphasize that (1) his role is to help the child say as much to her parents as she feels she comfortably can and (2) the objective of the individual sessions is to explore what the child wants to communicate directly to her parents and when and how she prefers to do so.

Contain and Switch

Rivett and Street (2009) described two specific interventions for managing a trauma-tized child's extreme emotions in a conjoint family session: *contain* and *switch*. First, *contain* refers to helping the child express her feelings while also paying attention to other family members' difficulty hearing these feelings. It is advisable to explain to the family that expressing and listening to painful feelings is a necessary step in the healing process (Rivett & Street, 2009). Second, *switch* refers to changing the subject or changing the approach in order to relieve tension when emotions are running high. Several SAFETY interventions in the SOFTA model reflect the switching technique: *therapist changes the topic to something pleasurable or non-anxiety arousing when there seems to be tension or anxiety* and *therapist asks one client (or a subgroup of clients) to leave the room in order to see one client alone for a portion of the session.*

Alliance-Empowering Strategies

Four Threats to Safety

Safety, a precondition for effective therapeutic work in virtually all contexts—and particularly important with challenging couple and family cases—has specific implications for work with survivors of relational trauma. In these cases, safety tends to be threatened on four interlocking levels, each of which needs to be handled carefully in order to build and sustain solid alliances with all participants in the therapy (see Fig. 5.2).

At the first level, relational trauma threatens safety within the person or *intraper-sonal safety*. Essentially, this kind of trauma is experienced as a break in a person's safe base. As discussed earlier, at a psychological level, extreme lack of safety causes denial and dissociation. To address this threat, therapists should hold individual sessions and use decision dialogues with child survivors of trauma. From the

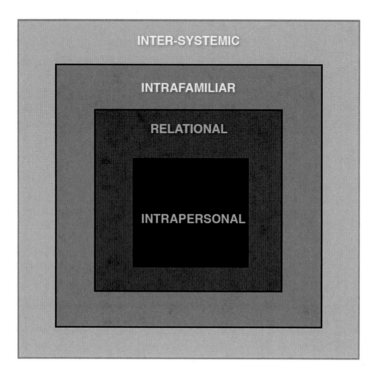

Fig. 5.2 Four interlocking safety threats experienced by maltreated youth

perspective of SOFTA, these sessions provide the space to generate an authentic emotional connection between child and therapist that can gradually facilitate engagement with other family members and, if necessary, with important professionals in the child's life, such as teachers, coaches, or religious leaders.

At the second level, relational trauma threatens safety in the child's social relationships, including the alliance with the therapist. We call this level *relational safety*. As noted earlier, the therapeutic relationship does not escape the serious challenges that survivors face in any personal relationship. When extreme resistance is evident, it is crucial to tread lightly. The therapist needs to avoid challenging the child to face the adversities and suffering caused by the trauma.

Safety at this level can be increased when the child sees the therapist as someone like herself. Although research on matching client and therapist demographic characteristics (gender, race/ethnicity, and so on) is not conclusive (e.g., Flaskerud, 1990), age is impossible to match when the client is a child. For this reason, when assigning therapists to cases, it is important to attend to any characteristics that *can* be matched, such as gender, religion, or cultural background. More important still is for the therapist to try to match the child's communication style, for example, as animated or as reserved and cautious.

The third safety level, *intrafamilial,* has to do with what we described earlier as the *big wall* between the maltreated child and the non-abusive parent or caregiver.

Several SOFTA indicators clearly reveal this wall, such as the child's reluctance or refusal to respond or make eye contact when directly addressed by another family member. To reduce this threat, therapists should use safety-specific interventions during separate sessions with the child and parent, such as providing structure and guidelines around confidentiality and pointing out that effective therapy involves taking emotional risks. In private sessions, the therapist needs to refrain the non-offending parent from trying to convince the child that the abuse did take place, since this attempt to break through the denial is misguided and likely to fail.

The fourth safety level has to do with the complex professional network that usually surrounds cases of relational trauma. We call this level *inter-systemic safety*. Not only the parents but also the child is affected by the authority and power that other professionals (educators, social services, probation officers, etc.) hold over their lives. For this reason, alliance empowerment involves facilitating the child's or the family's positive relationship with these other professionals. For example, the therapist can help a foster child prepare for an upcoming interview with a caseworker or help a parent write a letter explaining the family situation to the school psychologist.

To prevent an alliance rupture, the therapist should openly share all his communications, coordination of services, and initiatives with the network should be shared openly with the family. In other words, family members can only feel protected by the therapist if he frankly explains and clarifies all aspects of his communication with the other professionals or agencies that have authority over the family.

How should therapists manage the various safety threats? Which level should be prioritized? Is there a particular path to follow in order to build a safe therapeutic system? The four safety threats are interlocked, so that a shift in any level can positively or negatively influence a client's safety at any of the other levels.

Generally, it is preferable to focus first on the intrapersonal level in order to set the stage for a strong alliance and a productive therapeutic process at the second, relational level. However, it may not always be wise—or possible—to begin at the innermost level, depending on the characteristics of the case. By assessing the threat indicators at each of the four levels, the therapist can determine the safest first step for the child or family.

In many cases, the therapist can address the intrafamilial threat to safety by, for example, setting ground rules for the therapy (e.g., no screaming or physical contact in the session) or by interspersing conjoint sessions with individual ones for the most vulnerable member of the family. When a family's previous experience with social services or family court was negative or problematic, the therapist should work at the intersystemic level by clarifying the limits of confidentiality and promising transparency about his communications with officials and other professionals. In other words, although we recommend addressing intrapersonal safety first due to its potential impact on safety at the other three levels, therapists need to intervene at any level when a specific threat to safety is of concern to the family.

Optimally, therapeutic work at one safety level facilitates safety at another level. At the intrapersonal level, by not confronting a child's denial of abuse, the therapist promotes relational safety. Relational safety is also enhanced when the therapist is able to reduce inter-systemic threat by, for example, negotiating with social services to extend the parents' probationary period. Similarly, by containing hostile family interactions, the therapist enhances the child's intrapersonal safety.

Emotional Connection Cannot Be Prescribed

Although creating personal connections with clients is a particularly important aspect of the alliance in work with survivors of relational trauma, the emotional bond is not guaranteed, nor can it be prescribed. What are the practical implications of this limitation? Essentially, the therapist needs to adopt a humble and cautious attitude about the traumatized child's emotional response to him. While it is important to convey a sense of optimism about their work together, the therapist should not allow his own high expectations to discourage him. Rather, it is important to appreciate small, positive shifts in the traumatized child's bond and persevere even in the face of denial and dissociation.

In short, it is the maltreated child who will decide whether or not to accept the personal bond offered by the therapist. Similarly, the child is the one to decide whether she will engage emotionally with foster parents or with teachers and counselors in a residential setting. The therapist's challenge is an internal one: to recognize and accept the realistic difficulty of gaining the child's trust.

Nonetheless, much therapeutic work can be done to enhance the alliance, as long as the therapist monitors his own zealousness. Trust is established in therapeutic relationships just as it is between people in any other relationship—through accessibility, reliability, sensitive responses to bids for psychological comfort, and conversations that do not prompt emotional flooding.

Tread Lightly

Since difficulty in managing emotions is a major consequence of relational trauma and since working with emotions is an important aspect of therapeutic work with survivors, how this work is carried out invariably affects and is affected by the therapeutic alliance.

As a general guideline, the therapist must closely monitor the child's expression of emotions. In the SOFTA model, ignoring signs that a client is feeling vulnerable due to some intense emotion like frustration, anger, sadness, or fear can seriously compromise the alliance (e.g., the negative SAFETY indicator *therapist does not attend to overt expressions of client vulnerability, e.g., crying, defensiveness*). In contrast, reassuring or normalizing intense emotion and vulnerability contributes to a strong bond with the child, as long as the reassurance is not at the expense of other family members' sense of safety.

When a child expresses intense feelings in a conjoint session, such as harsh blame or rage toward a parent, the therapist can change the topic to something less anxiety provoking or invite the child to be seen alone in order to vent her feelings privately. Indeed, the most productive work with emotions often takes place in the child's individual sessions, where outbursts are less likely to hinder the family's healing process.

Therapists need to be sensitive to the consequences of emotional reactivity, by paying close attention to the safety of every participant in the session. After an emotionally intense moment has passed, the therapist should initiate a conversation about the meaning and impact of that moment on each family member by asking, for example, "What phrase or words that your mother used made you feel like crying just now?" and "Can you find a word to describe your reaction to your daughter's comment?"

Adapt to the Client's Attachment Style

Throughout this chapter we have emphasized that a client's difficulties in relationships invariably affect the therapeutic relationship, even more so in the context of relational trauma. It is also important to point out that ignoring the very real relationship difficulties of traumatized families can lead the therapist to make erroneous negative attributions about the clients' behavior. In other words, therapists should not give into pessimism when working with these families. It is particularly important to stay optimistic with the maltreated child and remain open to his bids for attachment.

Nonetheless, it is necessary to adjust one's expectations for emotional connection according to each child's characteristic attachment style. A disorganized attachment style tends to be associated with extreme relational trauma, neglect, and adversity. Children with this characteristic style are likely to feel highly threatened in therapy. They indicate their discomfort by, for example, avoiding eye contact, sitting with a closed posture, refusing to engage, or storming out of the room (all of which are negative SAFETY indicators). On the other hand, some highly disorganized children and adolescents minimize their problems or cooperate superficially.

For children with extreme attachment difficulties, playfulness and humor are particularly helpful for enhancing emotional connections. However, the main objective in working with these children is to reduce their fear of rejection or abandonment by staying "centered" and demonstrating a consistent level of care and concern.

Children with an anxious-ambivalent attachment style also demonstrate fluctuations in their response to the therapist. Typically, they show enthusiasm about the help they are receiving at some moments and, at other moments, demonstrate a clear disregard for the therapist by, for example, commenting on her incompetence or lack of skill or by initiating hostile or sarcastic interactions (negative CONNECTION indicators). Other ambivalent children express their anxiety nonverbally or make uneasy comments about some aspect of the therapy (recording equipment, one-way mirror, questionnaires, and the like). Generally, anxious-ambivalent attachment shows up not only when the child experiences the therapeutic interaction positively but also when she experiences the interaction as unsafe or threatening. With these children as well, the therapist needs to be a constant, stable presence by resisting the tendency to react to the child's inconsistent or challenging behavior.

Particularly when the child's attitude or behavior suggests an avoidant attachment style, the therapist has to closely monitor her expressions of care so as to avoid flooding. That is, the therapist needs to titrate her emotional distance so that any communications of interest or concern do not remind the child of the trauma she endured at the hands of another seemingly caring adult.

Avoid Amplifying Denial

Denial of problems or the need for therapy can occur regardless of the nature of a client's problems. However, in therapeutic work with maltreated children, we must not lose sight of the function of denial, which is to help people survive in situations of high threat. Since children, in particular, tend to experience profound psychological damage as a result of relational trauma (van der Kolk, 2014), their denial is highly adaptive.

Therefore, the first guideline for building a strong alliance with these children is to avoid any intervention that might amplify the traumatic response of denial. To maximize safety, the therapist should not confront the denial by insisting that the child (or the non-offending parent) acknowledge the abuse. Nor should the therapist request details about the traumatic events in the child's history or confront the family with evidence of the abuse. Further, the therapist should postpone any mandated interventions or requirements until the family is fully prepared for them.

All of these guidelines refer to what should *not* be done. So, what *should* be done? First and foremost, the therapist should intervene in any way that defuses the four threats to safety discussed earlier. Next, she should work toward enhancing strong personal connections with each family member, which will then allow her to—delicately—make change-oriented interventions focused on the child's emotion management and negative identity. Interventions like the decision dialogue have a dual function: promoting safety (so that the child knows she will not be pressured to share everything with her parents) and promoting the family's trust and faith in the therapist as an experienced, skilled, and caring adult. SOFTA interventions aimed at enhancing emotional connection include expressing confidence, trust, or belief in the client; showing interest in the client apart from the therapeutic discussion at hand; and reassuring or normalizing the client's emotional vulnerability.

To reiterate, it seems counterintuitive that the primary strategy in cases like these is to *not* do something. However, it is actually proactive to avoid intervening in a way that seems logical and is effective in other kinds of therapy cases. Therapists need to anticipate that even when maltreated children demonstrate improvement in EMOTIONAL CONNECTION and ENGAGEMENT behaviors, they are nonetheless prone to revert to negativity about the therapeutic process or about the therapist as a person. This unpredictability is predictable due to the intense fear and mistrust caused by relational trauma.

Create Separate Spaces

The strategy of alternately holding individual and conjoint sessions with different family subsystems applies more broadly than in the decision dialogues and ABFT tasks described earlier. This strategy is often the only way to create and maintain everyone's sense of safety due to the extreme difficulty of discussing child maltreatment in a frank and open manner. Indeed, alternating individual with family sessions is helpful not only for discussing the extent and consequences of the relational trauma but also for (a) containing any intense conflict between family members that the trauma discussion has produced and (b) joining with anyone who is having trouble connecting with the therapist due to the emotional interference of other family members.

SHARED SENSE OF PURPOSE is important here. That is, whenever the therapist suggests holding private sessions with an individual or subsystem (e.g., couple, one parent and child, sibling), it is essential to obtain everyone's agreement that the objective of varying the format is to "make the therapy be for everyone." If, however, family members interpret the therapist's suggestion to mean that she is recommending "different therapies for each of us," the family's sense of a Shared Purpose could be compromised. For this reason, it is essential to explain the rationale and obtain each and every family member's consent to proceed in this fashion before doing so.

Case Example: The Colangelo Family

Paz Colangelo, 14, was living in residential care when she was referred for psychotherapy by child protective services at the request of the facility director. Prior to meeting Paz, the therapist received a report explaining that this young adolescent had been repeatedly raped by her father when she lived with him after her parents separated.

In fact, Paz had witnessed her father's increasingly violent acts toward her mother, Soledad, for many years. The parents' separation took place when Paz was 12, following a particularly severe episode of violence. The next day, Soledad left the family home without making a formal complaint to the police, leaving Paz alone with her father.

In the 5 months following the parents' separation, Paz was beaten, tortured, and violated by her father. Following a call from the residential school, which Paz attended intermittently and with clear behavior problems, the police arrested the father. Eventually, the courts found him guilty of incest, rape, and child endangerment and sent him to prison.

The social worker in charge of the family determined that Soledad was extremely unstable and negligent with regard to Paz, due to having left her alone with the father. When asked, Paz rejected the offer of supervised visits with her mother. Paz also adamantly refused to consider foster care. Thus she wound up in a residential care facility for adolescents.

In his report, the facility director indicated that Soledad was available and willing to participate in conjoint sessions if family therapy was determined to be beneficial for Paz. The therapist decided to begin by seeing Paz individually.

At the start, he found it extremely difficult to engage the teenager, who rarely looked at him (negative EMOTIONAL CONNECTION[1]). Any attempt to explore Paz's emotions or her reactions to the events in her family was met with denial or silence and a closed body posture (negative SAFETY[2]). Next, the therapist tried simply asking about her daily life. Paz murmured that everything was "fine" (negative ENGAGEMENT[3]). She was only interested in complaining about the food at the residential center and about being angry that her roommate used her things without permission. Notably, unlike other teens at the center, Paz did not request free time outside or the freedom to organize her own schedule.

In responding to a brief questionnaire after each session, Paz indicated a neutral view about the usefulness of therapy. Her answers to the open-ended questions also showed a clear lack of interest.

The educator at the residential facility who brought Paz to the clinic each week informed the therapist that it was difficult to coax her to attend the therapy sessions. Paz seemed unmotivated, repeatedly asking the teacher the same question: "Why do I have to go?" (negative ENGAGEMENT[4]). When the therapist asked Paz about her reluctance to keep their appointments, she simply explained that she was "lazy," but "it's okay to come, even though I don't know what it's for."

This case exemplifies the difficulty that therapists often have engaging traumatized adolescents. Paz's negative attitude toward therapy and her denial of abuse blocked every attempt on the therapist's part to initiate a personal relationship with her. Simultaneously, the professionals who had referred Paz for help were exerting pressure on the therapist to "fix" her. The therapist also put pressure on himself, knowing the horrific torture and abuse this child had suffered. He found it daunting to sit with her due to her complete lack of interest in the therapeutic process. Active rebellion would have been preferable!

What to do? The therapist was aware of the importance of remaining positive and open with Paz. Knowing her history, the therapist also understood that it was much safer for Paz to deny what had happened to her than face the extent of her suffering until she was assured of the therapist's unconditional support and acceptance.

The therapist hoped that his patience and provision of safety might turn the tide. Two events marked the first step forward in Paz's therapy. First, the educator from the residential center requested a private meeting with the therapist to tell him that Paz had opened up to her about the abuse she had suffered at her father's hands. With obvious affection for the girl, the educator explained that after her mother left,

---

[1] Client avoids eye contact with the therapist.

[2] Client protects self in a nonverbal manner.

[3] Client shows indifference about the tasks or process of therapy.

[4] Client questions the value of therapy.

Paz decided to live with her father because she had fond memories of him from her early childhood. Very concerned, but unsure how to respond to these disclosures, the educator suggested that Paz discuss her feelings and memories with the therapist. When Paz hostilely rejected this idea, the educator became overwhelmed.

With the educator's permission, the therapist told Paz that her teacher was finding it hard to be the only person to hear her story. The therapist took this opportunity to explain that his priority was to keep Paz safe and that he would allow nothing she told him to threaten her safety (SAFETY[5]). The therapist followed up with these empathic remarks about Paz's conflicted emotions:

Therapist: I know it's very hard for anyone to understand that you have all kinds of memories besides having suffered all the damage your father did to you. But everything that you've lived through since you were born is very real for you—it's your life. I imagine it's hard for you to organize all your memories and feelings (EMOTIONAL CONNECTION[6]).

Paz: Organize? What do you mean?

Therapist: I mean, many people would like you to put your bad and good experiences in different "boxes." And these "boxes" should have clear labels glued on the outside.

Paz: I'd like to label those boxes, too, and throw some of them away!

Therapist: But that's very complicated…our life experiences can't be so easily put into a separate box and thrown away, don't you think?

Paz: Not everyone understands that. I feel like I'm a monster when I have bad or weird thoughts.

Therapist: I know how that works. For you, what kind of "weird" thoughts?

Paz: Well, I miss the life we had with my father when he was well … or feeling hate toward my mother.

Therapist: This doesn't seem strange or weird to me (EMOTIONAL CONNECTION[7]), but I understand it's hard for your teacher and others to know what to say when you tell them things like that.

Paz: I guess that's why my teacher asked me to explain it here. But I don't want to feel like a monster. I don't want a psychologist to remove my brain.

Therapist: I certainly don't want that either! In fact, I don't want you to explain anything to me that you don't want to (EMOTIONAL CONNECTION[8]).

Paz: Sure?

Therapist: Totally. So that there's no doubt on your part, I'll offer you a deal.

Paz: A deal?

Therapist: Yes. We can do therapy this way: You ask whatever questions you want and I'll answer you. You suggest what you want us to talk about, your

---

[5] Therapist provides structure for safety.

[6] Therapist expresses empathy for the client's struggle.

[7] Therapist discloses his personal reactions to the client or the situation.

[8] Therapist reassures or normalizes a client's emotional vulnerability.

doubts or your weird thoughts, and when you want us to stop, you can do something else…you can signal me (SAFETY[9]).

Paz: What kind of signal?

Therapist: Do you see this little red piece of cardboard? (hands it to her) Take it in your hand, and when you let it drop to the ground, I'll shut up and immediately stop talking about anything we've been discussing.

Paz took the red card and dropped it. The therapist remained silent. Then, with a surprised smile, Paz asked, "Is it really going to work like this?" The therapist nodded but stayed silent.

Paz (laughing as she picked up the cardboard):   Come on, this is fun. Let's talk a little, let's try (ENGAGEMENT[10]).

This dialogue does not require interpretation. It was direct and opened the door for Paz to have a new feeling of safety and power in the therapy. In fact, this was the beginning of a more productive phase of treatment.

The second event that marked another step forward in Paz's emotional bond with the therapist occurred a few sessions later. At that time there were many indicators of Paz's SAFETY, but she remained closed off to any suggestion about including her mother in the therapy.

In one particular session, Paz reverted to being highly anxious and silent, crossing her arms over her chest (negative SAFETY[11]). The therapist reminded her to take the red cardboard and suggest something for them to discuss in the session (ENGAGEMENT[12]). Paz replied that she had nothing to suggest, saying "everything is the same as always" (negative ENGAGEMENT[13]). Her tone suggested anxiety, but she did not appear sad or upset.

After some time suggesting possible topics, similar to those they had discussed in previous sessions (specifically her difficulties at school), the therapist realized that Paz was nervously twisting a piece of paper in her hands throughout the session. He decided to ask about the paper, simply to fill the time. Very nervously, Paz answered that the paper was sheet music for a song she was rehearsing:

Therapist: I didn't know you sing! What song is it (EMOTIONAL CONNECTION[14])?

Paz: Well, it's that famous song called Hallelujah, a soul-like version. My singing teacher asked to sing it at a school festival.

Therapist: What good news! I didn't know you sing! I imagine you must sing very well to be asked to be the soloist.

---

[9] Therapist provides structure for safety.

[10] Client indicates agreement with the therapist's goals.

[11] Client protects self in a nonverbal manner.

[12] Therapist asks what the client wants to talk about in the session.

[13] Client shows indifference about the process of therapy (e.g., paying lip service).

[14] Therapist expresses interest in the client apart from the therapeutic discussion at hand.

Paz:	I don't think I'll do it. I can't see myself climbing on stage, singing ...
Therapist:	Well, singing well is a gift. (pause) I sing very badly (EMOTIONAL CONNECTION[15]).
Paz (laughing):	You sing badly?
Therapist:	Fatally! Do you want me to prove it (EMOTIONAL CONNECTION[16])?
Paz (having fun):	Yes, prove it!

The therapist asked for the sheet music and began singing. As he was honest in disclosing that he sang terribly, Paz burst into laughter.

| *Therapist*: | I wouldn't go up on stage because the audience would throw all kinds of stuff at me when I open my mouth. (pause) Why don't you sing only the beginning of this song, so I can see if I recognize this version? |

What happened next was an amazing discovery, one that solidified the emotional bond between Paz and the therapist. As it turned out, she had great talent. The therapist was frankly in awe of her singing voice, which he expressed sincerely. For Paz, his admiration was very difficult to accept—to be valued, to be admired, and to feel special as a person were entirely new for her. The emotional connection fostered by this short exchange turned out to be the beginning of the "virtuous cycle" that turned around Paz's sense of self.

One consequence of the horrific abuse Paz had suffered was her negative identity, which caused her to oscillate between various extreme behaviors. As her self-image was quite poor, both about her abilities and her physical appearance, she was usually highly self-conscious and timid. While she had outbursts of shame whenever anyone made any remark about her, no matter how minor, she also frequented drug hangouts and engaged in promiscuous behavior with boys she barely knew. This stark contrast was very difficult for her caregivers to understand or prevent.

Fortunately, after the "music session" with the therapist, Paz wanted to discuss her contradictory behavior with him. An intervention that proved to be particularly effective involved discovering the basis for Paz's inhibition and shame. First, the therapist explored with her all the situations in which she felt unsafe. He also suggested some "homework," for example, trying out something that she thought would "shock" her peers, such as telling a joke or wearing a funny hat. After doing so (ENGAGEMENT[17]), Paz was baffled—her peers were not shocked by her behavior, nor did they see her as "ridiculous." Rather, her "shocking" behavior either went completely unnoticed or was praised by her friends.

In the midst of this therapeutic work, Paz asked the therapist a specific question:

---

[15] Therapist discloses some fact about his personal life.

[16] Therapist shares a lighthearted moment with the client.

[17] Client indicates having done homework or seeing it as useful.

Paz:	What would you call someone like me? What kind of person am I?
Therapist:	What do you think? You're the expert on "Paz" (EMOTIONAL CONNECTION[18]).
Paz:	I think I'm "indecisive."
Therapist:	Can you explain why? Give me an example.
Paz:	It always happens to me. Yesterday I was with [my friend] Maria, and we talked about what to do in the afternoon. She suggested going to a place where we have friends who usually smoke weed. Well, they're friends of Maria's brother. And I never say anything, I don't care. We can go there or any other place. Maria asks me and I don't say anything. I'm "indecisive." It's pretty clear, isn't it?
Therapist:	Did you really want to go there with her?
Paz:	No.
Therapist:	Did you want to go somewhere else?
Paz:	Yesterday I had some money and I would've gone to buy a T-shirt that I like.
Therapist:	Then you're not "indecisive."
Paz:	Why not?
Therapist:	"Indecisive" means you have doubts and don't know how to make a decision. But what happens to you is that you "don't say" what you already decided...you don't express what you really want or what you really think.
Paz:	You're right. I decide in my mind but I don't say it...I don't dare.
Therapist:	Maybe you're afraid of something?
Paz:	Yeah, I'm always afraid something'll happen, that other people won't like what I say and they'll punish me. I don't want them to see me as strange or leave me alone.
Therapist:	Well, we have to look for a word for that, but it's not "indecisive." You know how to decide, you know what you really want.

This simple intervention spiked Paz's interest and enthusiasm. In fact, it was the turning point in her sense of self. And from a therapeutic point of view, it was a huge step forward: learning to express what she wanted and what she honestly thought, as well as confronting her fear of rejection. These were healthy, attainable therapy goals.

Obviously, all of this work was tremendously meaningful. Having been abandoned by her mother and tortured and raped by her father, Paz had experienced a total negation and destruction of her will and her dignity as a human being. As she gradually allowed herself to feel liked and cared for by the therapist, she naturally began to increase her engagement in the therapeutic process. The sessions became highly productive, although the therapist paid close attention to any sign of Paz's vulnerability, loss of control, or lack of safety.

---

[18] Therapist expresses belief in the client.

All of these therapeutic advances led to another turning point when Paz's mother was invited to join the therapy. Before doing so, the therapist asked Paz if she would agree to allow him to hold a few individual sessions with Soledad (ENGAGEMENT[19]). Paz agreed. The therapist's next step was to interest her in some of her mother's concerns, those that Soledad had given him permission to share with her daughter (without breaking the mother's confidentiality or compromising her sense of safety). Finally, after some hard work to ensure safety and develop strong emotional bonds with both clients, the therapist initiated conjoint family sessions, which were interspersed with individual sessions for each family member.

From the beginning, however, the "big wall" between Paz and Soledad threatened to rupture the alliances that the therapist had carefully built with each client separately. The feelings behind the wall were easy to understand. Although both mother and daughter were abused by the same person, they both felt guilty. Soledad felt guilty for failing to protect her daughter and for having trusted that her husband would treat Paz well despite what he had done to her, Soledad. She described herself as a "martyr," saying that she had made a huge mistake by thinking that her husband's respect for Paz would keep him from harming her. For her part, Paz felt guilty for not wanting to live with Soledad and for having stayed with her father even after witnessing his violent mistreatment of her mother. Paz also felt guilty for having rejected her mother, knowing that Soledad suffered greatly from this rejection.

To approach the big wall, the therapist worked individually with Soledad to prepare her for the conjoint sessions, in particular to decide what she could do to show her love for Paz. The most difficult aspect of this work was helping Soledad figure out how to explain to Paz that it was not possible for them to live together. The therapist used reframing to construct a non-blaming perspective on the situation. That is, the limitations that prevented them from living together as a family were not incompatible with their mutual love for each other.

With Paz, the therapist's primary objective was to ensure that the conjoint sessions would feel safe and that any stressful conversations would be avoided or stopped altogether. Here is an excerpt from an individual session with Paz that focused on her sense of safety:

Therapist: What questions would you like to ask your mother? Is there something you don't dare ask or that you're afraid that would negatively affect her?
Paz: I want to know if she's afraid of my father.
Therapist: Do you mean afraid *now*, in the present, even though he's in prison? Or do you mean if she was afraid *before*, when she lived with him?
Paz: She was afraid then...me too, and I still am now.
Therapist: And you think it'll be good to ask her that? Do you want to do it? Or do you want me to do it for you in our joint session (ENGAGEMENT[20])?

Paz: No.

---

[19] Therapist asks client whether she is willing to follow a specific suggestion.

[20] Therapist asks client whether she is willing to do a specific in-session task (e.g., enactment).

Therapist: Well, then, we won't do it. What would you like us to do (ENGAGEMENT[21])?

Paz: You can just tell her it's a question I ask myself but I don't want to talk about it.

Therapist: So…in the family session I can tell your mom that you ask yourself if she's afraid of your father now, but also I'll say that you simply want to know her answer, and then you'll discuss it with me alone, in our individual session….what do you think?

Paz: Yes, that'd be perfect. Do you think she'll like it?

Therapist: I'm sure it'll go well, but I'll watch carefully if it's not.

Working together with two victims, both of whom feel guilty, tends to evoke terrible suffering. Great delicacy is needed in order to preserve a climate of safety. In one family session, a particularly poignant moment came when Soledad was able to verbalize what she felt for her daughter: "love and admiration." Paz looked shocked that her mother chose the word "admiration," so much so that the therapist asked, "Why 'admiration'?" Soledad's answer was specific and very sincere: She explained that she admired Paz for her strength, for having acceptable grades in school, and for her ability to "overcome" without blaming her mother.

Despite this progress, Paz and Soledad still had great difficulty communicating with one another outside therapy. In the conjoint sessions, each of them described helpful aspects of their respective individual work. Paz, for example, told her mother about how much everything she was doing with music was helping her and about how much better she felt when she was singing. They also talked about yoga, which each of them did separately. However, they had great difficulty spending time together comfortably. When they began sharing holidays and weekends, their conversations focused on daily events. Notably, they never discussed living together again.

In the final phase of treatment, the therapist asked Paz and Soledad about their affection for each other:

Therapist: I wonder if now that you are spending more time together, is it easier for you to express affection…I mean to give each other a hug or say things like "I love you"?

Soledad: I think we both know we love each other but we don't usually show it. We laugh together, make jokes, and touch each other, but it's rare to hug or say loving things.

Paz: Well, there's no need. But there *is* something we both have to tell you [therapist]. When we're together we don't say things like "I love you" or "I think of you" … We talk about more normal things, like school or friends. But when we're not together we chat a lot using WhatsApp, and that's where we say really nice things. Sometimes my mother makes me cry with her loving messages.

---

[21] Therapist encourages the client to articulate a goal for the therapy.

The communication barrier between mother and daughter resulted in a difficult decision, 2 years after Paz had begun therapy. Mother and daughter agreed to formalize the process of having Paz live with the parents of her best friend. It was decided that this foster home would best meet Paz's immediate needs, including continuing her studies with a scholarship she had won to advance her musical training.

Although in many ways this decision was the result of successful therapeutic work, it nonetheless reawakened a sense of guilt in both mother and daughter. For Paz, this "relapse into guilt" was more pronounced, expressed through some new psychosomatic symptoms and fears. When she began to value everything she had attained, specifically a stable family situation and recognition of her abilities and talent, and when she discovered value in herself and her body (taking care of her appearance, recognizing her attractiveness, etc.), she began having some phobic reactions. She became afraid of riding in a car or a bus, she became dizzy and had palpitations when she was with friends, and she became terrified of death for no apparent reason.

When treatment resumed due to this "relapse," Paz experienced no difficulty recreating a strong therapeutic relationship. She easily found her place in the therapy and experienced the therapist as a safe person who she trusted to respect her, her ideas, and her solutions to her problems. Paz even accepted Soledad's help and advice, finally recognizing her mother as someone who had also faced great hardships and thus had something worthwhile to offer her.

Final Thoughts

Creating therapeutic alliance with survivors of maltreatment is undoubtedly a major challenge. As we described in this chapter, the initial difficulty we encounter with these cases is the maltreated child's unwillingness or inability to relate with others. This difficulty occurs, to varying degrees, in anyone who directly or indirectly experienced relational trauma. For this reason, entering into a personal relationship with a therapist tends to be threatening, simply because the offer of help, care, and trust evokes painful memories of previous failed relationships.

Denial and dissociation are particularly characteristic of highly traumatized children. These defense mechanisms vary in intensity based on the magnitude of the psychological harm inflicted on the child. Consequently, development of a positive therapeutic alliance in these cases requires great perseverance.

Safety needs to be monitored carefully during each session and indeed during every minute of the treatment process. As shown in the case of Paz Colangelo, safety can simultaneously be threatened on different levels, from within the client to between the client and the broader professional network, as well as within the client's personal and familial relationships. By carefully addressing each of these threats, we can sometimes work miracles with the most vulnerable children in our care.

References

Castonguay, L., & Hill, C. E. (Eds.). (2011). *Transformation in psychotherapy: Corrective experiences across cognitive behavioral, humanistic, and psychodynamic approaches*. Washington, DC: American Psychological Association.

Diamond, G. S., Diamond, G. M., & Levy, S. A. (2014). *Attachment Based Family Therapy for depressed adolescents*. Washington, DC: American Psychological Association.

Escudero, V. (2013). *Guía Práctica de la Intervención Familiar II. Intervención en contextos cronificados o de especial dificultad*. Junta de Castilla y León.

Flaskerud, J. H. (1990). Matching client and therapist ethnicity, language and gender: A review of research. *Issues in Mental Health Nursing, 11*, 321–336.

Friedlander, M. L., Escudero, V., & Heatherington, L. (2006). *Therapeutic alliances with couples and families: An empirically-informed guide to practice*. Washington, DC: American Psychological Association.

Johnston, J. R. (1990). Role diffusion and role reversal: Structural variation in divorced families and children's functioning. *Family Relations, 39*, 405–413.

Miller, A. (1981). *The drama of the gifted child*. New York: Basic Books.

Rivett, M., & Street, E. (2009). *Family therapy: 100 key techniques*. London: Routledge.

Sheinberg, M. (1992). Navigating treatment impasses at the disclosure of incest: Combining ideas from feminism and social constructionism. *Family Process, 31*, 201–216.

Sheinberg, M., True, F., & Fraenkel, P. (1994). Treating the sexually abused child: A recursive, multimodal program. *Family Process, 33*, 263–276.

Sheinberg, M., & Fraenkel, P. (2001). *The relational trauma of incest: A family-based approach to treatment*. New York: Guilford Press.

Sheinberg, M., & True, F. (2008). Treating family relational trauma: A recursive process using a decision dialogue. *Family Process, 47*, 173–195.

Van der Kolk, B. A. (2005). Developmental trauma disorder: Toward a rational diagnosis for children with complex trauma histories. *Psychiatric Annals, 35*, 401–408.

Van der Kolk, B. A. (2014). *The body keeps the score: Brain, mind, and body in the healing of trauma*. New York: Viking.

Walsh, F. (2017). *Strengthening family resilience* (3rd ed.). New York: Guilford Press.

Chapter 6
Disadvantaged, Multi-Stressed Families Adrift in a Sea of Professional Helpers

> *If the misery of the poor be caused not by the laws of nature,*
> *but by our institutions, great is our sin.*

—Charles Darwin

Multi-stressed, disadvantaged families that experience moderate to severe difficulties socially, personally, and economically due to sociocultural deprivation (e.g., Bachler et al., 2016; Witkiewitz et al., 2013) often find it difficult to initiate or remain in therapy despite a pressing need for assistance. In many cases, these families seek psychological help only at the insistence of the judicial system, social services, school psychologist, or child protective services. Unfortunately, secondary gain complicates the therapy process when economic assistance comes with the stipulation that the family follow through on the treatment referral.

In this chapter, we describe ways to reduce resistance and facilitate a multi-stressed family's collaboration in the therapy process by providing safety and a "joining with." Note that we use Madsen's (2007) term *multi-stressed* to describe these families, even though the traditional term in the literature is *multiproblem.* In our view, *multi-stressed* is less pejorative because it acknowledges the pernicious interaction of psychological difficulties and external stressors in the lives of these families.

In part, the difficulty in trying to engage a multi-stressed family lies in the clash between the clients' sociocultural context and the professional context. For this reason, alliance empowerment begins by addressing the family's lack of safety. To do so, the therapist must first determine the family's relationship to the referring agency or institution and understand how the family views the therapist's role in relation to that agency. All too often the family, therapist, and referring professional have opposing views on the presenting problems, on how the problems should be approached, on the nature of the therapeutic relationship, or on the agency's authority over the family's life.

In large part, therapy with multi-stressed, disadvantaged families involves the same complexities described in previous chapters of this book. That is, in working with particularly stressed families, we often need to focus on difficulties in the couple's relationship or in the specific challenges of what we call *parenting in isolation.* Not uncommonly, multi-stressed families also require help to reduce an adolescent's risk behaviors or work through relational trauma.

© Springer International Publishing AG 2017   127

V. Escudero, M.L. Friedlander, *Therapeutic Alliances with Families,*
Focused Issues in Family Therapy, DOI 10.1007/978-3-319-59369-2_6

Despite the many varied problems a particular family may be experiencing, the common denominator is the challenge to the therapeutic alliance due to the referring agency's authority over the family. Although agencies and courts often recommend separate help for the parent(s) and the child(ren), we recommend against offering different therapies for individual family members. Rather, family empowerment requires a concerted treatment plan for the entire family system.

Unique Challenges

Multiproblem or Multi-Treated Families?

Before therapy begins, a disadvantaged family with multiple difficulties has likely received various forms of assistance from social services, the juvenile justice system, housing authorities, religious leaders, the children's school, and so on. In crisis situations, the family typically meets with many professionals—police officers, physicians, and school officials—who rush to intervene.

Some offers of help can either be accepted or rejected by the family, but often psychotherapy is obligatory, even coercive. The provision of economic assistance, for example, while not explicitly coercive, is often conditional on participation in a mental health intervention. Yet how can destitute parents decline participation in a "voluntary" parenting course when they are in dire need of financial help?

Due to this complexity, a multi-stressed family can rapidly become a multi-treated family. All too often, the influence of other professionals is an obstacle for the smooth initiation of family therapy. Indeed, the first challenge involves helping family members see that psychotherapy is unique and distinct from other professional contexts. However, it is often just as confusing for the therapist as it is for the family to sort out the objectives of each recommended or mandated intervention (e.g., individual counseling for the mother, anger management for the father, play therapy for the young child, residential care for the adolescent). In order to collaborate effectively with the various professionals who are already involved with the family, the therapist may not be able to recommend against a mandated intervention, such as anger management training, in favor of conjoint family therapy. To complicate matters further, the family's sense of safety is compromised if the therapist is required to send routine reports to an outside agency about the family's progress in treatment. Not surprisingly, this lack of privacy is a major source of confusion and frustration for the family.

Take the case of Emma, who was referred for family therapy by child protective services. Each of her three children had a different father, none of whom had any contact with Emma.

The first session was saturated with negative SAFETY indicators. Emma insisted that the social workers were wrong about their concerns for the 7- and 11-year-old boys—the "real problem" was her 17-year-old daughter. Responding to this remark, the therapist inquired about the teenage daughter's difficulties. Emma reacted defensively to these questions, explaining that her daughter did not need a therapist or the psychological evaluation that had apparently been prescribed by a psychiatrist. When the therapist persisted by trying to explore the mother-daughter relationship, Emma expressed mounting anger toward the residential center where her daughter was living. She was adamant that the counselor in the facility had already told the therapist about her conflicts with him over their handling of the daughter's risk behaviors. This was not the case, however.

Interestingly, although Emma thought the psychiatrist was wrong about the severity of her daughter's emotional problems, she was pleased that he was supportive of her fight against the facility. To complicate matters further, while the facility's counselor adamantly disagreed with Emma about how to handle her daughter's acting out, he shared Emma's view that the social workers from child protective services were in error about the vulnerability of the two boys.

The therapist asked Emma to explain her most immediate problem. She answered that since she had been unable to pay the rent on her apartment for several months, she feared that her boys would be removed from the home. The therapist's response to this disclosure prompted a positive shift in the therapeutic relationship:

Therapist:	I have to confess that this whole situation is overwhelming me and I'm lost (EMOTIONAL CONNECTION[1]). I wonder if you're feeling the same way?
Emma (leaning forward) (ENGAGEMENT[2]):	You feel lost?
Therapist:	Yes, and very overwhelmed with everything you must be going through. That's why I wonder how you can carry so much heavy weight on your shoulders (EMOTIONAL CONNECTION[3]).
Emma:	Well, there are days I feel like leaving this life of mine, running away, disappearing, I can't take any more...but I have to fight for my children (SAFETY[4]).

---

[1] Therapist discloses his or her personal reactions or feelings toward the client or the situation.

[2] Client leans forward (in response to a direct question from the therapist).

[3] Therapist (verbally or nonverbally) expresses empathy for the clients' struggle.

[4] Client shows vulnerability (e.g., discusses painful feelings).

Therapist:	I don't want to add to your burden (EMOTIONAL CONNECTION[5]). So I don't want the referral you got to come to the family therapy center to be one more hassle for you. I specially want to keep that from happening, but I don't know what to work on first. Can you help me out (ENGAGEMENT[6])?
Emma (softly)*:*	It's funny that you're asking *me* for help (SAFETY[7]). That's never happened before, and I've had to see a lot of professionals. I think I'd like to talk about what you just said.
Therapist:	How do you feel about all this?
Emma:	Yes, I need some peace of mind to explain how I feel, and about how scared I am about maybe losing my children, every one of them. They've all lost their relationship with their fathers, and I think they blame me.
Therapist:	Would you like me to meet your three children (ENGAGEMENT[8])? I *would* like to meet them.
Emma (fidgeting with her purse strap) (negative SAFETY[9])*:*	Okay, I think maybe you can help me find out how they feel too… ? But, what about the counselor from the [residential] center and the psychiatrist? Will CPS [Child Protective Services] make you write a report about me?
Therapist:	I'll go talk to all of them, but first I want to know about your family's background. And I'll tell you everything I say to them when the time comes—what do you think (SAFETY[10])?

[5] Therapist discloses his or her personal reactions or feelings toward the client or the situation.

[6] Therapist discusses or negotiates therapy goals with client(s).

[7] Client varies her emotional tone during the session.

[8] Therapist asks client(s) whether they are willing to follow a specific suggestion.

[9] Client expresses anxiety nonverbally (e.g., taps or shakes).

[10] Therapist provides structure and guidelines for safety and confidentiality.

Emma had a positive response to this simple exchange, the objective of which was simply to begin building a safe and personal therapeutic alliance, uncontaminated by multiple, contradictory professional opinions—at least, that was Emma's subjective experience of the "help" she had already been offered by others.

Therapy or Social Control?

Like in Emma's case, when the care of a minor child is considered "inadequate" or "negligent," the child protective system often takes on the responsibility normally entrusted to parents. This intervention is essentially one of social control. At the same time, however, when a lack of resources is seen as contributing to the parents' negligence, social services may also offer the family financial, social, and psychological assistance.

In cases of negligence, parents often fail to understand that psychological help involves support rather than control. For this reason, the therapist needs to acknowledge the coerciveness experienced by the family. However, even when the therapist empathizes with the pain caused by children's removal from the home, many parents respond defensively because they see the therapy as part of "what social services are doing to us."

It is particularly challenging to create a safe therapeutic environment when the therapist is required by the authorities to report the family's compliance with treatment to a judge. In other words, therapists are not exempt from some obligations that are meant to be protections but that parents understandably interpret as interference.

Chronic Stress

One characteristic that complicates therapeutic work with disadvantaged, multi-stressed families is the chronicity of these families' difficulties. Typically, the therapist comes into the picture long after the family has been exposed to multiple, repeated attempts at intervention. In an analysis of the patterns of chronicity in these types of families, Escudero (2013) found the following 7 features to be most common:

1. *Dependence on social services.* "Dependence" is a typical feature of the multi-stressed family's lifestyle, expressed as helplessness and external attributions for the family's problems. Dependence on the aid provided by social services often becomes part of the problem rather than a tool to cope with and resolve the family's difficulties.

   A pattern of dependence not only characterizes the family itself, but also it reflects the family's ongoing relationship with the social service system.

Unfortunately, social service professionals, who are typically overwhelmed by a large caseload of needy families, tend to develop a paternalistic attitude toward these families that only reinforces their dependence and lack of initiative. Understandably, it is all too easy for a family to transfer its dependent relationship with social services to the family therapist.

2. *Long-term disorders.* By their very nature, some psychological problems and characteristics of family dysfunction require long-term treatment. These difficulties include, among others, severe mental health disorders, addiction, social isolation, and intellectual challenges.

   Some risks to health and safety are repeated across three generations, particularly alcoholism, criminal activity, and violence and abuse. When these kinds of problems are transmitted intergenerationally through the family's values, norms, routines, and lifestyle, the problems tend to be invisible to the family and are thus extremely difficult to dislodge therapeutically.

3. *Sequence of negative life events.* According to Escudero (2013), it is common to discover in the history of multi-stressed families a lengthy chain of negative life events, such as deaths, imprisonments, job losses, evictions, and an urgent need to leave a community or neighborhood and move from one dwelling to another. Sometimes these negative life events are complicated by relational trauma experienced through two or even three generations. In these cases, therapists need to help families recover from a complex set of relational challenges, as described in Chap. 5.

4. *Poverty and social isolation.* Obviously poverty is not exclusively associated with social isolation or marginalization, but it is a common feature of multistressed families (Bachler et al., 2016; Witkiewitz et al., 2013). Research indicates that low socioeconomic status is associated with less engaged parental behavior, particularly less parental monitoring, thereby negatively affecting a parent-child attachment and the child's rate of development.

   In general, poverty is a risk factor that contributes to psychosocial disorders and increased vulnerability in the family system (Lund et al., 2011). When there is a lack of employment in the community, especially one in a rural area, many clients need mental health services throughout their lives simply to cope with the adversities that attend poverty (Friedlander, Austin, & Cabrera, 2014).

   In some cases, a family is isolated from the surrounding community. In other cases, the family is part of a marginalized community, a microculture, or an ethnic neighborhood. As discussed later in this chapter, immigrant and refugee families are particularly vulnerable, due to the acculturative stress that accompanies virtually every aspect of their daily life—language, employment, housing, education, and so on. For these families, the therapeutic context is especially threatening. Psychotherapy belongs to a world that is altogether foreign to them.

5. *Frustration with previous professional help.* When a family has a lengthy history of unsuccessful interventions, family members tend to be as frustrated as the professionals. Even when the intervention attempts have been prolonged, it is nonetheless quite common for them to be repeated, each time with similar negative outcomes. These repeated failure experiences logically lead to frustration on

the part of the family and pessimism on the part of the professionals. Invariably, this negativity carries over to the work of building a therapeutic alliance with the family.

6. *A lengthy history of conflict.* Some families have a specific profile in which conflict between the couple or among various family subsystems is perpetuated across two or three generations (Escudero, 2013). Unresolved conflict, involving coercive control as well as physical/sexual violence, often cycles throughout the extended family system, never receiving adequate professional attention.

   In other words, conflict can become a habitual characteristic of a multi-stressed family's lifestyle. In fact, some parents bring each of their children to see a therapist just as a matter of course, so that therapy is a kind of "generational norm" in the family (Friedlander et al., 2014, p. 588).

7. *History of parental rejection.* Often therapists discover evidence of neglect and abandonment in the families of origin of the parents whose children are referred for treatment. Not surprisingly, reactive attachment disorders show up in these children, mirroring the attachment disorders of their parents, who themselves were abandoned or neglected as children and placed in the care of social services.

Disorganization in the Professional Network

The confusion that challenges therapeutic progress is not only located within the multi-stressed families themselves. All too often, the various professionals working with a particular family experience a similar level of confusion, as well as frustration, due to the inherent difficulties of working together to foster change in multi-stressed clients (Escudero, 2013; Madsen, 2007). These difficulties are due to specific sources of disorganization in the network of professionals: lack of coordination, judicial power, negative expectations, and a dilution of responsibilities.

Lack of Coordination Perhaps the primary difficulty that accounts for professional disorganization is a lack of coordination between the professionals who represent the various social service and mental health agencies working with a specific family. Poor coordination occurs when recommendations or requirements in one arm of the network, such as the juvenile justice system or child protective services, are not adequately implemented by the other arm of the network. Indeed, it often seems that a lack of coordination in the lives of family members is mirrored in the network of professionals, as if systemic disorganization were contagious.

Judicial Power In some cases, interventions mandated by a judge are at odds with the therapist's attempts to unify the family, such as when parents can only see their children during supervised visits. The power of the courts can also stall the initiation of conjoint family therapy. Moreover, the social control wielded by family courts can contaminate a family's trust in the therapist and his ability to work effectively with the entire family system.

Consider this case example. A childcare worker in a residential facility for adolescents gained the trust of Saeeda, an "emotionally disturbed" adolescent. Fearfully, Saeeda told the worker that her mother was regularly prostituting herself to make ends meet. Learning this information from the childcare worker, the therapist recommended that Saeeda remain in residential care for the time being, at least until her mother agreed to participate in conjoint family sessions. Unfortunately, however, neither the therapist nor the facility administrator was able to dissuade the family court judge from sending Saeeda home to her mother. Judicial power trumps all.

Negative Expectations It is understandable that with all these constraints, professionals working with multi-stressed families tend to have negative expectations about the possibility of recovery. Unfortunately, negative expectations can become a self-fulfilling prophecy. For this reason, therapists often encounter burnout in the professionals who work with the family. When burnout is suspected, the therapist needs to communicate optimism about the family's potential for change when she coordinates services with these professionals.

Dilution of Responsibilities Dilution of responsibilities occurs when the people in charge of a case delay taking action, when professionals repeatedly evaluate and refer the family elsewhere, or when urgency is required, but it is unclear which agency should take the lead. Indeed, responsibilities can easily become diluted when people working in different areas of a family's life (psychological, economic, legal, educational, and so on) are trying to address urgent risk factors.

In Escudero's (2013) interviews and discussion groups with professionals, dilution of responsibilities emerged as a specific source of disorganization. In fact, rather than criticize the families for this problem, the professionals expressed a frank dissatisfaction with their own work.

No doubt the complexity of the risk factors and the various interventions required by each of these risks account for a dilution of responsibilities. As an example, consider the difficulty in evaluating risk, determining priorities, and coordinating services for a vulnerable family that is simultaneously experiencing addiction, intimate partner violence, child neglect, and school failure. Also, consider how easily family therapy can become stalled when a judicial decision about terminating parental rights delays the family's availability for mental health treatment or when a social worker's indecision about recommending a child's placement outside the home stalls the school psychologist's evaluation of the child's educational needs.

Accommodation to Chaos

Sometimes family members are so accustomed to crisis and chaos that they describe their experience as simply "our way of life." Indeed, when deprivation, conflict, and neglect are the only social context a child experiences, it is no wonder that as an adult he recreates the same kind of family environment.

Consider, for example, Marion, who "refused to see" her 11-year-old daughter's profound depression when it was urgently brought to her attention by the school psychologist. Due to her own history, Marion had no basis for understanding how the girl's suicidal ideation could have been resulted from the father's alcoholism, unpredictability, and abandonment of the family. Rather, Marion thought her daughter was "way better off" after the father left—after all, she herself grew up on the streets, with no parents to protect her.

This kind of denial or minimization of psychological problems is a natural accommodation to chaotic life conditions, including violence and chemical dependence. As explained in Chap. 5, in many cases denial is an unconscious defense mechanism that helps people survive chronic relational trauma. After all, when life's problems seem unsurmountable, denying their existence or the gravity of risk is fully understandable.

Therapists have a tendency to view accommodation to chaos as a perpetuation of "victimization." In therapy, the family presents as helpless in the face of overwhelming external stressors. The parents, feeling victimized despite recognizing their problems, exhibit a complete lack of initiative. Understandably, however, a life filled with unrelenting hardships makes it difficult for people to understand the need for a therapy referral or mandate.

Indeed, victimization is the lived reality for many families. All too many families suffer extreme economic and sociocultural deprivation. All too often racial bias and discrimination are traumatizing. All too often community violence claims the life of an innocent child.

Regardless of the kinds of stressors in a family's life, the therapist needs to explore how the family's worldview (Liu, Soleck, Hopps, Dunstan, & Pickett, 2004) prompted the entrenched external attributions that challenge the clients' engagement in therapy. That is, when family members are accustomed to seeing their problems as entirely caused by outside events or environmental hardships, they have difficulty viewing themselves as capable of finding solutions. A passive response to the therapy is the likely result.

Essentially, the culture of victimized families clashes with the culture of psychotherapy. It is therefore understandable when a multi-stressed family experiences extreme discomfort in the psychotherapeutic context. Not uncommonly, the parents conceal or minimize the extent of problems or psychological symptoms. When concealment is seen as intentional, the therapist is tempted to view the family as resistant. To the contrary, however, conscious concealment should be interpreted as a lack of SAFETY in the therapeutic context. Mistrust is a natural consequence when people are coerced to take part in something that has no meaning for them.

Intrafamilial Conflict Due to Acculturative Stress

In the present context of global migration, many families are creating new lives in countries whose social systems and religious traditions are difficult for them to understand. Invariably, the need to acculturate rapidly to a new culture has a strong impact on families. For many of these families, severe acculturative stress hinders the adjustment process, particularly when the parents are simultaneously under pressure to learn a new language, find employment and suitable housing, and make important decisions about their children's education.

Rates of acculturation vary across generations, due in part to the comparative rapidity by which children are able to learn a new language. Adolescents, who naturally turn to peers for acceptance, often reject the traditions, values, and norms of their immigrant parents and grandparents. In many cultures, adolescent rebellion is not only unacceptable but also is unexpected. Intense family arguments often arise over virtually any aspect of daily life, from the adolescent's clothing to his choice of friends, food, use of technology, and type of music.

Many immigrant and refugee families view therapists and the context of psychotherapy context with extreme mistrust, especially when the family was mandated by social services or family court to seek professional help. Resistance is not surprising when one family member interprets another family member's willingness to cooperate with the therapist as indicative of disrespect.

Not uncommonly, therapists need to rely on the children to act as translators for their parents. This power imbalance complicates therapeutic progress if the parents view their child's relationship with the therapist as a rejection of the heritage culture.

Multi-stressed families struggling with acculturative stress are likely to refuse the assistance of a therapist if they mistrust the resources offered to them by social services, the health system, or the educational system. Therapists need to recognize an immigrant family's resistance to follow through on a referral as due to the wariness that is a natural part of acculturation.

Often, a strong emotional connection with the family can be made by showing genuine interest in the family's cultural heritage and traditions. Before setting goals or recommending a specific course of action, the therapist can promote safety by explaining the private nature of therapy (within the limits to confidentiality imposed by referring agencies). The challenge of working with clients whose culture differs from that of the therapist is not, of course, exclusive to immigrant and refugee families. Whenever a family is required to seek professional help due to severe child neglect or maltreatment, cultural differences between the therapist and family can be an additional obstacle to overcome.

Recommendations from the Literature

Family Subtypes

Recently, Bodden and Deković (2016) identified characteristics common to families that professionals classify as "multiproblem." The authors sampled children referred for mental health services by their medical providers or other mental health professionals with families that voluntarily sought therapy. The first objective was to contrast the questionnaire responses of 85 families broadly defined as "multiproblem" (many of whom needed intensive supervision or home visits) with 150 families recruited for participation from the general population through the children's schools. The authors' second objective was to establish cutoff scores on the various measures to identify distinct characteristics of multiproblem families. A final objective was to use cluster analysis to identify subtypes of these families.

Bodden and Deković (2016) concluded that multiproblem families display a broad and complex pattern of stressors in seven domains: child factors, parental factors, child-rearing problems (i.e., inadequate or inconsistent parenting), family functioning problems, contextual problems, social network problems, and mental healthcare problems. Three fairly distinct types of families were identified: (1) *Community-problem families* experience difficulties due to the social context (e.g., financial problems, strained relations with the community, problems with the criminal justice system) rather than due to problems in child, parent, or family functioning. (2) *Multiproblem families* have mental health or behavioral problems, including severe parenting and family functioning difficulties. (3) *Child-focused mild-problem families* have less severe family functioning problems, although the children in these families exhibit externalizing difficulties such as aggressive or oppositional behavior and out-of-home placements (Bodden & Deković, 2016).

In our view, each of these domains presents a different and specific challenge to the therapeutic alliance. What seems most essential is first to identify how an individual family experiences the interaction of these diverse sources of stress and next to initiate therapeutic work in this area.

Collaborative Therapy

W. C. Madsen's (2007) *collaborative therapy model* is an essential reference for working with multi-stressed families. According to Madsen, it is incumbent on therapists to recognize the harsh realities in families' lives without overlooking their abilities, talents, and inherent wisdom for coping with adversity.

This constructive and optimistic perspective describes ways in which therapists can build strong helping relationships with families that are overwhelmed by multiple stressors and continual crises. The term *multi-stressed* communicates Madsen's (2007) empathic understanding of the difficulties and pressures on these families.

The collaborative therapy model has inspired our framework for creating therapeutic alliances from the perspective of SOFTA. In particular, several concepts in the model speak directly to alliance building with multi-stressed families who are also receiving services from other professionals or agencies.

According to Madsen (2007, 2011; Madsen & Gillespie, 2014), therapists first need to understand the other professionals' relational stance with the family. The term *relational stance* refers to the way in which the professional approaches the family or the position taken in relation to the clients. Optimally, this relational position is one that "strengthens respect, connection, curiosity and hope in the therapeutic relationship" (Madsen, 2007, p. 9).

Second, therapists need to help families view themselves as *in a relationship* with the problems in their lives rather than as *having* these problems. In other words, the family is not "the problem," but rather is separate from and "more than" the difficulties that prompt the need for mental health services.

Third, Madsen (2007) uses the term *collaborative inquiry*, which characterizes our fundamental strategy for empowering families through the therapeutic alliance. Basically, using collaborative inquiry, the therapist explores with family members (1) where they want to head in their lives, (2) the challenges that block their way, and (3) how they can best address those challenges. The premise is that the therapist is an *appreciative ally* who shows the family that she is "on their side."

Home-Based Therapy

Researchers studying effective therapeutic work with multi-stressed families have determined that home-based intervention can make a significant difference, especially in the treatment of child and adolescent mental health (Bachler et al., 2016). In many cases, conducting sessions in the family's home is unavoidable. Many multi-stressed parents are not able to take time off work for regular appointments, nor do they have the financial resources for transportation to the therapist's office or for childcare during the adult-only sessions.

Recognizing that achieving positive outcomes in traditional settings with multi-stressed families tends to be very difficult (Curtis, Ronan, & Borduin, 2004), the developers of several home-based family therapy approaches have demonstrated highly favorable client outcomes, with robust effect sizes. These approaches include Multisystemic Family Therapy (MST; Curtis et al., 2004), Multidimensional Family Therapy (MDFT; Liddle, Rowe, Dakof, Henderson, & Greenbaum, 2009), and outpatient therapeutic family care or Therapeutisch Ambulante Familienbetreuung (TAF; Bachler et al., 2016). Most of these approaches emphasize the working alliance as an essential ingredient of successful home-based treatment.

Focus on Resilience

Traditional psychotherapy overly emphasizes Problems (capitalization intended!), a focus that multi-stressed families tend to experience as defeating, even humiliating. Indeed, all too often problem-saturated therapy reinforces these families' sense of being paralyzed by the many stressors and hardships in their lives.

Over the past two decades, there has been a major shift in the field from a focus on deficits to a focus on resilience, a perspective that emphasizes recognizing and enhancing a family's strengths and resources as a core aspect of therapy (Walsh, 2003, 2017). Interventions are less about "what went wrong" and more about "what can be done" to improve a family's functioning. Research supports this approach as a powerful way to address the needs of multi-stressed, impoverished clients (e.g., Alexander, Waldron, Robbins, & Neeb, 2013; Coatsworth, Santisteban, McBride, & Szapocznik, 2001; Liddle et al., 2009).

The resilience perspective closely aligns with our model of alliance empowerment, since focusing on strengths and abilities encourages family members to become collaborators in the therapeutic process. In our view, the families most in need of feeling empowered are those that are multi-stressed, disorganized, and disadvantaged.

Building Alliances with Mandated or Otherwise Involuntary Clients

The multi-stressed, disadvantaged families we have been describing in this chapter are often mandated to treatment by an authority that has control over some aspect of their lives. Not uncommonly, an entire family is required to receive "family preservation" services following an official finding of negligent or risky parenting by child protective services. In other cases, the juvenile justice system mandates family therapy as part of the rehabilitation of an adolescent who broke the law or was violent in the home or at school.

Even in the absence of a mandate, many families do not voluntarily seek mental health services. Rather, they request therapy after receiving a "strong recommendation" to seek help from school personnel, a physician, community leader, or some other interested third party.

Is it possible to build a strong alliance with involuntary clients? While little research has been published on this topic, two recent studies (Sotero, Major, Escudero, & Relvas, 2016; Sotero, Cunha, Silva, Escudero, & Relvas, in press) used the SOFTA-o to compare alliance behavior in voluntary and involuntary families. Results were encouraging. In general, despite the finding that the involuntary clients had more observably problematic alliances at the start of the therapy, by the fourth session the two groups did not differ significantly. Interestingly, it was not only that the involuntary families had improved alliance-related behavior, but also ratings on the four SOFTA alliance dimensions became more similar over time across the two groups.

The first of the two studies was focused on client behavior (Sotero et al., 2016). A team of trained observers rated each SOFTA dimension from video recordings of Sessions 1 and 4. The sample consisted of 20 involuntary and 20 voluntary families seen in brief family therapy at a university center. Among the 20 involuntary families, 6 were legally mandated by the courts, and 5 were referred by the child's school, 5 by mental health services, and 4 by health centers. In contrast, all 20 voluntary families were self-referred. The problems described by the families in both groups were complex, including intrafamilial conflict and family ruptures due to separation, divorce, and death.

The researchers had a meticulous method for selecting comparable families from a large sample of clinical cases seen over 8 years. This process ensured that the only difference between the groups was the referral condition, i.e., self-referred versus referred by a third party. A second basis for inclusion in the study was a detailed analysis of the archived clinical record to determine how family members had described their reasons for seeking assistance. In the involuntary group, over half of the participating family members had clearly stated not wanting, needing, or believing in the usefulness of therapy. Inclusion in the voluntary group required that none of the participating family members expressed this sentiment.

Observations of the families' first session showed that the voluntary families demonstrated significantly more alliance-related behavior than did the involuntary clients on all four SOFTA dimensions (Sotero et al., 2016). That is, compared to the voluntary families, those that had been pressured to seek help demonstrated significantly less ENGAGEMENT, CONNECTION, SAFETY, and a more problematic SHARED PURPOSE or within-family alliance.

In the fourth session, however, the only group difference was the clients' observed levels of engagement in treatment. That is, ENGAGEMENT was significantly lower among the involuntary families, despite an average shift from negative to positive SOFTA-o ratings. Additionally, it was notable that the evolution of SAFETY differed for the two groups, with the voluntary families demonstrating more problematic behavior on this alliance dimension as therapy progressed. The authors concluded that in the first few sessions, feeling comfortable in the therapeutic context is as essential for voluntary clients as it is for involuntary clients (Sotero et al., 2016).

In the second study of the series, Sotero et al. (in press) used the same sample to compare the therapists' observable SOFTA behaviors across the two groups. In Session 1, therapists who worked with the involuntary families, compared with those who saw the voluntary families, were significantly more focused on building engagement and promoting a shared sense of purpose within the family. This result is not surprising. When clients are not motivated to participate in treatment, it is considerably more challenging to encourage and sustain their cooperation.

In Session 4, however, no therapist differences were found, similar to the convergence of client behaviors across the groups in the earlier study (Sotero et al., in press). That is, the group differences observed in the therapists' contributions to the alliance in Session 1 faded as the therapy went on. By the fourth session, the involuntary families apparently did not require a greater focus on alliance building than did the voluntary families.

This line of research with mandated or otherwise involuntary clients is still exploratory. Nonetheless, Sotero et al.'s (2016, in press) results underscore the importance of alliance building with particularly challenging cases. Taken together with Walsh's (2017) perspective on fostering resilience, Sotero et al.'s results suggest that by paying close attention to client engagement and within-family collaboration, therapists can make a major difference in the lives of multi-stressed families, even those who do not voluntarily seek professional help.

Alliance-Empowering Strategies

Create an "Affected Community"

To build alliances in a multi-stressed, disorganized context, the first priority is to help the family acquire a sense of unity about the therapeutic work. Typically, unity has two obstacles: (1) conflict within the family, resulting in the disengagement of one or more members (Minuchin, 1974), and (2) multiple and diverse issues simultaneously demanding the family's attention (parenting problems, a housing crisis, financial stress, health problems, dependence on social services, and so on). Together, these obstacles can compromise the development of a strong expanded or within-family alliance.

A felt unity within the family regarding the therapy is the essence of the SOFTA's Shared Sense of Purpose within the Family. Indeed, the SHARED PURPOSE behavioral indicators (see Tables 1.1 and 1.2) can serve as a guide for "joining with" in order to strengthen the within-family alliance. However, before focusing on family members' willingness to collaborate with one another, it is important to help them see that (a) in one way or another, everyone in the family is affected by its internal difficulties and external stressors and (b) even though the various problems affect each person differently, they can best be addressed through a shared effort.

This general strategy relies heavily on reframing in order to define common or shared goals and create what Escudero (2013) called the *affected community*. Essentially, this term refers to the sense that everyone is affected by the family's struggles and therefore has a unique perspective to share in overcoming the problems. The therapeutic objective is simply to promote an open and collaborative attitude within the family.

The task of creating an "affected community" is particularly challenging when working with multi-stressed families, since these clients typically have conflicting priorities for improvement or problem resolution. Within-family conflict and blame are also commonplace. Of course, each case is individual and thus has unique characteristics that facilitate or hinder an expansion of the alliance.

Friedlander, Escudero, and Heatherington (2006) recommended two interventions that can help family members develop a shared value about the therapy: (1) identify a common external "enemy" and (2) unite family members against any problem or situation that threatens to break up the family unit. First, by finding an external enemy, family members can ask for and receive help to handle some person (the bad landlord, the verbally abusive uncle) or some situation (impending eviction, acculturative stress) that is causing difficulties for the family. Optimally, everyone participating in the therapy will agree that coordinated action is necessary to confront the problematic person or circumstance. The therapist can then describe herself as the family's ally in this struggle.

One caveat is in order, however. This intervention is only effective if the family members do not use the "external enemy" (or scapegoat) as a justification for inaction and if they also recognize their own need to change. As an example, it would be counterproductive to align family members against the teenage son who is creating havoc with his antisocial behavior and illegal drug use. On the other hand, it would be helpful to unite family members around the need to understand the boy and contain his behavior, so that everyone has a stake in the outcome.

Another strategy involves suggesting to family members that avoiding a problematic situation can potentially break them apart (cf. Friedlander, Heatherington, Johnson, & Skowron, 1994). Since most families would rather stay together, pointing out the possibility of a rupture can facilitate a united sense of purpose about preventing the family's dissolution. Of course, the therapist must carefully convey the impression that the situation is an opportunity for action and growth, not one that will invariably destroy the family. As an example, multi-stressed families are all too often faced with the threatened removal of the children. When the therapist can help the parents see that this negative consequence is avoidable if they work together (to coordinate their parenting practices and better nurture the children), this common goal can be highly motivating.

Other traumatic contexts can also bring a family together, such as uniting family members to protect a survivor after the sexual predator has been imprisoned or to share their grief over the death of an important family member. When handled with sensitivity, all of these circumstances can generate a strong within-family alliance that keeps clients in treatment and facilitates their attainment of mutually agreed-upon goals.

Clarify Who Is the "Real Client"

Mandates to seek mental health services usually come from child protective services, family court, or some agency or institution outside the therapist's practice setting. Even when the therapist is an independent practitioner who accepts a mandated referral, the family will likely consider the referral source to be the therapist's "real client." This perception is reinforced when the therapist is employed by that agency or institution.

With mandated or "highly recommended" clients, it is essential to establish a safe start to the therapy. As mentioned earlier, the therapist needs to clarify her relationship with the family as well as her relationship with the agency or professionals who mandated, recommended, or prescribed the treatment. Even when the therapist provides details about the obligatory structure, such as the frequency of sessions, duration of treatment, and requirement to file routine reports, families usually need time to process the information before feeling safe enough to engage productively in the therapy.

Therapists should not interpret a family's request for details or repetition of the required procedures as evidence of "resistance" or "defensiveness." It is only natural to be wary of any situation that is coercive. Mandates are indeed coercive, since the consequence for not following through can break a family apart.

The therapist version of the SOFTA-o contains specific interventions that contribute to a family's ENGAGEMENT and SAFETY (see Table 1.2). These include explaining how therapy works, providing structure and guidelines for privacy and confidentiality, inviting family members to inquire about intimidating aspects of the therapy (e.g., recording equipment, reports to third parties, treatment team observation, one-way mirror, etc.), asking clients what they would prefer to discuss, and encouraging family members to articulate their goals for the therapy. In other words, the therapist needs to make it clear that the family is the "real client."

Visit the Family's Home

Compared to home visits, seeing families in a private consulting office or community clinic gives therapists more control over what takes place in treatment. However, offices are not comfortable for many disadvantaged families, especially if they are also required to see other professionals in buildings located at a distance from their communities. With families that are highly fearful of mental health interventions, providing therapy in the home may be the only way to engage them.

Regardless of the reason for home visits, this approach to family therapy has some distinct advantages. Meeting families where they live makes the therapeutic process seem natural. This is not a trivial point, since these families' typical experience of office visits tends to be quite impersonal. Children in particular are more comfortable at home, surrounded by their belongings and feeling free to move about during the sessions.

Perhaps the greatest advantage to meeting families at home is that it provides a window into the life of the family. That is, home visits allow the therapist to observe specific aspects of the family's functioning up close, including the parents' disciplinary practices, how the family organizes its time and space, the nature of the children's activities, and so on.

Nonetheless, sometimes unpredictable events that occur during a home visit are difficult to manage, even risky. Some clients are more likely to scream or engage in physical conflict at home than in an office. Some clients feel more free to get up and leave the room when they dislike what is being said about them. Some clients are rude to the therapist if they believe she is "spying" on them in order to report their shortcomings to authorities.

For this reason, therapists need to approach home visits with caution. Optimally, the therapist should meet the family in the office for the first session. If this is not possible, it is advisable to become familiar with the details of the case before visiting the home. Additionally, we recommend four tasks to facilitate a positive response to home-based therapy: (1) manage the time and duration of the appointments, (2) determine an appropriate space in which to hold the sessions, and set ground rules around (3) what can or cannot be done during the sessions (e.g., opening the door but not eating or texting) and (4) the technical aspects of the therapy (appropriate and inappropriate topics, taking turns to speak, etc.) (Escudero, 2009).

In other words, as the professional person in the situation, the therapist has a certain "authority" to structure the time, space, and content of the sessions. However, since the physical space belongs to the family, there is a kind of paradox: While the therapist is visiting the family for professional reasons, he is nonetheless a guest. Behaving like a good guest (arriving on time, complimenting the family on aspects of the home or its décor, inquiring about family pictures or unfamiliar objects, and so on) helps set family members at ease. A sense of comfort is readily observable when, for example, family members show up on time for the appointment or offer the therapist a cup of coffee.

With respect to alliance building, home visits have two other distinct advantages. First, holding sessions in the home allows family members to feel somewhat empowered, which can easily be observed through their natural and open interactions with one another (a positive SHARED PURPOSE indicator). Second, the inherent hierarchy in any therapeutic relationship is reduced somewhat when the therapist is the family's "guest." After all, the therapist is coming to the family rather than the reverse.

Convey Optimism

The lifestyle that accompanies a low social class has been described as a kind of microculture or worldview (e.g., Liu et al., 2004). In working with multi-stressed, disadvantaged clients, the therapist needs to understand this worldview in general as well as from each family's unique perspective.

When inquiring about the family's lifestyle, it is important to avoid being judgmental. Rather, as we emphasized in previous chapters, in order to foster strong emotional connections with clients, therapists need to approach their subjective experiences with respect, showing genuine interest in everything they endured in the past and how they choose to live in the present. Of course, showing interest is not equivalent to approving a client's risk behavior.

To empower the family through the alliance, the therapist needs to pay close attention to any aspect of the family's way of life that can serve as a resource. Despite the many obstacles and hardships, it is important to stay optimistic about the family's potential for change. When the problems are many and the professional helpers are many, a great deal of optimism is required.

Optimism is the conviction that not only "can" a family change but that it "will" change. For the therapist's optimism to be a motivating force for the family—and not seem unrealistic or naïve—the therapist needs to establish small, incremental goals and amplify any and all improvements.

Conveying optimism is especially difficult when a family has serious problems in multiple aspects of their lives. How, for example, can clients stay the course when they are on the verge of eviction from their home, where they are the sole caregivers for a disabled parent with dementia, and one of the teenagers has begun engaging in criminal activity? On the other hand, let's say that for the first time ever, the father joined the mother for a family conference at the children's school. If the therapist applauds the father's initiative, family members might protest that "it's not such a big deal" or that this small change can have no real impact on their many other problems.

This kind of pessimism is understandable, but the therapist cannot allow it to taint the therapeutic work. Rather, this is precisely the moment when the therapist's perseverance can have an impact. Optimism is conveyed by appreciating small changes and explaining to family members that what seems minor to them now can sow the seeds for a more meaningful change in the future.

When a therapist insists that meaningful change is gradual and the family's goals can be achieved, this optimistic perspective can create a "virtuous circle." That is, engagement in therapy requires positive emotional bonds, and small improvements that a family experiences as a result of the therapy can raise their hopes and improve their trust in and connection to the therapist. In other words, the downward spiral of a disorganized, disadvantaged lifestyle can be transformed into an upward spiral of improved family functioning.

One complication, however, is the frequent occurrence of crisis in the lives of disadvantaged, multi-stressed families. When life is progressing reasonably well, unexpected events can cause a crisis that throws off the therapist as well as the family. It is important to remember that crisis situations are common when a family is suffering multiple hardships and when the only response to stress they know is to increase their risk behaviors (e.g., alcohol or opioid use, sexual acting out, gambling). Crises may not ever be eliminated, but better coping strategies can be learned.

With respect to the alliance, when a crisis occurs, family members have a tendency to devalue everything they have achieved to date. In a crisis, the loss of a sense of safety is not only experienced by the family, but also by the therapist, who can easily begin to doubt himself and his ability to facilitate change. Not uncommonly, the therapist may also doubt the family's ability—or motivation—to make improvements.

Optimism can be regained, however. To do so, therapists need to stay current with best practices in working with poor and disadvantaged families, seek consultation and supervision, and attend relevant clinical trainings. By understanding the worldview of people from the lower social classes, the therapist can build a strong relationship with the family to sustain their collaboration whenever a new crisis occurs.

Serve as a Bridge for Specialized Treatment

The psychological and behavioral changes that result from therapy can generate a cascade of improvements in many areas of a family's life. Generally, when clients' motivation starts to pay off, they see some success in, for example, coordinating their parenting efforts or communicating with greater openness. At this point in treatment, family members often have the energy to turn their attention to external difficulties with finances, housing, employment, or education. It is natural for multi-stressed, disadvantaged families to expect the therapist's help in overcoming these kinds of outside obstacles. However, it is important to explain to the family the kinds of changes that can and cannot reasonably be attained in a psychotherapeutic context.

Nevertheless, families often bring urgent situations to the therapist's attention. The parents' immediate priority may be, for example, to attend to the 18-year-old's recent arrest in order to prevent his incarceration. Of course, the therapist can discuss this crisis with the family, exploring what may have contributed to the boy's criminal activity and discussing how the parents can address the situation without resuming their destructive patterns of aggressive conflict. In other words, the therapist can unite the parents around the new problem and help them increase the resolve to improve their parenting. The therapist needs to be clear, however, that he cannot intervene with judicial officials on the family's behalf in this situation or in any other legal matter.

Communicating the realistic limits of family therapy is essential when building alliances with multi-stressed families. However, some problems, like drug addiction and severe mental illness, naturally seem like they should be addressed in the conjoint therapy. When the therapist determines that a family member's problem is beyond his expertise or requires a specialized treatment that would be better addressed by another provider, how should he handle the referral without hindering the therapeutic alliance?

In our view, two responses need to be avoided: (1) withdrawing altogether after referring the family to a specialized service, such as a drug treatment facility, and (2) continuing the conjoint therapy without helping the family receive specialized care for the affected individual (Escudero, 2013). Naturally, any family would feel abandoned if the therapist "gives up" by discontinuing the conjoint treatment. On the other hand, any family would feel frustrated, even betrayed, if the therapist generates unrealistic expectations for improvement without helping the family obtain the kind of care that is clearly required.

In these circumstances, the most advisable strategy is to expand the alliance by creating an "affected community." As described earlier, the therapist can help family members understand that since everyone is affected by the severe difficulty experienced by one of them, concerted action is needed to address the situation. In doing so, the therapist can educate family members about the specialized intervention and arrange for the necessary services with professionals in the outside agency or treatment center. Facing the situation together is fully compatible with family empowerment, the goal of which is to improve family functioning without creating confusion about what psychotherapy can or cannot do.

Case Example: The Difús Family

The Difús family lived in a village in a rural area, where they rented a dwelling a short distance from the village center. The father, Begory (46), had always worked as a day laborer, while Aicha (38), the mother, worked at home, caring for their children and tending an orchard and some small farm animals.

The parents were from Haiti, where they had met as a young couple. Ten years previously, they immigrated with Begory's parents and their three children, Richo (a boy of 16), Kerline (a girl of 14), and Frandy (a boy of 9). The family lived in a mostly Haitian community but had little contact with neighbors.

Referred by social services, the family requested an appointment at a family therapy center located in the nearest town, about 10 miles from their home. Having a signed release of information from the parents, the social worker who made the referral informed the therapist about the parents' neglect of their two adolescents, Richo and Kerline, who were engaged in various risk behaviors. The worker emphasized the highly charged conflicts in the family, particularly between the teenagers and their father. Additionally, the worker mentioned that recently, in a state of emotional crisis, Aicha had been seen by emergency services at the local hospital. However, after a brief stay in the crisis unit, she did not follow through with the recommended psychiatric referral for a more thorough evaluation.

Over the past year, social services had been pressuring Aicha and Begory to seek help at the family therapy center, with no success. Now, however, several critical events had prompted the parents to accept the referral for treatment. These incidents were detailed in the social worker's formal report to the therapist. The report also outlined the family risks that social services expected to be targeted in therapy.

The first incident was an urgent call from Aicha on the social services' emergency line. She phoned because Richo, who had not been at home for the previous 8 days, was not responding to calls or texts on his cell phone. Responding to the emergency call, the local police opened a case file and searched for the boy. During the investigation, the police found out from the father, who was not aware of Aicha's call to the emergency line, that Richo had been working in a friend's warehouse and all was well.

After being informed of Richo's whereabouts, Aicha explained to the police that she was expected to meet with social services the following day and was afraid of the consequences if she count not account for Richo's whereabouts. The family was receiving financial assistance from social services, and the caseworkers were well aware that Richo was having serious difficulties at home and at school. In addition to conflicts with his parents, he had a habit of drinking and wandering the streets alone until very late at night. Although the parents had made several complaints about their son to the school and to social services, he continually refused to obey them. The parents felt helpless to discipline him due to the 16-year-old's size and physical strength.

The second incident detailed in the social worker's report was also a complaint, but this time it had to do with Kerline, the 14-year-old daughter. Two months earlier, Aicha had called the local police station to report that Kerline had disappeared for 3 days, she was truant from school, and the parents could not handle her. The police managed to reach the girl by phone, but she lied about her whereabouts. In short order, however, she was located at the home of her paternal grandparents, several miles away. According to the worker's report, on being informed that Kerline was found, Aicha asked the police to allow her daughter to stay with the grandparents.

The police report concluded that, based on all the evidence, including conversations with the grandparents and Kerline, the family's obvious disorganization had likely resulted in child neglect. More disturbing still, the worker's report revealed that Kerline had told the police officer that she was afraid to return home because Richo had threatened her with a knife.

The social worker's report also described the latest crisis that had led the parents—finally—to accept the referral for family therapy. Aicha had made yet another urgent call to police, reporting that her husband had hit Kerline during a disagreement about a TV show that the girl was watching. A formal investigation by child protective services resulted in the determination that a small bruise on Kerline's wrist was the result of child abuse.

The following day, Kerline was taken into foster care and Begory was detained by the police. However, after taking his sworn statement, the family court judge approved Begory's provisional release. Kerline returned home with an apparent lack of concern after having forcefully rejected the social worker's recommendation to keep her in foster care. Since both parents now accepted the referral for family therapy and indicated their commitment to follow through, it was decided to allow Kerline to remain at home.

The first therapy session involved the entire family. The therapist easily uncovered a longstanding pattern of conflict and chaotic communication among family members, particularly a great deal of verbal aggression between the two adolescents. Everyone showed a lack of respect for the mother, and the amount of hostility Kerline directed at her father was remarkable.

The father tended to downplay all of these problems and minimize the seriousness of the crisis events described above. The therapist had the impression that Begory's decision to attend the session was strongly influenced by his fear of the police.

For her part, Aicha came across as sincere and open but quite helpless and ineffective. It was clear that none of her attempts to impose rules was supported by her husband, who aligned with the children against her to disavow his own parental responsibilities.

During the initial session, it also became evident that 16-year-old Richo enjoyed a level of freedom that put him at great risk. He boasted that he knew about robberies and drug use in the community. He had no interest in studying but rather hoped to find a job as a gardener. He explained that on weekends he usually went to his grandparents' home—he had no rules there, and sometimes he slept elsewhere.

According to Aicha, Kerline's academic performance had been satisfactory until the previous year, when she began skipping classes and her grades dropped precipitously. Aicha also worried about Kerline's relationships with older boys who, like her daughter, also refused to study.

For her part, Kerline described feeling rebellious. She bitterly complained about the parents' differential treatment of her and Richo—while she was pressured "about everything," he was not expected to do anything. Notably, she denied having been abused by her father, stating that "what happened was just a simple discussion."

Frandy (9) was a mystery for the therapist. He had hardly been mentioned in the report from social services. In the session he was affectionate with his mother and seemed quite used to a way of life with little structure and much conflict. He was at grade level in school, according to Aicha. Although the teacher said that Frandy was "well behaved," she thought he was "overly anxious."

The therapist concluded the first conjoint session by thanking the family members for their participation and openness. She suggested that for the next appointment, her preference was to see them separately in two groups, the parents and then the children.

The family's response to this suggestion was somewhat discouraging. Begory asked if he were "required" to come, explaining that unless he took a job that was somewhat distant from the family center, they would have no money for food. Aicha asked what social services would "do" if Richo and Kerline kept fighting and refused to obey their parents. Richo said that since he was "self-sufficient," he did not need therapy, but he would come so as not to disappoint his father. Kerline warned that if Richo did not attend the session, she would not feel obliged to do so either. For his part, Frandy seemed complacent—he had no questions about any of it.

Begory did attend the next session after all. Alone with the parents, the therapist spent considerable time learning about their history as a couple and why they had decided to leave Haiti. The therapist's goal was to gain the parents' trust by demonstrating that she was not judging them.

Unfortunately, Aicha's responses to these questions seemed to provoke considerable anxiety in her husband. Silent throughout this conversation, Begory became more withdrawn nonverbally and seemed defensive when Aicha was describing their previous life in Haiti (negative SAFETY[11]). Recognizing the potential for a split alliance, the therapist focused on SAFETY and her personal connection with Begory in order to understand and then reduce his defensiveness:

Therapist: Begory (ENGAGEMENT[12]), it seems like the things your wife is telling me about your life in Haiti and your first years in this country are making you uncomfortable (SAFETY[13]). I don't want either of you to tell me something you'd rather not talk about. This isn't an investigation. We're here to help…I'm just a family therapist (EMOTIONAL CONNECTION[14]).

Begory: But I figure everything we talk about will have to be told to the police or to social services.

Therapist: I just have to make a report about seeing you and how the therapy is going, but that'll be in three months. And I have no problem telling you about the notes I take after each session. I don't need to file my first report for three months (SAFETY[15]). Does this help?

---

[11] Client expresses anxiety nonverbally.

[12] Therapist pulls in quiet client by addressing him specifically.

[13] Therapist acknowledges that therapy involves discussing private matters.

[14] Therapist reassures a client's emotional vulnerability.

[15] Therapist provides structure and guidelines for safety.

Begory:	Yes, thank you. When I did what Aicha wants, to discipline our children, I was taken to the police station!
Therapist:	You have my commitment to tell you, session by session, the observations I'm making and I'll read you my report before sending it (EMOTIONAL CONNECTION[16]). (pause) What you said about supporting Aicha and ending up getting detained by the police interests me a lot. Aicha, what do you think about that?
Aicha:	It's true. You (looks at Begory) *have* to work, but I need help to get more control over what the kids do. (to the therapist) And he's trying. But he's hard on them 'cause he's never had to deal with kids' problems before.
Begory:	We've had some very hard years, and it's true that Aicha has been handling the kids by herself.
Aicha:	I didn't want to talk about these problems, but I think I should [do so] *here*... (SAFETY[17]).
Therapist:	I get the idea that you feel helpless with all these crises the last few months and with all the fighting between Richo and Kerline.
Aicha:	Yes! we can't do it any more, and we worry that Frandy'll wind up getting hurt.
Begory (to Aicha)*:*	You're right (SHARED PURPOSE[18]). Actually it's gotten way out of hand. We've got lots of problems because I can't find work close to home. It's been a horrible year.
Therapist:	I understand. And it strikes me that you all feel a great affection and concern for Frandy. Even his brother and sister worry about him (SHARED PURPOSE[19]).
Aicha:	Yeah. We're actually a very close family. We just don't know how to keep calm when we're all together.
Begory:	I'm scared if I try to lay down the law with the kids, I'll get reported to the police or CPS.
Therapist:	I appreciate your honesty, Begory (EMOTIONAL CONNECTION[20]). Do you think we could use the therapy sessions to talk about how you can support each other to be more effective parents (ENGAGEMENT[21])?
Aicha:	I think we need it.

---

[16] Therapist reassures a client's emotional vulnerability.

[17] Client implies that therapy is a safe place.

[18] Family members validate each other's point of view.

[19] Therapist draws attention to clients' shared feelings.

[20] Therapist discloses her personal reactions to the client.

[21] Therapist asks clients whether they are willing to follow a specific suggestion.

Begory (to the therapist):	And do you have some ideas?
Therapist (to Begory):	Well, I think we could start by your finding out what exactly Aicha needs from you, what she is asking from you, since she's the one who's been most concerned about the children's problems. What do you think?
Aicha (excitedly SAFETY[22]):	I need you (Begory) to listen to me! *Nobody* listens to me... sometimes I feel invisible.
Therapist (to Aicha):	I think now Begory *is* listening to you. That's a first step, and here we're not going to judge what was done right or wrong in the past (SAFETY[23]). Our goal is simply to help you tell him what your needs are and what you want from him (ENGAGEMENT[24]).

Aicha felt very supported by this intervention, and Begory seemed reassured. This exchange resulted in a compromise between the parents about not blaming each other over past mistakes (SHARED PURPOSE[25]) and an agreement with the therapist to work on improving their effectiveness with the children (ENGAGEMENT[26]).

In doing so, the therapist pointed out the importance of telling her the family story in order to recall their dreams about leaving Haiti to start a new life for the family. It was quite poignant for the therapist to discover a true love story beneath all the stressors and problems.

In her first session with the three siblings, the therapist's objective was to find some common ground in order to strengthen their relationships with each other and build a within-system alliance about the therapy. Although the initial plan was to have Frandy attend only a portion of the session (so as not to burden this young child with the arguments between the teenagers), it turned out that he was key to creating an atmosphere of cooperation.

Surprisingly, the adolescents were much calmer with their parents absent from the session. The therapist began by asking Frandy to "introduce" her to Kerline and Richo by describing the best and worst aspects of his siblings' personalities. A very outgoing child, Frandy, found it amusing to play this role. With some help from the therapist, he spoke very highly of both teenagers, particularly when describing their unique talents. He had nothing to say about their negative attributes.

With good humor, Kerline and Richo acknowledged Frandy's positive descriptions of them (SHARED PURPOSE[27]). Next, the therapist asked the two teenagers

---

[22] Client varies her emotional tone during the session; client shows vulnerability (e.g., discusses painful feelings).

[23] Therapist helps clients talk truthfully and not defensively with one another.

[24] Therapist explains how therapy works.

[25] Family members offer to compromise.

[26] Clients indicate agreement with the therapist's goals.

[27] Family members share a lighthearted moment with each other.

how they saw their parents' desperation over the past year. Kerline responded by expressing tremendous guilt about her fights with Begory, explaining that she only wanted him to help her mother out a little more. Richo apparently did not realize that his mother was feeling overwhelmed:

Richo:	I guess it's because my dad works a lot and sometimes has to go far away to work. My mom has always taken care of everything, but now it's bad.
Kerline (angrily exclaiming, to Richo)*:*	It's that *you're* always saying you're going to leave home and you don't realize that makes *you* the problem (negative SHARED PURPOSE[28])!
Therapist (to Kerline)*:*	You mean Richo doesn't realize that you need him at home? Do you really need him (SAFETY[29])?
Richo (very surprised, to Kerline):	But how?! You're always fighting with *me* and you say everything I do bothers you.
Therapist (to Richo)*:*	I think Kerline's upset because you're thinking of leaving and not helping her out. Maybe your sister needs you more than you think.
Frandy (interrupting, to Richo):	I don't want you to go, either!
Kerline (to Richo):	See…Frandy needs an older brother, just like maybe I do, too (SHARED PURPOSE[30]). When you're not at home I get nervous that mom's overwhelmed and I don't know what to do (SAFETY[31]).
Therapist:	Richo! Did you ever think they'd be asking you for help (SAFETY[32])?
Richo:	No, and that's the truth!…But don't I get to look out for my own life? Who helps *me*?
Frandy (interrupting again):	Do you have problems with any gang?
Therapist (smiling)*:*	I have a great Therapy Assistant right here (pointing to Frandy) (EMOTIONAL CONNECTION[33])! Richo, do you want to talk about these problems now (ENGAGEMENT[34])? Or we could also do it another time.

---

[28] Family members blame each other.

[29] Therapist actively protects one family member from another (e.g., from blame).

[30] Family members validate each other's point of view.

[31] Client varies her emotional tone during the session.

[32] Therapist helps clients to talk truthfully and not defensively with each other.

[33] Therapist shares a lighthearted moment with the client(s).

[34] Therapist asks client(s) what they want to talk about in the session.

Richo:	Can I talk about them some other time?
Therapist:	Do you mean some other time "alone"?
Richo:	No, not alone. But only with Kerline.
Therapist:	If Frandy agrees (Frandy nods), we can do it next time. Is that okay with you, too, Kerline (ENGAGEMENT[35])?
Kerline:	Sure…(softly) When we were little, Richo always told me his problems.
Richo (to Kerline):	And you did too (SHARED PURPOSE[36])!
Therapist:	I really like the idea that we can use this therapy to get back the closeness you two had years before (SHARED PURPOSE[37]). Do you think it'll help with the tension you feel at home?
Kerline:	Right now, in our house you can't talk about anything. We argue for no reason. We need someone like you to trust (EMOTIONAL CONNECTION[38]).
Therapist:	Thank you, Kerline. Richo, do you feel the same way?
Richo:	I'd be embarrassed if my friends knew I came to therapy…they'd tell me I'm crazy. (pause) But it seems okay. (to Kerline) I didn't think Mom was in such a bad way.
Kerline (to Richo):	I'm not going to tell your friends.
Therapist:	Well, maybe today, with the help of my Assistant Therapist (smiling at Frandy, who nods with an amused expression), we could think of some little thing that during the week would help your mom out a little. Do you agree (ENGAGEMENT[39])? Any ideas?
Frandy (raising his hand):	Me! I want to be the one to find the "answer" (ENGAGEMENT[40]).

This was the beginning of a long and arduous therapy with the Difús family. The format involved varying the sessions with the parents and siblings, as well as holding individual sessions, mostly with Aicha and Richo. Early on, the therapist was able to convince Aicha to be evaluated by her physician to determine whether her emotional difficulties required pharmacological help. This referral turned out to be quite helpful.

---

[35] Therapist asks client(s) whether they are willing to follow a specific suggestion.

[36] Family members validate each other's point of view.

[37] Therapist draws attention to clients' shred experiences.

[38] Client verbalizes trust in the therapist.

[39] Therapist asks client(s) whether they are willing to do a specific homework assignment.

[40] Client agrees to do homework assignment.

Although each member of the family had different concerns and personal goals, the therapist facilitated an expanded alliance in which everyone agreed to be of help to everyone else. Richo, for example, pursued his desire to leave school and be officially emancipated, but he also accepted that his brother and sister needed him to stay close. Kerline wanted more freedom and for her parents to recognize her artistic talent, but she also agreed that she needed to negotiate the rules with her parents and then follow them.

The therapeutic work with Aicha and Begory was perhaps the most complicated part of the treatment. It took the parents quite a while to learn how to coordinate their efforts and share the household responsibilities. Begory came from a highly traditional family in terms of gender roles, whereas Aicha's family of origin was quite disorganized and chaotic. For this reason, the couple sessions focused a fair amount on their respective histories and, notably, on how their Haitian culture and experiences as immigrants affected each of them and their relationship.

Final Thoughts

Construction of a strong therapeutic alliance with a multi-stressed family requires a broad, systemic view of the treatment context. This perspective should cover not only the various areas of stress and difficulty in the family's life but also the history of previous interventions and the other professionals' ongoing relationship with the family.

Creating a safe, personal context for open and honest disclosures requires family members to fully understand the nature of therapy and how it differs from other professional assistance or therapeutic interventions they may have received in the past. Creating safety also often requires conflict management among all the professionals involved in the case so as not to dilute the conjoint family work.

The work to unite the family around a strong SHARED PURPOSE can best be done by creating an "affected community" to work with the therapist toward a common vision, such as maintaining the integrity and dignity of the family. The ENGAGEMENT dimension of the alliance, in particular, requires perseverance and optimism on the part of the therapist to sustain the family's willingness to do the hard work necessary for making therapeutic progress.

References

Alexander, J. F., Waldron, H. B., Robbins, M. S., & Neeb, A. A. (2013). *Functional family therapy for adolescent behavior problems*. Washington, DC: American Psychological Association.
Bachler, E., Frühmann, A., Bachler, H., Aas, B., Strunk, G., & Nickel, M. (2016). Differential effects of the working alliance in family therapeutic home-based treatment of multi problem families. *Journal of Family Therapy, 38*, 120–148.

Bodden, D. H. M., & Deković, M. (2016). Multiproblem families referred to youth mental health: What's in a name? *Family Process, 55*, 31–47.

Coatsworth, J. D., Santisteban, D. A., McBride, C. K., & Szapocznik, J. (2001). Brief strategic family therapy versus community control: Engagement, retention, and an exploration of the moderating role of adolescent symptom severity. *Family Process, 40*, 313–332.

Curtis, N. M., Ronan, K. R., & Borduin, C. M. (2004). Multisystemic treatment: A meta-analysis of outcome studies. *Journal of Family Psychology, 18*, 411–419.

Escudero, V. (2009). *Guía Práctica de la Intervención Familiar I*. Junta de Castilla y León.

Escudero, V. (2013). *Guía Práctica de la Intervención Familiar II. Intervención en contextos cronificados o de especial dificultad*. Junta de Castilla y León.

Friedlander, M. L., Austin, C. L., & Cabrera, P. (2014). When psychotherapy is indefinite and there is no final outcome: Case study of a community mental health clinic. *Psychotherapy, 51*, 580–594.

Friedlander, M. L., Escudero, V., & Heatherington, L. (2006). *Therapeutic alliances with couples and families: An empirically-informed guide to practice*. Washington, DC: American Psychological Association.

Friedlander, M. L., Heatherington, L., Johnson, B., & Skowron, E. A. (1994). "Sustaining engagement": A change event in family therapy. *Journal of Counseling Psychology, 41*, 438–448.

Liddle, H. A., Rowe, C. L., Dakof, G. A., Henderson, C. E., & Greenbaum, P. E. (2009). Multidimensional family therapy for young adolescent substance abuse: Twelve-month outcomes of a randomized controlled trial. *Journal of Consulting and Clinical Psychology, 77*, 12–25.

Liu, W. M., Soleck, G., Hopps, J., Dunstan, K., & Pickett, T., Jr. (2004). A new framework to understand social class in counseling: The social class worldview model and modern classism theory. *Journal of Multicultural Counseling and Development, 32*, 95–102.

Lund, C., De Silva, M., Plagerson, S., Cooper, S., Chisholm, D., Das, J., et al. (2011). Poverty and mental disorders: Breaking the cycle in low-income and middle-income countries. *Lancet, 378*, 1502–1514.

Madsen, W. C. (2007). *Collaborative therapy with multi-stressed families*. New York: Guilford Press.

Madsen, W. C. (2011). Collaborative helping maps: A tool to guide thinking and action in family-centered services. *Family Process, 50*, 529–543.

Madsen, W. C., & Gillespie, K. (2014). *Collaborative helping: A strengths framework for home-based services*. New York: Wiley.

Minuchin, S. (1974). *Families and family therapy*. Cambridge, MA: Harvard University Press.

Sotero, L., Cunha, D., Silva, T., Escudero, V. & Relvas, A.P. (in press). Building alliances with (in)voluntary clients: A study focused on therapists' observable behaviors. *Family Process*.

Sotero, L., Major, S., Escudero, V., & Relvas, A. P. (2016). The therapeutic alliance with involuntary clients: How does it work? *Journal of Family Therapy, 38*, 36–58.

Walsh, F. (2003). Family resilience: A framework for clinical practice. *Family Process, 42*, 1–18.

Walsh, F. (2017). *Strengthening family resilience* (3rd ed.). New York: Guilford Press.

Witkiewitz, K., King, K., McMahon, R. J., Wu, J., Luk, J., Bierman, K. L., et al. (2013). Evidence for a multi-dimensional latent structural model of externalizing disorders. *Journal of Abnormal Child Psychology, 41*, 223–237.

Chapter 7
Empowering Through the Alliance: A Practical Formulation

> The two most powerful warriors are patience and time
>
> —Leo Tolstoy

In this final chapter we describe a general strategy for navigating multiple alliances in particularly challenging therapeutic contexts. Despite many relevant differences among the various clinical cases described in previous chapters, there are nonetheless some important commonalities in working with difficult couple and family cases.

We propose that the commonalities can be organized schematically as a kind of road map. In the sections that follow, we explain and illustrate this map, which is essentially an operative framework, to be read like a flowchart, for building and sustaining strong family alliances. As shown in Fig. 7.1, the map has three sequential steps, each of which relies on specific therapeutic strategies to leverage alliances in the service of family empowerment.

We call the first step *Safety to Connect.* By this, we mean that the Safety within the Therapeutic System dimension of the working alliance is an essential precondition ("Safety first") for ensuring a productive therapeutic process regardless of the intervention context. From the perspective of alliance empowerment, therapists should use specific SAFETY strategies (e.g., explaining confidentiality, acknowledging that it is difficult to reveal private matters to a stranger, and so on) early in therapy to create a non-defensive, non-intrusive relational environment. In other words, SAFETY is the crucial first step in facilitating strong emotional bonds between the therapist and each member of the family.

The second step is *Connect to Engage.* Essentially, this step involves the deliberate use of interventions to strengthen family members' individual emotional connections with the therapist, the objective of which is to facilitate every participant's meaningful engagement in the therapy. To do so, the therapist should closely observe each family member's behaviors reflective of the therapeutic bond and then use explicit CONNECTION strategies (e.g., empathy, normalizing, self-disclosure, immediacy, and so on) to bring everyone into the collaborative process. The basic idea is that effective engagement of all clients in the therapy is largely achieved through strong personal connections with the therapist. After all, in order to risk committing to therapeutic goals and tasks, clients need to feel understood by the

© Springer International Publishing AG 2017

V. Escudero, M.L. Friedlander, *Therapeutic Alliances with Families*, Focused Issues in Family Therapy, DOI 10.1007/978-3-319-59369-2_7

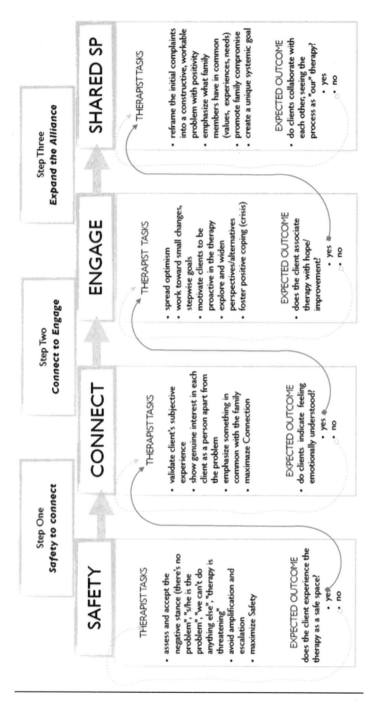

Fig. 7.1 Three-step operative framework for building and sustaining strong family alliances

therapist on an emotional level, trusting him to protect them from further harm. Simply put, emotional connection is the platform that motivates family members to risk changing.

The third and final step involves nurturing a productive *Expanded Alliance* which, in the SOFTA model (Friedlander, Escudero, & Heatherington, 2006), refers to a strong Shared Sense of Purpose within the Family. This within-family alliance, empirically shown to be the strongest predictor of therapeutic success, can be observed in the quality of family members' interactions with one another. Examples of positive interactions include family members offering to compromise, validating one another's point of view in the face of disagreement, sharing a lighthearted moment with one another, and so on. Negative interactions include blaming, trying to align with the therapist against another family member, and so on. Therapeutic strategies to facilitate a SHARED PURPOSE include pointing out commonalities in family members' needs, feelings, or experiences; prompting compromise; encouraging clients to ask each other for feedback; and so on. In work with challenging cases, the "expanded alliance" tends to become strong only when each family member is genuinely connected to the therapist and feels that therapy is a context of comfort and safety.

In short, our framework can be summarized by this axiom: alliance empowerment, the primary characteristic of successful conjoint therapy with challenging cases, is achieved through the use of specific strategies to strengthen the within-family alliance, which requires deliberate enhancement (and constant monitoring) of each family member's levels of safety, emotional connection, and engagement.

Step One: Safety to Connect

A Schema to Address the Initial Challenge

The circumstance that most impedes a strong start to conjoint therapy occurs when one or more family members have fears, secrets, or other difficulties that make the therapeutic context feel threatening. A simple classification of these difficulties suggests three non-mutually exclusive categories: *denial of the problem* (hence, denial of the need for professional help), *drowning in the problem* (hence, helplessness/hopelessness and feeling a lack of control), and *a traumatic reaction to the helping relationship* (hence, avoidance and/or rejection of the therapy).

When the Russell family—Meryl (45), Mark (52), and their son Kevin (15)—stepped into the therapy room for the first time, the parents' full attention was on Kevin. After 15 min of being questioned, the parents had been unable to provide even a basic description of themselves. Kevin, silent, focused all his attention on the therapist. It was particularly a defiant kind of attention, though. His gaze conveyed hypervigilance—just the attitude one would expect before a battle begins.

Actually, Kevin's parents had a similar defensive posture. Like soldiers, their bodies radiated tension, intense wariness about a possible attack, essentially a psychophysiological stance of self-defense. There was one difference: Kevin's eyes were riveted on the therapist, while the parents only had eyes for Kevin. All of the observable SOFTA behaviors were indicators of poor SAFETY and poor SHARED PURPOSE.

Here, then, is a good case for illustrating the implementation of the first step in our model—the need to build a secure base for the therapy. Let's assume that the therapist's theoretical approach prompts her to start off by asking the Russells about the problem that brought them to treatment and/or about their goals for change. For example, she could ask for a description of the family violence that prompted the referral for family therapy. She might further inquire about the family's relationship with the referring agency. Alternately, she could explore, from a solution-focused perspective, what had changed for them since they made the initial call for an appointment.

However, if the therapist ignores the clear negative indicators of SAFETY, she will likely find it difficult to foster a positive start to the therapy. Indeed, the therapy may never *start*.

Here is an excerpt from the actual intake with the Russells, several minutes into the session:

Therapist (to Kevin):	Based on these first few minutes, I'm getting the impression that you are a little angry or that there's something that doesn't work for you (CONNECTION[1]). I don't know if it has to do with the explanation you were given about coming to therapy…or maybe you'd like to ask me something…maybe about my intention or my role here … is that it (ENGAGEMENT[2])?
Kevin (still defensive):	I don't know why you say that.
Therapist:	It's just an impression. I'm very eager to get to know you and your parents (CONNECTION[3]). I'd like to be of help, whatever the difficulty that brings you here.
Kevin:	Difficulty? Nothing. I shouldn't have to be here, as *they're* the ones who want this (negative

---

[1] Therapist discloses his or her personal reactions or feelings toward the client(s) or the situation.

[2] Therapist pulls in quiet client(s), e.g., by addressing them specifically.

[3] Therapist discloses his or her personal reactions or feelings toward the client(s) or the situation.

Therapist:

ENGAGEMENT[4]). So they're the ones who should come.

I understand that being here without wanting to is a bit like feeling trapped, right (CONNECTION[5])?

Kevin (glaring at his parents):

Trapped! Hmph! See! Even he agrees with me (negative SHARED PURPOSE[6])!

Therapist:

What do you think your parents have been feeling all this time that they've been sitting here (SAFETY[7])? I think neither of them is comfortable…I would even say they don't like having to be here (SHARED PURPOSE[8]).

Kevin:

I don't know *what* they feel…well, I don't care.

Therapist:

So what do you think they expect from all this?

Father (interrupting):

Can I explain?

Therapist:

First, I'd rather give Kevin an opportunity to… Kevin (SAFETY[9])?

Kevin (avoiding eye contact with his parents—negative SHARED PURPOSE[10]):

If I'm "trapped," it'll be because they want to make you think I'm a problem and everything is going to hell because of my so-called lack of control. That's what they're going to say.

Therapist:

Thanks, Kevin. I don't want you to feel trapped (CONNECTION[11]). I just need some help to understand how I can help all of you. (to the parents) What do you feel about what you can do or what you can get from this therapy?

---

[4] Client questions the value of therapy.

[5] Therapist expresses empathy.

[6] Family members try to align with the therapist against each other.

[7] Therapist helps clients to talk truthfully and nondefensively.

[8] Therapist draws attention to clients' shared feelings.

[9] Therapist actively protects one family member from another (e.g., from blame).

[10] Family members avoid eye contact with one another.

[11] Therapist discloses his or her personal reactions or feelings toward the client(s) or the situation.

Mother: I think Kevin's acting like he always does, belligerent (negative SHARED PURPOSE[12])… he doesn't want…

Therapist: Sorry to interrupt you, and I am of course very interested in what you have to say about Kevin, but it would be of much more help if you could first tell me how *you* feel about being here today (SAFETY[13]).

Mother: We're very tired and afraid that Kevin doesn't accept anything. It was hard to get him to come here today.

Father: We've done all…I can tell you the details, and it'll take the whole appointment. We spend all year making all kinds of sacrifices, handling unacceptable situations, putting our life aside for Kevin, trying to make Kevin understand the problem. He won't take responsibility for any of it (negative SHARED PURPOSE[14])!

Therapist: Thanks you, both. I think I understand the situation a little better now. I'd like to find a starting point that's not so hard on everyone. I understand that Kevin feels trapped because he's afraid that coming here is a judgment about his behavior. But it won't be that at all. Kevin, for now I'm very interested in your point of view about the conflict that your parents mentioned, but I'd also need to know a little more about your mindset, your view on things and who *you* are (CONNECTION[15]). As well (looking at the parents), I'd like to know the whole story…what brought about this tired feeling, the

---

[12] Family members blame each other.

[13] Therapist actively protects one family member from another (e.g., from blame).

[14] Family members blame each other.

[15] Therapist expresses interest in the client apart from the therapeutic discussion at hand.

> feeling that you've done everything possible. I have to confess that I may need a small guarantee of confidence or trust on your part, from the three of you. I sense that today it'd be uncomfortable for Kevin to hear your story about fatigue and frustration, and also that it wouldn't be nice for you to listen to Kevin's anger...

The therapist closely observes Kevin's reaction and the reactions of his parents to these comments. She continues only after all three family members nod their heads, confirming the sense of discomfort that was blatantly obvious.

Therapist (to the parents):   So, would you give me a chance to talk to Kevin alone for a few minutes about his anger? (looking at Kevin) And then I could speak with your parents for a while? I'm sure after that it'll be easier to decide together how we could approach this therapy (SAFETY[16]).

This excerpt illustrates one way to initiate conjoint therapy with a defiant teenager by focusing on ensuring SAFETY and CONNECTION. What was crucial about how this therapist approached the family?

On the one hand, she focused her attention on the *relational level of communication,* not solely on the content. Specifically, she did not elicit details of the conflict that the three family members identified, nor did she focus on the "lack of control" that Kevin mentioned was his parents' main "accusation" of him. Rather, the therapist was particularly attentive to Kevin's expression of anger and to the fear and apprehension that Meryl and Mark were exhibiting as they observed Kevin's reaction to the therapist and the therapy, all the while blaming him.

On the other hand, the therapist had a working model in which *safety is imperative* for both subsystems (parent(s) and child(ren)) to be heard and feel secure in the therapy. Blame and conflict make it almost impossible for family members to feel understood by one another. For this reason, SAFETY interventions are essential. As noted above, the therapist's most powerful SAFETY intervention was the request to see Kevin and then his parents alone for a portion of the session, which allowed each subsystem to express frustration in a private space with the therapist without fear of retaliation.

In this example, what specific dilemma did the therapist face in trying to build a safe and collaborative working relationship with this family? Basically, she was faced with the same kinds of contradictions that we described in the previous

---

[16] Therapist asks one client (or a subgroup of clients) to leave the room in order to see one client alone for a portion of the session.

chapters of this book. In this particular case, Kevin began by denying that he had a problem. At this point, the therapist was unclear whether his attitude was a visceral refusal to engage in any helping relationship, that is, with her or with any other person who might try to help him. The parents indicated that they had lost all control over the problem. In a sense, they felt almost completely incapable of influencing Kevin's attitude or behavior.

So how can a therapist work effectively with a child or adolescent who denies that there is a problem and whose adult caregivers make it clear that they can do nothing to effect a change? The alternative is transparent: Like the family, the therapist cannot do it alone either—she has to empower change by building alliances with each individual client and with the family as a unit.

Let's begin by classifying and deconstructing three kinds of contradictions that pose a challenge to Safety in the therapeutic context:

1. *Denial of the problem* ("we don't have a problem," "the problem is my parents," "the problem is my husband," "the problem is social services," "the problem is *you*, the therapist")
2. *Drowning in the problem*, which refers to a feeling of lack of control or helplessness/hopelessness in relation to the problem ("we can't do anything else," "this has no remedy," "maybe we deserve all this")
3. *Traumatic response to the helping relationship*, i.e., the intent to help is itself the problem, or the therapeutic context reveals the client's insecure attachment

While the therapist's awareness of these three types of difficulties may be practically useful, *the dynamic interaction of these difficulties in a particular family is even more essential to understand*. In the Russell family, the parents' sense of impotence pushed them to focus all their energy on forcing Kevin to admit his aggressiveness, which they saw as the first step to changing his behavior. However, their intense "tunnel vision" only served to increase the boy's denial and defensiveness. The result was a vicious cycle in which the therapist had little maneuverability.

Other kinds of family dynamics can also challenge the initiation of therapy. As one other example, consider a mother who begins the first session by insisting that her daughter acknowledge a lack of control following a traumatic sexual assault, so therefore she *should* be open to being helped by a therapist. Unfortunately, the mother is unaware that her daughter experiences the therapeutic context as another assault on her integrity. The mother's failure to recognize her daughter's intense fear of entering into a therapeutic relationship generates a demand/withdraw cycle. That is, the more the mother demands the daughter to comply therapy, the more the daughter withdraws, and seeing her daughter withdraw, the mother makes even more demands for compliance.

In another case, a woman complains that while her husband denies all the problems in their relationship, she is ready to leave him because the problems are "insurmountable." Forced into the first session by the threat of abandonment, the husband is experiencing a keen sense of helplessness. In the first few minutes, he tells the therapist that since he has "no control whatsoever" over his wife's "decision" to end the marriage, "she may as well go ahead and do it – therapy is a waste of time."

Understanding and Working with Denial

Without a doubt, the first approach to a couple or family that is experiencing a lack of safety requires developing an understanding of the problem denial and rejection of the implication that psychotherapy is required. As explained below, three factors tend to be associated with a stance of denial: (1) relational antagonism, (2) not seeing or experiencing the problem, and (3) unconscious defense mechanisms.

Relational Antagonism Often the "I don't have a problem" attitude (Madsen, 2007) or location of the problem in someone else (my husband, my parents, my partner, etc.) is an indication that the client rejects the problem definition that others are promoting about him. For example, an adolescent rejects the conclusion of official evaluators (teacher, social services, probation officer, etc.) that he has problems requiring professional help, or he comes to the first session having experienced the referral process as pejorative or demeaning. Alternately, he may reject the authority of the person or system that located the problem in him. Examples include the teenager who resists virtually all adult figures (his parents, teachers, religious leader) and the woman who resists pressure from significant others (her partner, parents, friends). Not surprisingly, relational antagonism is most likely to occur when a system external to the family mandates psychotherapy as a condition for some desired outcome, such as avoiding imprisonment or the termination of parental rights.

Not Seeing or Experiencing the Problem As explained in Chap. 6, some families have been exposed to such a chronically high level of negligence or conflict that they legitimately fail to recognize what the larger community views as clear "risk behaviors." It is particularly challenging to work with violent or near-violent couples who do "not see any problems" because their entire lives are spent in a kind of microculture where conflict is the norm.

In these kinds of families, extreme conflict is commonplace, not only in the parents' personal histories but also in their families of origin. When a case is further complicated by the exposure or involvement of minor children to domestic conflict, it is not surprising that the parents fail to recognize the problems that the therapist (and referring agency) view as indicative of serious risk.

Working with families that live in impoverished communities where socio-educational deficits are common has taught us that negligence is almost invariably denied as a legitimate reason for family therapy, even with documented evidence to the contrary. One way to approach these families is to explore—with empathy—the life stories of the parents or caregivers in order to understand their personal experience as children. In almost every case, the history shows that as children, the parents were neglected, abused, or otherwise maltreated by their own parents. Hearing the parents' stories can help the therapist understand, with empathy, why they are failing to recognize the severity of the family problem and the critical need for therapeutic help.

It is particularly difficult to break through a family's resistance when there is an extreme lack of safety. Essentially, receiving a referral for psychological treatment implies that the parents must address risks or deficits—even dangerous neglect of their children—that are simply the norm for them.

This is not to imply that child negligence is solely caused by living in poverty. Sometimes neglect is transmitted trans-generationally, even in affluent families when the parents, as children, had received inadequate attention from their own parents.

A lack of problem recognition may also be a reflection of the family's ethnicity, inasmuch as culturally based norms around parenting, marriage, and child-rearing differ widely. Behavior that is considered normative in some cultures, such as the corporal punishment of children or the forced marriage of young teens, is seen as highly problematic in other cultures. Living as we are in an increasingly diverse society, therapists need to be aware of their own biases. To understand the world-view of families in minority cultures, therapists should seek the help of community leaders or professionals as needed so as to avoid causing further harm.

Defense Mechanisms In some cases, the denial of a problem that prompted a referral for couple or family therapy by an external agency is rooted in an unconscious defense mechanism. In these instances, the display of defensiveness does not result from a serious psychological disorder but rather is due to the client's perception that therapy is unsafe. After all, as therapists we invite—even urge—people to face very painful situations that may exceed their capacity to cope.

Denial and rationalization are two common defense mechanisms often seen in the earliest stages of therapy, even in otherwise well-functioning couples and families. Nonetheless, denial of a problem due to an unconscious defense requires the same attention to safety as the other factors underlying the all-too-common resistance to treatment.

Take the case of Guadalupe, an 11-year-old girl who began therapy with her mother a few weeks after the suicide of her father. The parents had divorced 3 years previously. When Guadalupe and her mother came for their first session, the girl could not respond to any question that the therapist asked about her mood or behavior. Instead, she made every effort imaginable to divert attention from herself, claiming that she had no idea what her mother meant by her "extreme behavior."

The therapist decided to concentrate solely on creating a safe base for Guadalupe, understanding that the chronically poor relationship between her parents prevented Guadalupe from accepting comfort from her mother or even from asking her mother about her father's death. To create safety, the therapist made it clear that he would not force her to talk about the suicide but rather invited her to spend some time alone with him playing (age-appropriate) games.

This approach resulted in a strong emotional bond between Guadalupe and the therapist. Feeling deeply understood and trusting the therapist, Guadalupe gradually brought down her defenses. Eventually it became apparent that denial was an unconscious way for this traumatized child to protect herself from guilt. Tearfully she told the therapist that she "should have done something" after she received a farewell text message from her father indicating his suicidal intent.

Guidelines for Creating Safety in a Context of Denial

Simply put, therapists need to avoid creating a vicious cycle with families in denial. The more people are pressed to acknowledge their problems (as defined by external agencies or by others who are demanding change), the more they tend to increase their resistance (conscious or unconscious) by denying the problem. Actually, denial is a natural response to the tension and pressure applied by others, including well-intentioned friends and professionals. To avoid becoming caught up in a cycle of demanding/denying the need for change, therapist can use three Safety to Connect strategies: avoid confrontation, enhance emotional connections, and define the problem systemically.

Avoid Confrontation   The most important guideline is to avoid amplifying the client's defensive position of denial by, for example, insisting that she "obviously" has a problem and presenting "evidence" of the problem's existence. In other words, therapists need to carefully avoid engaging in behaviors (questions, explanations, challenges) that prompt an oppositional response. Opposition, which tends to occur when a person feels judged or threatened in some way, is particularly likely to occur when other professionals previously failed to convince the family that therapy is necessary.

Rather, it is critically important to explore all the circumstances surrounding the three patterns of denial described earlier. If the client's behavior suggests a "relational antagonism" to the context of professional help, the therapist should normalize the client's hostile response (e.g., "Of course, it's natural to resent being forced to talk such personal matters when you'd rather not"). If the client's behavior suggests not recognizing risk due to living with chronic conflict or neglect, the therapist should carefully explore these culturally bound limitations. Finally, if the client seems to be defending against an acknowledgment of the problem, the therapist should pace her interventions carefully so as not to exacerbate the client's unconscious fears.

Several SOFTA SAFETY interventions are particularly helpful in the context of problem denial. These include providing structure and guidelines for safety and confidentiality, inviting the client to discuss any elements in the therapeutic context that might seem intimidating (e.g., audio- or video-recording equipment, mandated reports to third parties, observation by a treatment team, a one-way mirror, research questionnaires, etc.), and acknowledging the fact that therapy requires taking risks and discussing very private matters with a stranger.

Enhance Emotional Connections   By focusing on each family member's subjective experiences and personal history, therapists are able to distinguish the *person* from the *problem*. From the perspective of alliance creation, therapists need to approach each family member empathically. Other SOFTA interventions to enhance CONNECTION include expressing confidence, trust, or belief in the client; showing interest in the client apart from the therapeutic discussion at hand; disclosing personal reactions or feelings toward the client or the situation; and reassuring or normalizing the client's emotional vulnerability, not only his hurt feelings but also his anger.

Redefine the Problem Systemically To take the burden off the partner or family member whom others have defined as the problem, therapists can reinterpret the difficulty as one shared by the entire family system. In doing so, therapists need to approach clients' fears or deficiencies with sensitivity. Empowerment can happen when a therapist identifies something that "worries" the family as a whole and is a "common problem" that "I often see in families."

In previous chapters of this book, we discussed the importance of reframing as a valuable technique for involving the entire family in setting goals and negotiating tasks for the therapy. Reframing is particularly helpful for defining a problem systemically. Examples include "getting back on track as a family, now that Jamie has come home from jail," "adapting to an empty nest by reinvigorating your relationship as a couple," or "supporting each person as an individual, while still respecting the family's Muslim traditions."

When faced with strong problem denial, the therapist urgently needs to construct a problem definition other than the one previously imposed on the family by others. Optimally, the desired system-wide change is identified and prioritized by the clients themselves. When this occurs, families are more likely to feel validated and therefore accepting of therapeutic help.

Guidelines for Creating Safety When Clients Are Drowning in Problems

Many challenging couples and families described in the previous chapters have one characteristic in common: a feeling of dependence or helplessness/hopelessness. Overwhelmed, they have no faith in their ability to cope with and solve their problems. Unfortunately, when this characteristic is interpreted by professionals as *passivity*, it is extremely difficult to create a strong working alliance with the family. Rather, it is more effective to understand this challenge as due to a lack of safety in the therapeutic context.

Usually, by the time overwhelmed families come to their first therapy appointment, other professionals have done everything in their power to convince them that they *can* and *should* address their problems; further, it is only *logical* that they accept the help being offered to them. Typically, families have responded to this pressure with statements like "We can't do anything more," "We've already tried everything," "No matter what I think, they'll do what *they* want," and so on. Therapists should avoid interpreting these comments as avoidance of responsibility or minimization of the problem's severity.

If the therapist continues to pressure the family to change, a vicious cycle is likely to entrench the problems even further: That is, the more the therapist magnifies the problems and justifies the need for family members to do something to address them, the more they respond with helplessness and hopelessness.

When a therapist is frustrated in the face of the family's helplessness, her well-intentioned pressure for the clients to "do something" tends to be delivered with a critical tone that generates an even greater feeling of helplessness and being "out of control." Not surprisingly, the family's response to a frustrated, critical therapist is likely to be an increase in defensiveness or avoidance. These responses on the part of family members are observable in negative SAFETY indicators, such as expressing anxiety nonverbally (e.g., tapping, shaking), avoiding eye contact with the therapist, or being reluctant to respond to the therapist's questions. Unfortunately, therapists who find themselves caught up in this dynamic often fail to attend to their clients' sense of vulnerability.

In Chaps. 5 and 6, we described a variety of factors influencing the attitude of feeling out of control or helpless and hopeless that can lead clients to behave passively in the initial stages of therapy. In cases like these, it is important to thoroughly explore (a) what was not helpful or frustrating in previous therapy experiences, (b) the history of the family's unsuccessful search for a solution to the problem, and (c) their fear of any situation that might generate more family conflict or violence.

Understanding these factors will help the therapist understand the nuances in the family's circumstances, which she can then use to leverage a positive therapeutic alliance. In doing so, the therapist can determine whether family members are in a pre-contemplation stage of change (Prochaska & DiClemente, 1982) and therefore weakly (at best) committed to the therapeutic process or if family members desire change but are experiencing a post-traumatic stress response to the therapy, feeling like victims rather than like people capable of working toward change.

We suggest three useful guidelines for empowering families that enter therapy overwhelmed and helpless in the face of their problems. These include respecting the feeling of drowning, connecting emotionally by eliciting the history, and conveying patience.

Respect the Feeling of Drowning As in the context of problem denial, it is critically important to avoid enhancing or amplifying a family's negative stance on the problem or their participation in therapy by, for example, insisting that they *can* change or by advising specifically what they *should* do to change. SAFETY interventions that are particularly helpful in this context include explicitly acknowledging that therapy involves taking risks or discussing private matters, providing structure and guidelines for safety and confidentiality, and helping clients talk truthfully and nondefensively with each other.

Connect Emotionally by Eliciting the History Rather than focusing efforts on change talk, therapists should listen with respect and interest to the family's history of resignation and helplessness. The objective is not to respond with compassion but rather to convey that it is understandable that they feel tired and "out of control" and that the family's response to the situation is a logical one given its seriousness. Further, the therapist should make it clear that due the many complex problems, he has some familiarity with the kind of circumstances the family has been describing.

Convey Patience Engagement in therapy is likely to be a gradual process with families like these. Often one member of the family feels victimized by the others, such as parents of a very troubled teenager who has been violent with his siblings or a woman who was abandoned by her partner after the birth of their disabled child. Sometimes the family feels victimized by outsiders, such as parents whose children have been removed from the home by child protective services.

Patience is key. Before the family can become "clients" in a therapeutic sense, they need to feel comfortable with the therapist. They need to see her as a caring person who is helping them recover from the traumatic events that occurred or are still occurring in their lives. Generally, this stance of "convalescence" precedes a family's acceptance of the role of "client," i.e., as active partners with the therapist in negotiating therapeutic goals and tasks for change. In other words, the objective is to maximize safety so as to help the "drowning" couple or family connect with the therapist on an emotional level.

Guidelines for Creating Safety When Clients Have a Traumatic Response to Therapy

In previous chapters of this book, we described challenges to the construction of the alliance due to relational trauma in the family system. In Chap. 3, we noted that difficulties in a family can arise due to an insecure attachment style (or disorder) in one or both parents. In Chap. 5, we discussed the challenge of establishing a therapeutic relationship with clients who have suffered a relational trauma that damaged their ability to trust others, even those who are offering them care and concern.

At this point, we want to emphasize that relational trauma poses a specific kind of challenge to the creation of therapeutic alliances. Unfortunately, in some cases, a severe trauma history—or ongoing, chronic trauma—can make it impossible to form a strong alliance with an individual or a family. Sometimes dropout is unavoidable. However, as we explained in Chap. 5, uncovering a family's relational traumatic history requires an even more deliberate strategy to build a secure basis in the therapy. The following are some important guidelines for using the alliance to empower clients who enter therapy having suffered relational trauma.

Accepting the Contradictions In the face of trauma, a client's response to the helping relationship is likely to seem contradictory. That is, when the alliance improves, the client may feel more threatened, even to the point of "boycotting" the therapy or seemingly trying to destroy the basis of trust already established with the therapist. Recognizing the client's pullback, the therapist should avoid the understandable reaction to be frustrated or disappointed. Rather, he needs to realize, and then help the client understand, that her distancing from their close, personal relationship is a natural response to having been traumatized by someone else.

Adapt to the Client's Attachment Style   Having a traumatic response to the therapeutic relationship is most likely to occur with clients who have a disorganized
attachment style and/or have suffered extreme abuse. Clients who feel threatened
tend to demonstrate their extreme lack of safety by, for example, avoiding eye contact or refusing to answer questions. Alternately, these clients may engage in
pseudo-collaboration or minimize their problems. In terms of SOFTA behavior, clients with ambivalent attachment tend to demonstrate their lack of SAFETY by
expressing their anxiety nonverbally, making uneasy references to some aspects of
the therapy context (e.g., video camera, observation, supervision, research). In more
extreme cases, these clients tend to show their lack of SAFETY by commenting on
the therapist's incompetence or inadequacy or by initiating hostile or sarcastic interactions with the therapist.

When a client's behavior suggests an ambivalent attachment style, the therapist
needs to be a constant, stable presence in the face of the client's volatility. On the
other hand, when the client's relational positioning with the therapist suggests an
avoidant attachment style, the therapist should keep an appropriate emotional distance so that his caring concern is not viewed as threatening.

However, regardless of the type of attachment disorganization exhibited by the
client, when it seems that the therapeutic context is prompting a trauma response,
the first therapeutic objective should be to increase the client's trust by enhancing
CONNECTION. Only by demonstrating a constant level of care and concern can a
therapist reduce the client's fears of abandonment.

Step Two: Connect to Engage

After some degree of Safety has been established, the therapist should closely
observe each client's SOFTA indicators of emotional connection, which reflect the
quality of his personal alliance with the therapist. Particularly when the therapeutic
bonds are weak, therapists should deliberately use CONNECTION interventions to
facilitate each family member's active involvement in the therapy. The objective is
for everyone to feel that his personal perspective is deeply understood by the therapist, even when there are striking differences in family members' views on the problem and the potential solutions.

Feeling emotionally understood tends to have several favorable consequences.
Not only does it promote the belief that the therapist fully comprehends the presenting concerns, but also it promotes a feeling of relief. In general, clients are less tense
when they feel partnered with a therapist who understands their unique perspective,
their subjective experience. Moreover, having a strong emotional bond with the
therapist helps family members feel accepted rather than judged. This feeling of
unconditional acceptance is essential, so that later on clients are not resistant when
the therapist challenges their problematic behaviors or attitudes.

Feeling Emotionally Understood

Below we highlight some aspects that, in our experience, are determinants of positive emotional connection as reflected in SOFTA behavioral indicators.

First, family members act as if they do not feel judged, even when their initial attitudes are contradictory or at odds with a therapeutic context of change. These attitudes include the previously described positions of denial, drowning in problems, and a traumatic response to being helped or cared for.

Second, each client's subjective experience in relation to the problem—his anger, hopelessness, feeling of abandonment, betrayal, or injustice—is explicitly validated by the therapist in front of the rest of the family. Therapists should not lose sight of the fact that in conjoint therapy, a strong alliance is empowering for the very reason that each client observes the developing relationship between the therapist and the other clients.

Validation does not imply a justification of the client's behavior, nor does it imply that the therapist is aligning with one client against the other members of the family. In fact, therapists can—and should—validate the subjective experiences of family members whose views or positions on the problem are in direct opposition with one another.

Third, family members recognize the therapist's genuine interest in them as people apart from the problems or difficulties that brought them to therapy. Emotional connection strategies are also useful to draw attention to any personal characteristics that the therapist may have in common with the family. For example, using a judiciously timed self-disclosure, a therapist might mention that being an adoptive father himself, he fully appreciates the issues the family is facing.

Enhancing Engagement

In our family empowerment framework, fostering emotional connections is a powerful way to motivate each partner or family member to become actively involved in the therapeutic process. Regardless of the therapist's theoretical approach, style, or technique, ENGAGEMENT can be enhanced by using specific alliance strategies to empower the family to embrace change. Five therapeutic attitudes or skills are particularly facilitative of engagement: optimism, amplification, exploration, motivation, and resistance to crisis, as described below:

1. *Optimism.* Fundamentally, an optimistic attitude conveys the therapist's strong conviction that it is possible for the family to make improvements or resolve their problems. It is essential to communicate optimism about even small changes that result from family members' active engagement in therapeutic tasks, such as having completed a homework assignment or having made a minor shift in behavior (e.g., making eye contact with each other in the session).

2. *Amplification*. This skill refers to the therapist's ability to value small possibilities or instances of change. By developing scaled objectives or stepwise therapeutic goals and then amplifying them as each small success is achieved, the therapist can avoid overwhelming the family with the enormity of change. When working with a highly conflictual couple, for example, the therapist might suggest that each partner give the other 15 min of quiet time after returning home from work before asking questions or making requests. Even if the couple sees this "assignment" to be rather naïve in the context of their drama, the therapist could explain that once this small shift becomes habitual, she will suggest something a bit more challenging.

3. *Exploration*. An exploratory stance can widen family members' perspectives on their difficulties and open them up to considering alternatives. By demonstrating curiosity and interest in all of the family's shared experiences, the therapist can suggest trying some creative alternatives that are not routine. Suggestions that are just slightly out of the clients' comfort zone are most likely to be well received. For example, the therapist could help the parents of an angry teenager (like Kevin) to make a list of out-of-the ordinary, even absurd, responses they could make in the face of his defiance.

4. *Motivation*. The therapist needs to motivate family members to discover and then implement unique solutions to their difficulties. By valuing and encouraging all possible changes suggested by the family, the therapist's positive attitude can sustain them even in the face of failure. For example, the therapist can reframe an unsuccessful change attempt as a "trial-and-error learning experience."

5. *Resistance to crisis*. A therapist's resistance to acting precipitously in the face of a crisis is essential for creating safety and facilitating the family to cope, particularly when their emotions are highly volatile. Essentially, to promote ENGAGEMENT, therapists need to remain "centered" when faced with a sudden instability arising from either (a) the family's life circumstances (e.g., loss of employment or eviction from an apartment), (b) a relational crisis in the family (e.g., a child runs away from home), or (c) a rupture to the therapeutic alliance (e.g., a partner storms out of the therapy session in anger).

Let's return to the case of Kevin Russell. When he, and then his parents, met alone with the therapist, she found it much less difficult to create a bond with the teenager than with Meryl and Mark. This ease of connection surprised the therapist. It seemed to come as a surprise to Kevin as well.

Basically, the initial bond began when the therapist showed great interest in Kevin's personal life and the reasons behind his anger. She expressed curiosity when asking him to recall previous episodes of aggression. The therapist's lack of judgment was a stark contrast to all that Kevin had experienced in the previous months with other adults.

In response to her questions, Kevin described the tension at home as an environment of contagious fear, since all three family members reacted with either aggression or panic whenever they had the least disagreement. At school, Kevin experienced a great deal of stress as well, from peers as well as teachers. Further, Kevin had "survived" several stressful interviews with various representatives of social services.

Undoubtedly, all of these negative experiences were in striking contrast to the therapist's initial approach to Kevin. The result was that the initiation of therapy was far less conflictual than expected.

In a subsequent individual session, Kevin mentioned the decisive moment that convinced him not to storm out of the first therapy appointment. He recalled that the therapist had asked him if he was curious about his own explosions of violence, a conversation that the therapist remembered perfectly but had not seen as particularly important at the time. Kevin reminded the therapist of their conversation on this topic (ENGAGEMENT[17]), in which she had said the following:

Therapist:	I see you're telling me how you're being called an "aggressive boy," a teenager who can't or doesn't want to live with other people, even worse. You're also telling me that you're being crudely described as a kid who mistreats and despises his own parents....But I'd like you to forget about all that and just tell me if you're curious to understand how you *really* are, and how your reactions that are full of rage sometimes turn into aggression...?
Kevin:	...if I'm curious? I am who I am. I know how my stuff happens.
Therapist:	But you said that you're not that person described by your parents and social services, right?
Kevin:	No, I can't stand all that shit.
Therapist:	So, explain to me...or better, *show* me how you are.
Kevin:	Hmm...I'm quiet and strong.
Therapist:	Quiet?! Well, right now I see a calm guy, yes, maybe (CONNECTION[18]). And yet it seems that this Kevin is not very strong.
Kevin:	What do you mean?
Therapist:	Everything happening to you lately is burying this calm guy that you say you are. I mean, you're not able

---

[17] Client mentions the treatment, the therapeutic process, or a specific session.

[18] Therapist discloses her personal reaction to the client.

	to call up that calm version of Kevin…in fact, you can't avoid the Kevin who winds up becoming involved in a fight… so this doesn't show you to be strong.
Kevin:	I've never had that thought. I never saw it that way…
Therapist:	So, are you curious enough to explore what gets you going so that you wind up full of rage (ENGAGEMENT[19])?
Kevin (leaning forward, ENGAGEMENT[20]):	Do you mean talk about it in therapy? …I have some ideas. Yes, I think it'd be good to figure that out.
Therapist:	And what other things are unknown parts of you, Kevin? For example, are you sensitive…or romantic (CONNECTION[21])?
Kevin:	I don't think so! If you find that out about me, THAT would be a surprise!(Bothlaugh.CONNECTION[22])

This segment had as its therapeutic objective to strengthen the emotional bond with the client. Interestingly, it was Kevin himself who mentioned this moment as a significant turning point in his engagement in the therapy. We can take this example as a lesson about how a therapist's genuine, respectful, and humble curiosity about an adolescent can promote a notable shift in his engagement in the therapeutic process.

With the Russell parents, however, the therapist was surprised to find it much more difficult to promote their involvement. In fact, only Meryl displayed any behaviors indicative of positive ENGAGEMENT.

In a few sessions alone with the parents, the therapist fulfilled her promise to hear them out fully. She demonstrated a keen interest in their perspective and invested much time listening to the parents explain their many unsuccessful attempts to help Kevin over the previous 3 years. This failure included not only their own strategies to change him but also their constant search for professional helpers to "make" Kevin behave less impulsively and become more mature and communicative. They never got very far with any of these attempts. In fact, no one had ever given them a

---

[19] Therapist asks client(s) whether they are willing to do a specific in-session task.

[20] Client leans forward (in direct response to a question from the therapist); client indicates agreement with the therapist's goals.

[21] Therapist shows interest in the client apart from the therapeutic discussion at hand.

[22] Client and therapist share a lighthearted moment.

clear psychiatric diagnosis to explain their son's problematic behaviors, and despite Kevin's high intelligence, he had been expelled from several high schools.

Recognizing that these parents were "drowning" in their problems, the therapist insisted that they had the right and a strong need for self-care. Throughout the discussion, she adopted a friendly attitude, respecting their great fatigue and overwhelming frustrations.

During a couple of early sessions, Mark opened up quite well, explaining that because his father had been very authoritarian and aggressive, he had a deep abhorrence of violence. After this disclosure, however, his participation in the therapy was very spotty. He only attended another couple of sessions in the final phase of therapy, after Kevin's behavior had improved markedly, and he had begun attending a rehabilitative day program.

For her part, Meryl found the therapy to be a space for self-reflection. She easily expressed her emotions, particularly her fears for her son. Feeling deeply understood by the therapist, she became progressively more involved in the therapy. In conjoint sessions with Kevin, mother and son made some minor but important commitments to change which greatly improved the emotional atmosphere at home.

Step Three: Nurturing the Expanded Alliance

The third and final step of our framework for building and sustaining working alliances is to develop a productive "expanded alliance," the goal of which—in SOFTA terminology—is to achieve a strong Shared Sense of Purpose within the Family. As mentioned earlier and illustrated in previous chapters, the within-family alliance is a significant predictor of therapy success which, in difficult cases, tends to improve in the middle stage of successful conjoint therapy. In our operative model, we see the within-family alliance strengthening over the course of therapy due to continual monitoring of SAFETY, emotional CONNECTION, and all family members' ENGAGEMENT in the therapeutic process.

Nurturing an expanded alliance was key to successful therapy for Guadalupe and her mother, who had sought help to cope with the father's suicide. How did the within-family alliance come about with this grieving family?

In her alone time with the therapist, Guadalupe quickly developed a strong emotional connection with him, which was helped along by his playful and humorous attitude toward her. The therapist also held a few sessions alone with the mother, which she used productively to explore her guilt over her ex-husband's suicide. In response to these disclosures, the therapist demonstrated empathy and normalized her conflicted feelings. In other words, the therapist took the time in individual sessions with both mother and daughter to create SAFETY and a strong emotional CONNECTION to ensure that each individual felt deeply understood.

When the conjoint sessions began, however, Guadalupe and her mother had a serious relational difficulty. They found it impossible to discuss the father, even less his dramatic death. Recognizing their extreme lack of safety with one another, the therapist carefully approached the expansion of the alliance in a way that was least threatening. Using SHARED PURPOSE interventions (emphasizing commonalities in the clients' feelings and experiences), he explained that both family members were afraid they could not help each other. They both felt sad. They both felt angry. They both felt guilty. Driven by a strong need to be protected, each felt incapable of protecting the other. The result was that they both experienced the same unbearable solitude. Expanding the alliance further, the therapist reframed the goal of their work together as "you two supporting each another to come to terms with the traumatic loss you've suffered."

Perhaps the most powerful intervention, however, was the following. When it became clear that the first conjoint session was not working, the therapist asked Guadalupe and her mother to agree to a plan, whereby each of them would simply observe the therapist conversing with the other. The therapist took turns, speaking first with Guadalupe while her mother watched and then vice versa. These one-on-one conversations were aimed at eliciting feelings about how hard it was to talk about their loss.

In proposing this plan, the therapist suggested that each client should write him a note after the session describing her reactions to what she had heard from the other. The objective was to enhance Safety while cautiously approaching the fearful topic of the father's suicide.

Although both mother and daughter agreed to this plan, the notes proved to be unnecessary. Instead, they naturally began interacting directly with one another in the session, which carried over at home. After finally disclosing her "secret" (about her father's farewell text message) to her mother, Guadalupe had little trouble becoming an active participant in the conjoint therapy process.

Guidelines for Expanding the Alliance

Of particular importance related to the expanded or within-family alliance are the following four points. First, the therapist needs to emphasize all that family members have in common with one another. To do so, she can elicit the family's history, focusing particularly on family members' shared values, emotional experiences, and the suffering caused by the problems that brought them to treatment. In doing so, she can point out that there are some solutions to which all family members are aspiring, such as "improved communication," "respect for each person as an individual," and so on.

Second, the therapist can make liberal use of reframing to provide the family with a more hopeful perspective to help them consider alternatives for approaching and overcoming their difficulties. A two-step therapeutic intervention is particularly helpful in this regard. The therapist can begin by emphasizing positive experiences, emotions, and memories that had become buried by the current conflicts or other problems. With Guadalupe and her mother, for example, the therapist pointed out their good intentions, to protect each other from further pain. Then, she can use all of the information about shared experiences to help the family create a new perspective on their lives, one in which good intentions are valued.

Third, the therapist needs to work toward creating a therapeutic goal for the entire family. For the expanded alliance to be a powerful force in change, therapy cannot simply be a series of individual solutions for different family members. Optimally through reframing, the therapist helps the family construct a shared goal, one that allows each client to benefit personally but that also reflects the sense that the therapy can benefit everyone in the family.

Fourth, the therapist should promote compromise and commitment. Early on, family members tend to agree to work together as a compromise with the therapist. However, the most important strategy is for the therapist to facilitate commitments to change between the family members themselves.

In brief, expanding the alliance is the sine qua non of successful conjoint therapy. When we consider that a crucial aspect of therapeutic work is to provide families with the tools they need to solve their current problems—such as respectfully listening to and validating each other, compromising instead of blaming, and so on—a shared sense of purpose has the added benefit of giving families a blueprint for confronting future difficulties. As one woman replied when asked why she thought couple therapy had been successful in saving her marriage, "My husband saw the therapist take me seriously. So he started doing that, too!"

A Schematic Understanding of Couple and Family Alliances

To provide a visual representation of the intersection of individual and expanded alliances at a single point in time, we created a two-dimensional graph (see Fig. 7.2). Along one dimension, we consider the individual alliance, globally speaking from problematic to strong. Along the other dimension, we consider the expanded alliance, also from problematic to strong. Thus, at the uppermost extreme, we have a very strong/positive individual alliance, whereas at the lowest extreme, we have a very weak or problematic alliance. Similarly, on the left side of the horizontal axis, we have a very problematic expanded alliance, with a very strong expanded alliance on the right side of the axis.

The dots in the four quadrants of the graph depict four different alliance positions, Individual X Shared. The dots could either represent different clients, different families, or one family at different points in the therapy. For example, the dot labeled #1 depicts the alliances for a couple in which both partners' individual alliances in Session 1 are strong, with highly problematic expanded alliance. In other words, both partners are highly engaged, feel safe in the therapeutic context, and have a positive emotional bond with the therapist. However, they express dissimilar views on the goals and purpose of the therapy (she thinks he should change, he thinks she should change). Their poor shared sense of purpose is reflected behaviorally in their mutual blame and refusal to compromise or validate one another.

Fig. 7.2 Individual by expanded alliances

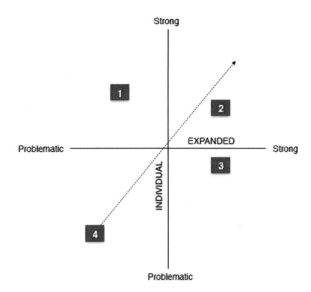

As another example, in the Russell family, Kevin's and Meryl's alliances gradually improved over time in treatment, especially as they each felt safer and became more engaged and connected with the therapist. However, the within-family alliance took much longer to develop; indeed, it never became particularly strong. Early in treatment, mother and son were located at point #1, representing highly positive individual alliances but a problematic expanded alliance. However, by the end of therapy, their alliances would be depicted by point #2, which represents more favorable individual alliances as well as a stronger shared alliance.

Point #3 represents a strong within-family alliance but a relatively weaker individual alliance. This point depicts, for example, the alliance of one family member who agrees with the others on the goals and value of therapy but has a relatively weak personal alliance in terms of ENGAGEMENT, SAFETY, and CONNECTION.

Finally, point #4 represents the most challenging clinical situation, one that reflects many of the families described in this book. The alliances of all family members are negative and highly individual, that is, with a very problematic within-family alliance.

The diagonal arrow in the figure depicts the ideal alliance trajectory for challenging couples and families. The arrow points to the upper right quadrant of the graph, showing that over the course of successful therapy with challenging cases, alliances tend to move from very negative or weak individual alliances to an increasingly strong expanded alliance within the family.

Of course, this figure is merely a hypothetical representation of alliances, one that needs to be empirically investigated. However, alliance research as well as our clinical experience suggests that while families begin therapy at different points in this spatial representation, the most successful cases demonstrate increasingly positive individual and shared alliances, the latter typically developing more slowly and deliberately over time in treatment.

Concluding Thoughts

Many of the common denominators we described also apply to less complex cases. *All* couples and families need to feel safe and deeply understood by the therapist, even when they begin therapy with a clear, shared vision of their problems and aspirations for the future.

The strategies described in this chapter and in earlier chapters are particularly relevant for working with particularly challenging therapy cases. In our view, it is not the couple or family that is "challenging." Rather, it is the work itself that is challenging.

In many families, individuals' characteristics and environmental stressors are so extreme that while change is desired, it also is feared. Letting any stranger, much less a psychotherapist, into the family's private world of suffering can elicit strong feelings of shame. With shame comes defensiveness.

Creating a strong working alliance with each family member and the system as a whole requires us to appreciate the conflicting feelings that underlie clients' denial and defensiveness. We assume that even if mandated to treatment, all family members who show up for a therapy appointment have some hope that life can change for the better.

Therapeutic work with highly stressed families can indeed be life changing. And witnessing profound changes in our most vulnerable clients has no parallel. Challenge can bring joy.

References

Friedlander, M. L., Escudero, V., & Heatherington, L. (2006). *Therapeutic alliances with couples and families: An empirically-informed guide to practice*. Washington, DC: American Psychological Association.

Madsen, W. C. (2007). *Collaborative therapy with multi-stressed families*. New York, NY: Guilford Press.

Prochaska, J. O., & DiClemente, C. C. (1982). Trans-theoretical therapy: Toward a more integrative model of change. *Psychotherapy: Theory, Research and Practice, 19*, 276–288.

Appendix A: Operational Definitions of the SOFTA Indicators (Clients and Therapist)

Client Item Descriptors

ENGAGEMENT IN THE THERAPEUTIC PROCESS[1]

Client indicates agreement with the therapist's goals.
After the therapist has explicitly identified or described the purpose for therapy or the goals for the treatment, the client says something that indicates acceptance of the therapist's perspective. The client might explicitly ("Yes, that's good") or more implicitly agree (e.g., "Well, that makes sense because..." or "Let's get started then").

Client describes or discusses a plan for improving the situation.
With or without prompting from the therapist, the client explicitly describes what he or she will do or think in working toward improvement. It could be an elaborate plan, such as "making sure to give each family member a compliment every day," or a more diffuse idea, such as "trying to look on the bright side of the situation." The client must explicitly articulate what he/she will do, *not* merely agree with the therapist's plan or suggestion in order for this item to be checked. This would not include situations where the client is telling others what to do.

Client introduces a problem for discussion.
With or without prompting from the therapist, the client explicitly identifies something specific that he/she would like to deal with in the session (e.g., "I think we need to talk more about how we communicate when we are angry"). The client must initiate the topic, *not* merely agree with the therapist's suggestion or identification of a problem in order for this item to be checked.

---

*Indicates that there is a parallel item under client behaviors

[1] Adapted from the *System for Observing Family Therapy Alliances* (SOFTA-o) *Training Manual—Revised,* by M. L. Friedlander, V. Escudero, L. Heatherington, L. Diehl et al., 2004, unpublished manuscript. Available from http://www.softa-soatif.net. Adapted with permission of the authors.

© Springer International Publishing AG 2017
V. Escudero, M.L. Friedlander, *Therapeutic Alliances with Families*, Focused Issues in Family Therapy, DOI 10.1007/978-3-319-59369-2

Client agrees to do homework assignments.

A "homework assignment" might be specifically prescribed by the therapist (e.g., "Over the next week, I'd like you to...") or might be a more general suggestion (e.g., "One thing you might try that has helped other people in your situation is to..."). The client must explicitly say something to indicate he or she will carry out the "assignment." A mere head nod or "mhmm" is *not* sufficient to check this item. If, however, the client asks a question about the homework that suggests that he/she plans to do it, such as "Should I also write down everything my wife does?," this item can be checked.

Client indicates having done homework or seeing it as useful.

This item is checked either in response to the therapist's questioning about the "homework" assignment (a specific plan or a general suggestion) or without being asked, the client mentions the value of the homework or at least indicates having attempted it. If the client indicates that he/she decided not to do the homework or could not find time to do it, this item should *not* be checked.

Client expresses optimism or indicates that a positive change has taken place.

With or without questions from the therapist, the client describes feeling hopeful or seeing that change is possible, either for himself/herself, for other family members, or for the family as a whole. This item can be checked if there is a straightforward expression of "Things are looking up," "We can make a change," or "We're getting somewhere now" or if the reference to optimism is indirect, such as "Well, I always think about the positives." Optimism implies hope for positive change, whether it be a small behavioral difference, saving a marriage, or keeping a teen out of trouble. This item can also be checked if the client's comment relates to a positive sense about the therapy, such as "Now that we're here, we can really work on this."

Client complies with therapist's requests for enactments.

In response to the therapist explicitly asking a client or some clients to do something *in the session*, the client does so. This might involve specific behaviors, such as changing chairs to face each other or talking with another family member about something that the therapist suggests (e.g., "Why don't you two talk and try to come to some understanding about how you are going to deal with..."). The "enactment" need not be an elaborate technique, like family sculpting, but simply following the therapist's suggestion to do something or try something differently in the session (e.g., breathing deeply before speaking, holding hands, looking in each other's eyes).

Client leans forward.

This item is only checked when the client *moves to lean forward* in response to something being discussed in the session or when being asked a question by the therapist or another family member. If the client is sitting forward throughout all or most of the session, this item is checked only once. If the client moves back and forth in the seat in response to what is being discussed, each discrete forward movement is checked.

Client mentions the treatment, the therapeutic process, or a specific session.

This item is to be checked when the client brings up the therapy as a topic (its value, the need for it, what is going on in the process, etc.). Examples would include remarking that the previous session brought up a lot of issues or that the client looks forward to the session or asks how long the therapist thinks the therapy will need to continue. If the client has negative things to say about the therapy, this item is *not* checked (see negative item about "feeling stuck"). Further, the item is *not* checked when the client merely responds to questions the therapist asks regarding the therapy (e.g., "How did you feel about last week's session?" or "How do you think this process is going for you?" or "What would you like to talk about today?"). Note that if the client mentions in the treatment in the context of improvement or optimism (e.g., "Things have been better since we started coming here"), the item "client expresses optimism..." should take priority.

Client expresses feeling "stuck," questions the value of therapy, or states that therapy is not or has not been helpful.
This negative item is checked when the client explicitly mentions dissatisfaction with the way the therapy is going, the need for it, or the direction it is taking. This expression of negative attitude or emotion may or may not be in response to the therapist's question or to the question of some other family member. This item is *not* checked if the client's response is vague, such as "I don't know" or "Okay, I guess," even if a negative attitude is suspected. Such vague expressions might be indicators of another negative item, i.e., showing indifference. That is, for this item to be checked, the expression of dissatisfaction must be clear and overt.

Client shows indifference about the tasks or process of therapy (e.g., paying lip service, "I don't know," tuning out).
Paying lip service refers to superficial compliance with what is being asked or suggested by the therapist or other family members. Indifference may be shown nonverbally, as in doing something else (e.g., cleaning out a pocketbook, filing nails), not following the flow of conversation, and looking around the room at what's in the office. As with other nonverbal items, it is more than just a momentary lack of attention, and for this item to be checked, nonverbal behaviors need to be fairly obvious. Verbally, people can show indifference by a notable lack of energy or enthusiasm (e.g., "Sure, if you like, we can try that"). Indifference tends to be inferred from the tone of voice. More obvious comments might be, for example, "Okay, but I doubt it will make any difference in the long run." This item should *not* be checked for young children, who can be expected to let their attention wander during a session, showing a lack of investment in participating in the session.

EMOTIONAL CONNECTION TO THE THERAPIST

Client shares a lighthearted moment or joke with the therapist.
This item refers to a behavioral connection through humor or good will, typically signaled by laughter. The comment could be initiated by the therapist or by the client, but both parties need to be simultaneously amused for this item to be checked.

Client verbalizes trust in the therapist.
The client's comment might be an overt statement like "I trust you" or a more implicit remark that suggests trust, such as "I know whatever I say here stays in this room" or "This is something I couldn't talk about with other people." The comment is more than an indicator of feeling safe in the therapy context; it needs to connote a personal sense of trust in the therapist, a recognition that the therapist is a trustworthy individual. Other examples include "I believe what you're telling me." In distinguishing between this item and "feels understood or accepted," the crucial element is trusting the therapist or trusting that what is said in therapy will be held in confidence. If the comment indicates that the clients *feel* trusted *by the therapist*, consider the item "feels understood or accepted."

Client expresses interest in the therapist's personal life.
Clients sometimes ask questions about the therapist's situation, such as whether he or she is married or has children, whether the therapist is spiritual or religious, or where the therapist grew up. This item can be checked if a direct question is asked or if, in response to the therapist's self-disclosure, the client follows up with a comment that suggests interest in the therapist as a person. As one example, the therapist talks about his grief when his father died, and the client asks, "Was he very old?" This item is *not* to be checked if the client asks about the therapist's credentials or professional experience or if the question is delivered in a manner that suggests defensiveness, a lack of confidence, or testing ("How do you feel about gays?").

Client indicates feeling understood or accepted by the therapist.
This item implies more than a sense of safety and comfort in therapy; it requires some indication that the client feels valued, respected, or trusted by the therapist. An explicit verbal comment might be made, such as "I know *you* don't judge me like other people do" or "I could tell YOU, but no one else." Alternately, the client's response might be nonverbal, such as tearing up after the therapist makes an empathic comment. Nonverbal responses like these, however, should only be checked if there is a clear implication of feeling understood or accepted.

Client expresses physical affection or caring for the therapist.
This item is checked when, for example, the client offers his/her hand at the end of a session or asks for a hug. Caring can be inferred from comments like "Are you feeling better? You were sick when we were here last week" or "What you think means a lot to our family."

Client mirrors the therapist's body posture.
For this item to be checked, the arms and the legs must be placed similarly. It is not necessary to try to determine whether the therapist mirrors the client or vice versa. (That is, a connection between client and therapist is reflected in the mirroring, regardless of who mirrors whom.) This item should only be checked once during a session, unless the client is clearly and obviously mirroring every move of the therapist. Mirroring can be associated with specific body posture changes, as when the therapist shifts body position notably when the discussion becomes more intense and the client mirrors that movement. When working with adolescents, it is common for therapists to mirror the adolescent's informal body posture.

Client avoids eye contact with the therapist.
For this nonverbal item to be checked, the client must, clearly and consistently, avoid eye contact with the therapist. There can be momentary "peeking" at the therapist, however. If the client avoids eye contact for a substantial period of time (minutes, *not* seconds), this item can be checked. Also, when the therapist asks a question ("Do you want to continue our sessions?") or says something directly to the client in a context in which eye contact is expected, if the client avoids making eye contact, the item should be checked.

Client refuses or is reluctant to respond to the therapist.
This item is checked when, either verbally or nonverbally, a client fails to respond to a direct request (question or remark) from the therapist, indicating either a negative reaction to the therapist or not wanting to comment. A lengthy silence in response to a question is one example if, in context, the silence suggests a clear reluctance or refusal to engage when invited to do so. Silence that occurs because the client is thinking hard about what to say should *not* be checked. Verbal expressions of reluctance include "I'd rather not talk about it," "It's none of your business," or "That's personal." If the client is clearly reluctant but later relents and does respond hesitatingly, the item can be checked if the reluctance was notable or prolonged.

Client has hostile or sarcastic interactions with the therapist.
This item is checked only if there is tension in the room and/or anger is expressed, *not* merely a disagreement about what was meant or what should be done. Essentially, this item connotes a disrespect or devaluing of the therapist on the part of the client.

Client comments on the therapist's incompetence or inadequacy.
Typically, it is client "hostages" who make cutting remarks about a therapist's competence. This item is checked when the client's comments suggest a belief that the therapist is not behaving therapeutically and ethically, doesn't know what he/she is doing, can't possibly understand, doesn't have sound credentials, and so forth. This item speaks more to the therapist's ability to work with the client than to feelings about the therapist as a person. Deprecating personal remarks are indicated by the item "hostile or sarcastic interactions with the therapist."

SAFETY WITHIN THE THERAPEUTIC CONTEXT

Client implies or states that therapy is a safe place.
The client might not necessarily use the word "safe," but the implication in his/her words is that he/she feels safe. This item requires some kind of verbal indicator; nonverbal indicators are *not* sufficient for this item to be checked. Implicit examples are when someone says he/she decided to wait until the therapy session to discuss something with a family member or says something like "It's okay to cry in here," "I didn't know whether I would have the courage to tell you, but...," or "I'm glad we finally made it here." The point is that the client suggests that the therapeutic environment is valued for its safety, not only as a place to solve problems. At times the indicator may be quite subtle, as "I don't know quite how to say this,

but I'll just take the plunge" or "I hope you [other family member] don't mind my saying this, but...."

Client varies his/her emotional tone during the session.

This item refers to a non-subtle tone variation. Of course, all clients vary their tone over the course of a session, but this item suggests variability with emotions like anger, sadness, fear, and happiness, which is signaled by tears, laughing, angry words, or tone of voice. This item is *not* checked if the client is fairly neutral or calm throughout the entire session or if the client is crying *or* hostile and angry throughout it all. Also, this item is *not* checked if the tone is simply excitement. In other words, emotion refers to feelings of sadness, anger, happiness, or fear. Note that this item can only be checked once, *not* every time the tone varies because it refers to the presence of a plasticity of emotions.

Client shows vulnerability (e.g., discusses painful feelings, cries).

For this item to be checked, either the process of the session is a difficult one for the client (shown by crying, for example) or the content of what the client is discussing is difficult and painful (shown by hesitation, anxiety, or verbal expressions of how hard it is to talk about something). Sometimes the content of the client's messages alone suggest vulnerability, as when one family member asks another if he loves her or when one family member asks another for help or forgiveness (i.e., the client is clearly "going one-down" in interaction with another client or the therapist). Some clinical judgment may be needed with this item. The judgment here is whether the communication seems to be difficult *for the client*. For some clients, admitting depression or anxiety would be a sign of vulnerability (shown by tone of voice or nonverbal manifestations of unease), whereas for others, such an admission is *not* a sign of vulnerability.

Client has an open upper body posture.

Although some people naturally sit in an open position, this item is checked when *in response to what is occurring in the session*, the client shifts to an open upper body position. The item is also checked (once) if the client sits that way naturally throughout the session. If the client moves back and forth from open to closed body posture in response to the surrounding interaction, each time he/she opens up, the item should be checked.

Client reveals a secret or something that other family members didn't know.

For this item to be checked, it must be clear that the client is saying something that is news to other family members. (The "something" needs to be something meaningful, not mundane, such as what the client had for dinner.) The information may or may not be a SECRET that has been deliberately withheld (e.g., the father's alcoholism, the wife's affair, the child's failing grade) but some important piece of information, a fact, that was not common knowledge, such as the daughter having reached puberty or the fact that the son doesn't respect his father. For this item to be checked, the revelation of material is significant enough to signal that the speaker feels safe enough to tell others something that was previously hidden or private, i.e., something it did not feel safe to disclose at home.

Client encourages another family member to "open up" or to tell the truth.
Commonly, this item is checked when a parent gently (not harshly) urges a child to speak, but it may also be a statement between adults like "It's okay. You can tell [therapist]," "This is the place to discuss it," "We won't get anywhere if you don't tell me how you really feel," and so forth. For this item to be checked, the tone of voice must be one that encourages rather than demands disclosures, i.e., suggesting that it is safe to talk about these things in therapy.

Client directly asks other family member(s) for feedback about his/her behavior or about herself/himself as a person.
It is risky to ask other people for their candid impressions of oneself. This item is checked only when the client explicitly asks for feedback about behavior, as in "Do you think I'm doing better?," or about how he/she is perceived by others, "Do you think I'm overweight? Attractive? A good parent? Nice enough to my mother?" Questions could also include how the other person construes the speaker's behavior, as in, "Why do you think I did that?"

Client expresses anxiety nonverbally (e.g., taps or shakes).
This negative item implies a lack of safety in the therapy environment. Although some people are naturally more anxious than others, this item is to be checked only when there is a clear, overt sign of anxiety, such as fidgeting, shaking, quavering voice, and so forth. If the anxiety persists at the same level throughout the session, it should be checked only once, unless the anxiety is so heightened or disruptive that it warrants additional check marks. If the anxiety is demonstrated in response to something that is said or takes place in the session, the item should be checked each time the overt anxiety is manifest. Note that this item only refers to *nonverbally* communicated anxiety. If the client talks about how anxious he/she feels in the session, the item "shows vulnerability" should be considered instead.

Client protects self in a nonverbal manner (e.g., crosses arms over chest, doesn't take off jacket or put down purse, sits far away from the group, etc.).
Self-protecting behavior can have many meanings, and this item should only be checked when the context of the session suggests defensiveness. For example, many people cross their arms over their chest for comfort. But the item should be checked when the arms crossing is clearly in relation to what is being said in the session. As an example, the father crosses his arms when the therapist asks the daughter, "How would you describe your relationship with your father?" Another example would be the wife crossing her arms as the husband starts to talk about her lack of sexual interest. At times a client might cross his/her arms on arrival in the therapy room, and this is a defensive pose. Thus, if the arms crossing is not clearly in relation to what is going on, this item should *not* be checked. If the arms crossing occurs throughout the session *and* there are *other* clear, nonverbal signs of defensiveness (hand on the forehead while looking down, legs crossed in the air as if to create a barrier, looking anywhere but at other family members, coat overlap), this item should be checked. Clinical judgment can be used here; if the behavior seems defensive or self-protective in the context of the session (keeping coat on, purse over

chest, umbrella in hands, or moving one's seat away from the group), this item can be checked.

Client refuses or is reluctant to respond when directly addressed by another family member.

This item is checked when, either verbally or nonverbally, a client fails to respond to a direct request (question or remark) from another client. A lengthy silence in response to a question is one example, if the silence indicates either a negative reaction to the other family member's request. Silence that occurs because the client is thinking hard about what to say should *not* be checked. If verbal, the response must clearly indicate a reluctance or refusal to engage when invited to do so. Verbal expressions of reluctance include "I'd rather not talk about it," "It's none of your business," or "That's personal." If the client is clearly reluctant but later relents and does respond hesitatingly, the item can be checked if the reluctance is notable. Reluctance can be signaled when a client avoids answering a question by turning to a third person, as in:

Husband (to wife):   "Tell me why you don't want to go out with my sister."
Wife (to therapist):   "You should just MEET his sister, wow! She is so obnoxious to me!"

Client responds defensively to another family member.

Defensiveness is indicated when, in a nonhostile manner, the client uses clearly complaining or criticism in response to another family member who is demanding explanations or justifications for his/her behavior. Often, defensive responses are part of a communication pattern called "cross-complaining": one family member complains about the behavior of another, and the target of the complaint responds by complaining about any behavior of the first one. If the defensiveness is directed toward the therapist, this item should not be checked. If the client's tone is angry or hostile, the item *Family members blame each other* should be checked instead, and if the comment is not hostile but is devaluing or disrespecting the other person, the item *Family members devalue each other's opinions or perspectives* should be checked. In other words, defensiveness is indicated when the client has been put on the spot by another family member to explain or justify his or her own attitude, behavior, or choices and answers back by complaining defensively about any behavior of the other (instead of explaining his/her own behaviors). Examples include (without overt hostility) "You are asking me about my behavior with your son but you do not say anything about your behavior with YOUR sister" or "You are saying you do not understand my hostility but last week YOU were very aggressive with me too, you yelled me three times."

Client makes an uneasy or anxious reference to the camera, observation, supervisor, or research procedures.

This item is indicated if the client spontaneously mentions these extra-therapy procedures in a way that suggests uneasiness. Examples might be, "Do you tell your supervisor everything we say?" or "I wish we could turn the camera off sometimes" or "How do I know that you won't send the tape to Child Protective Services?"

A nonverbal indicator might be looking warily at the camera and then deliberately leaning forward and speaking much more softly.

SHARED SENSE OF PURPOSE WITHIN THE FAMILY

Family members offer to compromise.
The offer may or may not be in response to the therapist's request for a compromise. Sometimes the client's offer to another is clear, as in "Well, if I do [this], will you do [that]?" A client might only make one part of the offer, such as "I could [do this]" or "I'm willing to...." Typically people compromise on something behavioral, but the compromise could also be cognitive, such as "I'll try to stop looking for the negative in everything, if you do." The therapist might ask each member of the family to think of something positive to do in relation to other family members, and if the client comes up with something, that could be considered a compromise, such as "I'll help Mom with the dishes." These statements need to be considered in a context of quid pro quo. That is, if a client merely offers to do something different without an implicit or explicit expectation that another family member will also do something in return, the item "Client offers a plan for improving the situation" (Engagement) should be considered instead.

Family members share a joke or a lighthearted moment with each other.
This item is checked only if the humor is evoked during the session, not before it gets started or as people are leaving. The humorous moment may or may not involve the therapist, but for this item to be checked, there needs to be some connection among the family members, i.e., joking *with* each other or making eye contact while laughing together. One exception is when a joke reflects negatively on another member or when family members joke together at another's expense (see the item "Client makes hostile or sarcastic comments to family members").

Family members ask each other for their perspective.
This item is often a precursor to an offer to compromise. For the item to be checked, family members must explicitly speak with one another, and one person needs to ask another what he/she thinks, feels, or wants to do. Examples include "How do you see it?" or "What do you think is causing this problem?" or "How would you suggest we solve it?" However, for simple questions about agreement regarding information or something prosaic ("Was it Wednesday or Thursday that you...?" or "Who said that, Mom?"), this item should *not* be checked. Also, if spoken sarcastically, however, this item should *not* be checked. This behavior is also *not* checked when it was prompted by the therapist, asking, for example, "Why don't you ask your dad and mom how they see your plan?" (see "complies with therapist's requests for enactment").

Family members validate each other's perspective.
Although validation tends to be thought of as positive (e.g., "I can see where you're coming from" or "That makes a lot of sense"), positive content is *not* required for

this item to be checked. A couple might agree in the session with each other, for example, that their marriage is over and that they need to separate. The validation might be mixed with other messages, such as "Although as your mother, I'm hurt by this decision, I recognize your right to do what you want." This item requires some verbalization, *not* merely head nods or "mhmm."

Family members mirror each other's body posture.
Doing so is generally unconscious rather than deliberate. For this item to be checked, at least two family members must be positioned similarly with respect to both arms and legs. It is important to pay attention to specific moments in which somebody changes his/her body position in response to what is being discussed and another family member mirrors that shift.

Family members avoid eye contact with each other.
Eye contact is a personal and cultural experience. Some people maintain good eye contact with everyone, so that doing so does not necessarily mean there's a connection. However, the avoidance of eye contact with other family members throughout the session, such as when everyone looks at the therapist and never at each other, is notable. Thus, for this item to be checked, the avoidance needs to be notable, consistent, or prolonged. Avoidance of eye contact among family members is particularly notable when one family member is speaking and others do not look at him/her.

Family members blame each other.
In determining whether or not blame is present, a distinction needs to be made between expressing blame and simple responsibility for an action or problem. Blame is usually carried in the tone of voice and implies fault. Further, blame tends to be indicated when the client describes a specific event or problem as clearly avoidable, intentionally caused, or due to another client's negative attitude. Terms like "blame," "fault," and "if only you had[n't]..." may or may not be present. Blame may also be expressed through a highly negative, accusatory, or pejorative manner. For this item to be distinguished from the items "devalue each other's point of view" and "makes hostile or sarcastic comments," the client must be blaming another client *for something*, typically for the problem under discussion, or for having done or not done something, for having made a poor decision, and so forth. Examples include "Your drinking caused all our problems!", "My son lost his job because he seems to think he can come in late and the boss won't mind!", or "You screwed up as much as I did when it came to parenting."

Family members devalue each other's opinions or perspectives.
This item is checked if the client verbally says something to contradict another client's point of view in a way that suggests disrespect. The item can be checked if the statement is made angrily, but *not* if it is made sarcastically or in a mean-spirited way (see item "makes hostile or sarcastic comments"). Examples include "You don't have the right to ask me that!", "That may be *your* point of view, but that's just because you don't give a damn!", or "Who gives you the right to talk to me that way?" The essential point of this item is that clients are not listening to each other in an accepting way. The key feature is disrespect rather than hostility. Note that if blame (i.e., ascribing fault for having done or said something) is expressed, consider

the item "family members blame each other." Note that devaluing is different from simple disagreement ("That may be *your* point of view, but I think you're wrong!").

Family members try to align with the therapist against each other.
Verbal expressions of this item include a client asking the therapist for an opinion in the midst of an argument with another family member; directly asking the therapist to choose sides, to decide who is right, or to intervene in a specific way with someone else; or joking with the therapist at another client's expense. The meaning of "against" is not necessarily a disagreement, however. It may simply be that one family member accentuates a controversy by including the therapist on his/her side. Examples of these less overt behaviors include saying to the therapist, "Can you tell him again what you told him last week?" or "My father needs to be told that he has to see a doctor for his heart." As another example, one adolescent may tell another in his mother's presence, "You need to listen to [therapist], not to mom!"

Client makes hostile or sarcastic comments to family members.
For this item to be checked, there needs to be a mean-spirited exchange, not merely an argument. Name calling, cursing, or threats are examples. The interchange must suggest not only disrespect (see item "devalue each other's opinions") but also rage, condescension, contempt, or disgust. If blame (i.e., fault for having done or said something) is expressed, consider the item "family members blame each other." Joking with one family member at another's expense could be also an example of this behavior when the joke implies hostility.

Family members disagree with each other about the value, purpose, goals, or tasks of therapy or about who should be included in the sessions.
The argument or disagreement needs to be clear, *not* implicit or simply nonverbal. Further, this item is only checked if the disagreement or argument is among the clients, *not* between one client and the therapist (see item "questions the value of therapy" under Engagement). This item should be checked rather than the item "Family members try to align with the therapist against each other" when the disagreement or argument is about the goals, tasks, or value of therapy, as in "You heard what [therapist] said! We need to be here!" Other common examples include "If you don't take this seriously, it doesn't make sense to come here" and "Why is HE coming? He NEVER does his part in anything!"

Therapist Item Descriptions

THERAPIST CONTRIBUTIONS TO ENGAGEMENT IN THE THERAPEUTIC PROCESS

Therapist explains how therapy works.
This behavior includes all types of explanations about the therapy process: time (duration of sessions, length of treatment, intervals between sessions), activities, theoretical models or methods, formats (individual, group, family), teamwork,

consent forms, legal/institutional obligations, use of recording or observation by others, etc. The item should only be checked when an explanation is given in some detail and actively, although it may be in response to a client's question. Incomplete or hesitant descriptions of therapy should not be checked, nor should the item be checked if the therapist makes a vague response to the client's question, as in:

Client: Do my parents always have to come?
Therapist: We'll see. Therapy can be with parents or not.

If, however, the therapist were to respond as follows, the behavior would be checked:

"It may be that it's not always necessary. In the course of therapy, we can all decide together which people can contribute something in a session depending on what we all consider useful. In that case no one feels obliged if they decide they shouldn't or don't want to come" or "Our kind of work implies that these decisions are made with everyone's agreement. Your participation is very important in how we work here." Note: If consent forms or the use of recording/observation is simply mentioned in explaining how therapy is done in the setting, this item should be checked. If privacy or confidentiality is specifically discussed, stressed, or explained in response to a client's question, check instead the Safety item, "Therapist provides structure and guidelines for safety and confidentiality."

*Therapist asks client(s) what they want to talk about in the session.
With this behavior, the therapist helps clients see that they have a role in deciding what to work on in session. The behavior can either be an open question ("What would you like to work on today?") or an invitation to comment on the therapist's plan for the session, i.e., offering clients the option of modifying the agenda or introducing new topics for discussion ("I had thought that today's session would be devoted to talking over John's change in schools, but I'd like to ask if you think that's enough, or is there something else you think we should do today?").

Therapist encourages client(s) to articulate their goals for therapy.
The therapist can accomplish this goal in the initial phase of treatment, e.g., by asking family members what they'd like to achieve in therapy or what needs to change for them to consider therapy useful, e.g., "What would you have to see taking place in order to feel that it's worthwhile to come here?" In more advanced stages of treatment, the therapist may ask clients for their participation in defining, redefining, or simply recording the goals, e.g., "Now that you've ruled out the possibility that your son is using heroin, what would you like us to focus on in therapy?" The difference between this behavior and the previous one is that here the therapist is encouraging articulation of a treatment goal, objective, or outcome, not merely a topic of discussion in the session at hand.

Therapist asks client(s) whether they are willing to do a specific in-session task (e.g., enactment).
By asking clients if they are ready to do something specific in the session before doing proceeding, the therapist is implying that the final decision is the clients'.

Examples include "I'd like you to recreate here and now the same conversation that you had at home. What do you think? Do you think you can do this?" and "There's something I think would be helpful, if you're willing to go along? It's something different that..." The item should not be marked if the therapist is simply asking a question rhetorically or for courtesy when, in reality, the client is not being given the option to refuse, e.g., "We're going to recreate your discussion at home right now. Maria, please sit in the chair next to your husband and...." or "What would you say to trying it again, but this time more forcefully? Go on, try it again."

Note: Mark this item only once if the therapist asks the same question repeatedly, i.e., about the same task. If, however, the therapist proposes the task again later on in the session, the item could be marked again.

*Therapist asks client(s) whether they are willing to follow a specific suggestion or do a specific homework assignment.

With this behavior, the therapist asks or implies a clear interest in the client's opinions about his/her suggestion for something new to be thought about or done between sessions or about a specific homework assignment that he/she is proposing. (If the suggestion is about something to do in the session itself, the previous item should be checked instead.) This comment usually takes place after the therapist has offered a concrete assignment or suggestion ("We're considering your going together to pick your daughter up as a way to show interest in her. How do you feel about that suggestion?"). On occasion, the therapist may accomplish this objective while defining or describing the homework task ("The team suggested a specific task for this week, but it requires both of you to be together on it. Are you prepared to come together to do something? Would you like to hear what the team suggested to me?").

Note: Mark this item only once if the therapist asks the same question repeatedly, i.e., about the same homework assignment. If, however, the therapist proposes the assignment again later on in the session, the item could be marked again.

*Therapist asks client(s) about the impact or value of a prior homework assignment.

Examples include the following: "Last session we talked about a task to do during the week. How did it go? Or what happened?" "Last time it seemed to me that you found my suggestion to plan a trip with your son interesting. Did you follow through with that idea?" "How helpful was the homework?" Occasionally, clients may indicate that they did not do the specific assignment or suggestion that was made in the previous session. The item should be checked nonetheless if the therapist asks about the impact or value of the task, as in: "Although you didn't do it, did you think or talk about it together?" "You didn't find it useful, or maybe you thought it was overly complicated or stressful?" "Could it be that this was somewhat scary for one of you?"

*Therapist expresses optimism or notes that a positive change has taken place or can take place.

Optimism about change can take many forms, e.g., "Incredible! You're saying that [the problem] hasn't happened again?" "It's a small change, but I've no doubt that it's a clear sign of improvement." "What you say suggests an improvement.

This week it's only happened twice but, earlier, it always happened three or four times in a week." "That makes me certain that you're going to get there." Sometimes the therapist may offer hope explicitly, e.g., "Even though things are really rough right now, I can see a spark between you, and that means there is still something growing in your relationship. I'm hopeful that we can make a difference for you in our work together."

Therapist pulls in quiet client(s) (e.g., by deliberately leaning forward, calling them by name, addressing them specifically).
For this item to be checked, the client or clients who are addressed must have been silent or withdrawn for a noticeable period of time or clients who are only superficially responding, e.g., one-word answers. However, if the therapist leans forward or addresses a client who has been talking (or crying), this item should not be checked. The behavior is meant explicitly to involve someone or some group of clients who have been silent or uninvolved. If the therapist's behavior is nonverbal, it must be a discrete change in body posture. By leaning forward, the therapist clearly communicates attention and concentration, an interest in what the client(s) is saying or experiencing in the moment, highlighting the relevance of this communication. The behavior should not be checked if the change in posture suggests tiredness or motives other than drawing in someone who has been quiet, as when the therapist leans forward to write something down, pick up an object, etc.

Therapist asks if the client(s) have any questions.
This behavior refers to all kinds of clear and direct offers to the client to ask questions related to the content or process of therapy, e.g., "Before we go any further, do you have any questions or concerns we should discuss?" This item should not be marked if the therapist simply asks for general reactions (e.g., "How's that plan for you?" "Are you okay with what we've been talking about?"). Even when the therapist asks if there are questions right after having done one of the other engagement behaviors (i.e., in the same speaking turn), this item should be checked, as in "Therapy works when... Do you have any questions about what I've just explained?" or "So, are you willing to try this at home? Is there anything you want to ask about this before we stop today?" As in this last example, because the therapist first asks about the client's willingness to do a homework assignment and then asks if the client has any questions, both items should be checked.

Therapist praises client motivation for engagement or change.
With this behavior, the therapist praises all direct or indirect expressions of motivation to get involved in the therapy or to work toward a change. The client's motivation can be expressed explicitly ("We're really excited about what we're doing here") or implicitly ("We're willing to come more often if that will help things along"). The therapist's praise must be patently clear in order for this item to be checked, e.g., "Excellent! This is essential for our work to get done," "Very good! Your participation and willingness to compromise is the most important thing," and "It makes me happy to see you happy and so ready to work."

Therapist defines therapeutic goals or imposes tasks or procedures without asking the client(s) for their collaboration.

For this item to be checked, there must not be a direct question from the therapist asking for the client's input. The essence of this item is that in giving instructions for an assignment at home, for an enactment in session, or for some other proceeding in the treatment, the therapist imposes his/her will without considering the opinion or well-being of the client. For this item to be checked, the therapist must not explain his/her reasoning, not ask if clients understand, and not use a questioning tone of voice. For example, "Next session I'll see you separately. I want one of you to come in the morning and one in the afternoon" would be marked, but "Next session, could I see each of you separately?" would not be marked. Other examples include the following: "Good, after consulting with the team, here is the assignment for you this week: You go pick up John every day at work and after..."; "In what remains of this session you'll take turns answering me, and I don't want you to speak to one another." An important precaution to keep in mind: the failure to ask for collaboration may be based on a prior agreement with the clients that allow the therapist to use his/her discretion in imposing tasks and procedures. In these cases, the item should not be marked. That is, on occasion, a previous conversation or some understanding established earlier in the session (or in a prior session) has given the therapist permission to offer directives or instructions without consulting the clients. As an example, working with a highly conflictual, troubled couple, a therapist and couple agreed that if the level of conflict seemed untenable to the therapist, he/she would see them individually. Thus, when he/she informs the clients that they will be seen separately in the next session, there is no need to consult them because a previous agreement to do so was already in force.

Essentially, this descriptor refers to moments or episodes in which the therapist references the goals of therapy in a unilateral or highly assertive (or even aggressive) manner. As an example, a therapist working with an adolescent and his parents says, "What we have to achieve in therapy is increase your ability to discipline John around his study habits, so he doesn't fail in school." In this case, the therapist asserted the goal of treatment without asking for the opinion or for confirmation from the clients. When, however, the therapist has already actively negotiated the goals of therapy with the clients and finally asserts a summary of what will be accomplished, this item is not marked, as in "Okay, I understand that you all want this therapy to eliminate the conflicts you're having over John's education."

*Therapist argues with the client(s) about the nature, purpose, or value of therapy.

This item requires subjectivity. Naturally a therapist's opinion can differ from the client's about the nature, purpose, or value of therapy. Typically, the item is marked when one client devalues what is occurring or the need for therapy, and the therapist tells the client he/she is wrong or that therapy is the only way changes can be made and so forth. The point is that client participation is negatively affected when there is an open confrontation (even if not particularly hostile) with the client about the process of treatment, as in:

Client: I don't see how therapy can change what someone does. That depends on a person's personality, and I think people's basic personalities never change.
Therapist: Therapy works to change people. As a professional, I know that's what's needed here.
Client: I don't think that can occur through therapy.
Therapist: Without trying it, you can't know what therapy does.

There are situations in which the therapist paints a different picture of the treatment process but avoids getting into a confrontation with the client. In cases like these, the item should not be marked:

Client: I don't see how therapy can change what someone does. That depends on a person's personality, and I think people's basic personalities never change.
Therapist: Yes, change is complex, but we can talk about what you think should change and how you see personality. What changes have you experienced since the problem started?

Therapist shames or criticizes how clients did (or did not do) a prior homework assignment.
Even if the therapist does not clearly criticize the clients for failing to do the homework (as in, "You should have done this. It's for your own good."), the blame can be subtle but nonetheless harmful. Examples include "Well, I know that you had a busy week, but isn't that an excuse?"; "We're not going to get anywhere without your full cooperation"; and "I'm going to insist that you do the assignment for the next week." There may even be a threat that therapy will be terminated without the client's cooperation, as in: "There is no point in your coming here if you're not going to follow through at home." When the client has attempted the homework and either not completed it or did it incorrectly, the item should be checked if there is implied criticism, as in "That's not what was expected. Next time, be sure you understand the assignment before you start" or "Well, you got it partially right. Try harder next week."

THERAPIST CONTRIBUTIONS TO EMOTIONAL CONNECTIONS

Therapist shares a lighthearted moment or joke with the client(s).
This item refers to the therapist's rapport with client(s) through humor or good will, typically signaled by laughter. The comment could be initiated by the therapist or by the client, but both parties need to be simultaneously amused for this item to be checked. Typically the markers are smiling, giggling, or laughter.

*Therapist expresses confidence, trust, or belief in the client(s).
The therapist verbally encourages the client(s) with comments that express general confidence in the family members' ability to achieve a goal or try a new behavior. Examples include the following: "I know you can do it"; "This is hard, but I have

faith in you"; "I've seen you do this in the past"; or "One aspect of your family that continues to impress me is your strength. With that strength, I have no doubt that you will be able to make these changes for each other."

Therapist expresses interest in the client(s) apart from the therapeutic discussion at hand.
Sometimes this occurs when a therapist recalls a detail that that client shared in a previous session. For example, "I remember your father was going in for surgery. How did it go?" or "You vacationed there before, didn't you?" The item should not be checked when during casual conversation the therapist is engaged but he/she does not specifically express interest in the client(s). For example, if the clients report that they went to a new restaurant for dinner and the therapist asks about the restaurant, the item would not be endorsed. If the therapist asks about the clients' reaction to the evening (e.g., "What was your experience like there? Did you enjoy the restaurant?"), the item would be marked. If the therapist initiates or changes the topic to something non-therapy related in an attempt to alleviate anxiety, mark instead the item "Therapist changes the topic to something pleasurable or non-anxiety-arousing" under Safety.

*Therapist expresses caring or touches client(s) affectionately yet appropriately (e.g., handshake, pat on the head).
In addition to handshakes and pats, this item includes other affectionate expressions by the therapist, such as reaching out to take or touch something (e.g., a picture, photograph, journal, hat) that a client brings into a session. This item would also be marked if the therapist uses terms of endearment (e.g., "sweetie" or "honey") with children. If the therapist makes the same gesture (e.g., handshake) with more than one family member at the beginning or end of the session, the item is marked only once. If there are separate gestures with different family members (e.g., pats child on the head at the beginning of session and shakes the parent's hand to celebrate an accomplishment during the session), the item can be marked for each behavior.

Therapist discloses his or her personal reactions or feelings toward the client(s) or the situation.
This item reflects the therapist's self-involvement in the session. The therapist reveals something about his or her inner experience during the family session. Examples include "I felt close to you while you were crying," "As we talk about this I feel sadder and sadder," or "I'm excited by what I hear. You all seem to have a lot of energy to work together to get more of what you want for your family life." Other examples include "I'm confused by your silence this week. I'm wondering if you are upset with me" or "I'm concerned that you have cancelled several sessions in the last few weeks. What's happening?" This item should be distinguished from the one below, which has to do with disclosure about something personal in the therapist's life.

*Therapist discloses some fact about his or her personal life.
For this item to be marked, the therapist must disclose some personal information that would not have been known to the client(s) otherwise. The self-disclosure can be spontaneous or in response to a question from the client(s). For example, "I grew up in a large family. I had seven siblings," "I grew up in the south," "I have two

children," "I'm going to _____ for vacation," or "We went to see the fireworks last evening." If the disclosure includes similarity to the client's experience, even something non-therapy related, check instead the item below.

Note: This item should not be marked when the therapist gives information about his/her orientation to therapy unless it includes personal data, such as where he/she went to graduate school.

Therapist remarks on or describes how his or her values or experiences are similar to the clients'.
When the therapist shares some personal experience or personal values and comments on how he or she is similar to the client, this item would be marked. This item takes precedent over the previous item ("discloses some fact") if the disclosure includes some connection to the clients' experience. Examples include the following: "When I was in college, I got pretty nervous and upset about tests too"; "I wanted some privacy when I was your age"; "I agree, I think it is important that the parents are in charge of the household rules"; or "I remember when my own children were toddlers, like you, I sometimes felt overwhelmed by the need to constantly watch them. I really valued conversation with and support from other adults in my life at that time." When the therapist's comment is non-therapy related but does express a similarity with the client (e.g., "I've eaten there before, too. What a restaurant!"), check the previous item instead ("discloses some fact about his/her personal life").

*Therapist (verbally or nonverbally) expresses empathy for the clients' struggle (e.g., "I know this is hard," "I feel your pain," crying with client).
Empathy is generally an expression of understanding of the experience of another person. The critical element in this item is the therapist conveying the message that he or she understands the experience of the client. In addition to the examples above (e.g., crying with client), the therapist could make any statement that reflects understanding of the clients' struggle. Examples include the following: "It's humiliating for you to have to go to court about these private family matters"; "You really didn't have any support from your parents when you were growing up, and you don't want it to be that way for your children"; or "It's scary when your mom yells like that." Nonverbal expressions that are clear and discrete can also be marked, as leaning forward or crying when a client relates painful material and patting a shoulder. If the nonverbal behavior is ambiguous (not clearly related to the clients' struggle or pain), the item should not be marked. Note: If the therapist's message in a single speaking turn includes reassurance or normalization, a decision should be made about whether to check this item or the following one, depending on which aspect of the speaking turn seems most salient. (However, both items could be checked if empathy and normalization occurred in different speaking turns.)

Therapist reassures or normalizes a client's emotional vulnerability (e.g., crying, hurt feelings).
Reassuring or normalizing a client's emotional vulnerability differs from empathy in that the therapist's statements explicitly affirm that the client's reaction is understandable, expected, or "normal" considering the circumstances. The therapist may

talk, in general terms, about how other families have expressed similar emotions. Some examples include the following:

"[To a single mother] I've worked with many single mothers over the years and a common theme has been their desire to have more time for themselves. It is understandable that you would wish for a break from the constant responsibility of parenting."

"[To a new stepparent] Becoming a stepparent when the children are adolescents has unique challenges. It's understandable that you are feeling confused and frustrated about what your role should be."

"[To one or both members in a couple] I see these disagreements about discipline bring tears to your eyes. That's okay – I hear that this is really painful for you. It seems important to give those feelings expression."

"Often individuals in a couple will feel more angry with each other than with their children when there are disagreements about discipline. Many parents have expressed those feelings in here."

"[To a teenager] You feel like you don't have any power or influence in your family. You want your parents to notice that you are growing up and can handle more. I can understand that you are frustrated. It's hard to figure out how to convince your parents to trust you."

Note: When the reassurance is nonverbal, consider instead the above item. If the therapist's message in a single speaking turn includes empathy, a decision should be made about whether to check this item or the preceding one, depending on which aspect of the speaking turn seems most salient. (However, both items could be checked if normalization and empathy occurred in different speaking turns.)

*Therapist has hostile, sarcastic, or critical interactions with the client(s).
Essentially, this item connotes disrespect or devaluing of the client(s) by the therapist. For this item to be checked, the therapist's communication needs to be mean-spirited, bitter, or contemptuous. For example, a therapist might sarcastically ask a family that has attended therapy irregularly if they planned to skip the next meeting: "Now, I'm not going to be sitting here alone again next week, am I?" The therapist's communication might be directed at one family member, but if his/her tone is hostile, critical, or sarcastic, the item should be marked. An example is [in an exasperated tone] "I wonder if ____ [child] will ever stay in [his/her] seat for the whole session without having to be reminded repeatedly." This behavior should not be checked if the therapist is sarcastic in a playful way, smiling, for example. If the therapist criticizes the client not doing homework, the Engagement item, "Therapist shames or criticizes how clients did (or did not do) a prior homework assignment," is checked instead.

Therapist does not respond to clients' expressions of personal interest or caring for him or her.
This item is checked when the therapist fails to respond to a direct question or statement connoting personal interest or caring for the therapist, such as questions

and comments by the client about the therapist's health, well-being, work, etc. Endorse this item when the therapist either ignores or shuts down the client's comment. Alternately, the therapist may react with silence or with a statement of reluctance to respond to the client(s). Statements of reluctance to respond include "It's none of your business," "That's personal," or "We're talking about you right now." This item would not be indicated if the therapist initially asks the client(s) to expand on his/her question or statement before the therapist replies. As long as the therapist acknowledges the client's interest, e.g., implying "I recognize or appreciate that you care about me," the item would not be marked, even if the therapist's response does not include a significant personal self-disclosure.

Note: Even if the client's expression of personal interest is not appropriate (e.g., asking the therapist for a date, asking the therapist about something highly personal), ignoring the client's comment should be marked. However, if the therapist gives a polite or didactic response ("Although I appreciate your interest, as a professional I am going to decline to answer your question about my private life"), the item would not be marked.

THERAPIST CONTRIBUTIONS TO SAFETY WITHIN THE THERAPEUTIC SYSTEM

*Therapist acknowledges that therapy involves taking risks or discussing private matters.

The therapist may make this statement at the outset of treatment when explaining the therapeutic approach and discussing how therapy works or do so whenever clients are reluctant to discuss upsetting issues or concerns. Examples include the following: "I know it's hard to expose your private life to a stranger"; "I know that talking about private matters can be difficult"; "I may ask you to try to talk with each other in different ways, ways that you may not talk with each other at home, and that may feel difficult and even risky at times. I want to encourage you to talk about how you are experiencing these challenges in therapy"; or, to a couple, "I know this is really personal, but can we talk about your sex life?" In essence, the therapist acknowledges that addressing personal feelings and problems in therapy may result in feelings of vulnerability and exposure. Normalization may also be intended, as when the therapist explains that concerns about exposing one's private life are common. For example, "Sometimes families end up fighting with each other before finding new ways to talk with each other" or "Sometimes the going can be rough. You may find that conflicts and problems can seem to get worse before getting better."

Therapist provides structure and guidelines for safety and confidentiality.

If the therapist discusses how the therapy sessions are to be structured in order to keep the clients safe (e.g., no name calling, yelling, physical contact), this item should be marked. The item is also checked when the therapist explains confidentiality, its limits, and privacy issues related to informed consent for release of information, recording sessions, research, and/or observing teams. Sometimes the therapist delineates and explains what type of information will be shared with third parties (e.g., Child Protective Services or other court-affiliated agencies). If the therapist also encourages the family to express reactions to these elements, also mark the next item, "Therapist invites discussion about the intimidating elements in the therapeutic context." Note: For this item to be checked, the therapist needs to discuss or explain confidentiality or privacy. If the use of consent forms, recording, or observation is simply mentioned in the context of what is done in therapy or in this setting, check instead the Engagement item, "Therapist explains how therapy works."

*Therapist invites discussion about intimidating elements in the therapeutic context (e.g., recording equipment, reports to third parties, treatment team observation, one-way mirror, research, etc.).
Simply reporting these extra-therapy procedures (e.g., "We're using the camera today") is not sufficient. The therapist must invite discussion about the intimidating elements in the therapeutic context. At a minimum, the therapist must offer the clients an opportunity to talk about their reactions to these conditions. Examples include "Most people feel a little uncomfortable with the camera [or observers] initially. We can talk about your concerns" or "Tell me more about what makes you uncomfortable. Can I answer any questions about it?" The client may ask a specific question about reports to third parties, but in order to mark this item, the therapist must do more than simply respond to the question; he/she must invite further discussion.

*Therapist helps clients to talk truthfully and nondefensively with each other.
This behavior can occur when one family member demands explanations or justifications from another. Rather than simply witnessing demands and defensive reactions, the therapist intervenes to ask family members to talk about their own upset and hurt feelings. The therapist may intervene in a number of ways to discourage defensive communications or to promote open, honest, and truthful self-disclosures. For example, "Speak from your heart" or "Say what's true for you." Speaking to one person about another, "She's not looking at you right now. Talk to her in a way that she'll want to look at you" or "Tell it like it is. Be open with him." The therapist may encourage family members to communicate differently in therapy than they might typically do at home. "Can you for just this moment be real and genuine with your parents?" or "Don't hold back. He needs to hear what you are saying." "Let her show you that she can handle what you're thinking." Note: This item can be marked even if the client was speaking directly to the therapist (i.e., not specifically addressing another family member) because the other clients overhear the therapist's intervention.

Therapist attempts to contain, control, or manage overt hostility between clients.
Overt hostility may include name calling, verbal abuse, and threatening remarks. The therapist does not necessarily have to be successful at controlling or managing the hostility, but this item is marked if he/she at least makes an attempt to do so. Sometimes therapists tell families that in order to help create a safe environment for everyone, he/she will stop the session if hostility or aggression emerges. Later, the therapist may remind the family of the no aggression contract or intervene directly

when hostility surfaces. Examples include the following: "Is this how it goes at home? Let's see if we can do it differently in here"; "I don't want to make therapy a place for you just to hurt each other"; "If you just keep rehashing this fight, it will go to another fight. It's unlikely that it will go problem solving"; or "This isn't going anywhere – can we try something different?"

Note: This item should be endorsed only once for interventions during a single hostile episode. If there are repeated hostile episodes separated by calm discussion, the item should be marked each time it occurs. If the therapist explicitly intervenes on behalf of one family member (e.g., mentions one family member by name, age, or other specific identification) to protect him or her from another family member, consider marking instead the item "Therapist actively protects one family member from another (e.g., from blame, hostility, or emotional intrusiveness)." Both items could be indicated during the same session.

If there is hostility and there is no therapist attempt to control it, consider whether the therapist allowed the conflict to escalate unchecked during the session. If so, mark the negative indicator ("Therapist allows family conflict to escalate to verbal abuse, threats, or intimidation").

Therapist actively protects one family member from another (e.g., from blame, hostility, or emotional intrusiveness).

For this item to be endorsed, the therapist must intervene directly and specifically to "rescue" one or more family members who is "under attack." The therapist must mention the client(s) by name or in other ways (e.g., by age or nonverbally, as by pointing). Examples include "Your wife needs a break," "It's too hard for a 10-year-old to say who he wants to live with," "I can see she's not ready to talk about this," or "I'm not sure it's safe for him to answer while you're so angry." The therapist can also intervene by proposing separate meetings (e.g., parents alone and child alone). If one client is clearly under attack during the session (rather than at some future date), check this item rather than the item "Therapist asks one or more clients to leave the room in order to see one client alone for a portion of the session."

Note: This item should be endorsed only once for repeated interventions in the same episode. For repeated episodes, separated by periods of calm communication, the item may be marked each time it occurs. Also, if the therapist stops the blaming or aggressive communication without specifying one or more clients, mark the above item instead ("Therapist contains, controls, or manages overt hostility between clients").

Therapist changes the topic to something pleasurable or non-anxiety arousing (e.g., small talk about the weather, room decor, TV shows, etc.) when there seems to be tension or anxiety.

This item should only be checked when the therapist initiates or changes the topic of conversation to a more casual, pleasurable, or relaxing one in order to reduce tension or anxiety:

Father [to son]:   You're failing all your major courses!
Son: [lengthy, uncomfortable silence]

Therapist: Well, before going into all the school problems, Johnny, I wanted to show you my new fish tank, that one over in the corner... Do you like fish tanks? Have you ever had one?

Note that it is not necessary for anxiety to actually be reduced in order for this item to be marked.

Also note that the item is not marked if the therapist uses these kinds of interventions at the very beginning or very end of the session simply as a bridge, e.g., "Is it still raining outside?" Moreover, if the small talk does not seem to be in response to tension or anxiety yet does refer to the clients' likes, dislikes, hobbies, etc., mark instead the Emotional Connection item, "Therapist expresses interest in the client(s) apart from the therapeutic discussion at hand." When both therapist and client(s) laugh at a joke or funny incident in the absence of tension/anxiety, mark instead the Emotional Connection item, "Therapist shares a lighthearted moment or joke with client(s)."

Therapist asks one client (or a subgroup of clients) to leave the room in order to see one client alone for a portion of the session.
This item is marked when the therapist asks to see one client or one subgroup of clients (e.g., parents, children) alone, even if requested by the client. By providing this private opportunity, the therapist allows discussion of personal matters that the client(s) may not wish to discuss in the presence of other family members. For example, the therapist notices that answering questions about sex or other intimate or private matters may be hard for an adolescent in the presence of her mother; the therapist decides to ask the mother to leave the room. This behavior essentially promotes safety by drawing boundaries and giving client(s) the space to speak freely. The item is not marked, however, when a client simply walks out of the session or when the therapist asks someone to leave in order to control hostility or to protect one client from others (consider instead the items, "Therapist contains, controls, or manages overt hostility between clients" or "Therapist actively protects one family member from another").

Therapist allows family conflict to escalate to verbal abuse, threats, or intimidation.
Some expressions of anger and blaming communication are likely to occur during the course of therapy as problems are aired and addressed appropriately and with measured control. This item should only be marked in situations where the therapist is lax or negligent about the ongoing hostility. As an example, a family member threatens, "You will do this or I will make you wish you had," and the therapist says nothing about the implied threat. Similarly, a family member uses extremely pejorative language toward another family member, and the therapist does not intervene. Moreover, this item is marked if any aggression (verbal or physical) ends of its own accord, that is, without the intervention of the therapist (e.g., someone walks out, family members shut down, the session is over).

Note: This item should not be marked when a therapist makes a direct intervention to control or manage hostility but is not successful at doing so. (In this case, mark instead "Therapist attempts to contain, control, or manage overt hostility between clients.")

Therapist does not attend to overt expressions of client vulnerability (e.g., crying, defensiveness).
For this item to be marked, client vulnerability expressed through crying or overt defensiveness is not acknowledged by the therapist. If the therapist does acknowledge the client's difficulty (e.g., by a softening tone of voice, leaning forward, offering tissues, or reassuring comments like, "I know this is tough to talk about"), mark instead the item "Therapist explicitly expresses empathy for the clients' struggle" (Emotional Connection). To mark this item, the therapist must essentially ignore noticeable client vulnerability.

THERAPIST CONTRIBUTIONS TO SHARED SENSE OF PURPOSE WITHIN THE FAMILY

*Therapist encourages clients to compromise with each other.
Compromise involves some contribution by each party to reach an agreement about the relationship or about specific course of action. The therapist may explicitly ask family members if a compromise is possible and what each person would be willing to do to reach a compromise. An example is, "Is there one small step that each of you could take to move closer to a compromise?" The therapist may also refer to compromise indirectly, as in, "Is there anything that each of you is willing to do to move closer to an agreement, something that each of you would feel better about?" The therapist could also suggest a specific compromise to a problem that is being discussed. In other words, the therapist encourages compromise through a suggested solution where each individual is asked to give something for the other, implying "If you do _____ for him, maybe he'd do _____ for you." Compromise should be distinguished from a concession when only one person is asked to give in to the other person. Asking one person, "Would you do this for her?" is asking for a concession not a compromise, and in this case the item should not be marked.

*Therapist encourages clients to ask each other for their perspective.
This item is often a precursor to the discussion of a compromise. The therapist may encourage any family member to check with one or more other family members about their perception of the problem or their perspective on possible solutions. In other words, the therapist's intervention involves family members in seeking to find out how everyone views a situation or problem. An example is "[Child], would you be willing to ask your parents to share their ideas about when things started becoming a problem at school? Mom and Dad, have you asked [child] what is going well in school? Why don't you see if you can help him say those things now, in here?" Note: The item should not be checked when the therapist directly asks another family member for input (e.g., "Mom, what do you think about [child's] difficulties at school?").

*Therapist praises clients for respecting each other's point of view.
Family members do not necessarily have to be in agreement for the therapist to acknowledge and recognize their show of respect for each other's views. For example, the therapist might say, "Even though you two have different opinions about this,

you each listened carefully to each other and seemed to show that you appreciate that the other person may have a reason for differing with your opinion"; "Wow, even though there are still differences in how each person sees things, I can't help but notice how you were willing to listen to each other. There seems to be some openness and respect for each other that I'm sure is going to be helpful in solving this problem"; or "It's important that you understand and acknowledge that you both have valid reasons for what you think. Even though you don't agree, I see there is some basic respect for each person's point of view in this family."

Therapist emphasizes commonalities among clients' perspectives on the problem or solution.

This item focuses more on the cognitive aspect of the clients' perspectives, the way people are looking at the problem as opposed to their underlying values, needs, or feelings (which are referred to in the item below). In order to check this item, the therapist must do more than summarize various perspectives. Rather, the therapist must make explicit statements about connections and common themes among the various family members' perspectives. For example, "Mom and [child], you both agree that the problem seemed to start with the change to a new school"; "It's clear that ultimately you both want [child] to have more responsibility. She wants to be trusted to do some things on her own and Mom wants her to act in a way, by making good choices and considering the family's rules, that she can trust her to handle this responsibility with maturity "; or "So, you all want child protective services out of your lives. It seems that you agree that part of the solution will be to figure out how to make that happen."

Note: A therapist might simultaneously address commonalities among perspectives and point out shared experiences among family members, i.e., in one intervention: "You both agree that [child] is not showing respect {point of view, perspective} and both of you feel scared that you've lost control with him {shared experience, feelings}." In this example, this item as well as the following item, "Therapist draws attention to shared values, experiences, needs, or feelings," would be marked.

Therapist draws attention to clients' shared values, experiences, needs, or feelings.

This item differs from the above item by its focus on values, experiences, needs, or feelings; the previous item focuses on similarities in perspectives on the problem or solution. In other words, to mark this item, the therapist must be discussing the clients' affective experience, needs, or values, not their views on a situation. An example of a shared value is family loyalty, as in: "Each of you has described your family as a family that sticks together through tough times" or "Both of you want the best for your children, although you go about getting it in different ways." The therapist may point out a specific instance in the session when two or more family members expressed similar feelings (e.g., wish for change, frustration, anger, distrust, loneliness). When discussing a specific problem, the therapist may point out how family members experience the situation in a similar way (even though they may not see the problem similarly), as in "You both feel like victims of the other," "You're both hurting a lot," or "Both of you feel trapped."

Therapist encourages clients to show caring, concern, or support for each other.

The therapist may encourage expression of caring, concern, or support among family members by suggesting a specific action that the clients do for each other. For example, the therapist could request that a family member pass the tissues to another family member who is crying. The therapist may say, "Can you reach out your hand to him, while he's saying that?" or "It looks like your child needs a hug" or "Could you let her know that you care about her, even though you are upset with the trouble that she's in at school" or "Say more about why you are concerned for her" or "What are you willing to do to support your child as he tries to change?" Note: When emotions are running high, the therapist may propose an in-session task, like "give him a hug" without asking if the clients are willing. If the purpose of the therapist's intervention is for support, do not mark the negative Engagement item, "Therapist defines therapeutic goals or imposes tasks or procedures without asking the client(s) for their collaboration."

*Therapist encourages client(s) to ask each other for feedback.

To distinguish this item from the item "Encourages family members to ask each other for their perspectives," mark this behavior only when the therapist explicitly encourages family members to ask each other for feedback in the session. The therapist might encourage all family members to ask each other how they feel about talking about the problems and possible solutions, for example. Other examples include "You want to convince your parents that they should consider your request. Why don't you ask your mom and dad how you came across?" or "Find out if your parents have other concerns about you?" In couple therapy, a therapist may ask, "Are you willing to ask each other how your partner sees you at home? Does your partner see you as trying to do things differently?" The item should only be marked if the therapist wants the clients to ask each other in the session, not if this is an assignment to do at home between sessions.

*Therapist fails to intervene when family members argue with each other about the goals, value, or need for therapy.

In contrast to the Safety items related to conflict or hostility between clients, the conflict in this item refers to conflict about coming to therapy. To mark this item, the family argument or disagreement about the value of treatment needs to be clear, not implicit or simply nonverbal. The clients might say, "You heard what [therapist] said! We need to be here!" or "This is useless, we don't want the same thing. He's not willing to take this seriously." If the therapist fails to address the conflict, this item should be marked. This item should not be checked if the therapist acknowledges the disagreement and points out that some family members are uncertain about the benefits of therapy. Also, if the therapist invites discussion of the client's doubts and searches for possible points of agreement among family members, this item would not be marked.

Therapist fails to address one client's stated concerns by only discussing another client's concerns.

Essentially, this item is marked at the end of the session when it is clear that although more than one client stated a concern, the therapist only addresses one concern, not the other(s). For example, at some point in the session, a parent raises a concern about an adolescent child's failure to complete homework and repeated disciplinary referrals in school for disrupting class, while the adolescent complains that the parent never gives him/her credit for helping out at home. This item would be marked if the therapist focuses the conversation on the school behavior problems but ignores or fails to address the adolescent child's complaint about lack of recognition for contributing at home. However, if the therapist comments at the end of the session, "We never got to your [one family member] concern, so we'll pick it up next time," the item should not be checked. Note: The client must specifically request a discussion on a topic, not just bring something up in cross-blaming. In the following example, this item would not be checked because the son is trying to deflect his mother rather than initiate a new topic:

Mother: Let's talk about your refusing to do anything I ask you to do!
Son: Well, you don't give me an allowance like other kids get!

If the conversation were to go as follows, the item should be marked:

Mother: Let's talk about your refusing to do anything I ask you to do!
Son: Can we also talk about why you don't give me an allowance like other kids get?

Appendix B: SOFTA-s Self-Report Questionnaires[2]

SOFTA-s (client)

Evaluate the following phrases, and indicate your level of agreement by circling the appropriate number:

	Not at all	A little	Moderately	A lot	Very much
1. What happens in therapy can solve our problems	1	2	3	4	5
2. The therapist understands me	1	2	3	4	5
3. The therapy sessions help me open up (share my feelings, try new things, etc.)	1	2	3	4	5
4. All my family members who come for therapy want the best for our family and to resolve our problems	1	2	3	4	5
5. It is hard for me to discuss with the therapist what we should work on in therapy	1	2	3	4	5
6. The therapist is doing everything possible to help me	1	2	3	4	5
7. I feel comfortable and relaxed in the therapy sessions	1	2	3	4	5
8. All of us who come for therapy sessions value the time and effort we all put in	1	2	3	4	5
9. The therapist and I work together as a team	1	2	3	4	5
10. The therapist has become an important person in my life	1	2	3	4	5
11. There are some topics I am afraid to discuss in therapy	1	2	3	4	5

(continued)

[2] SOFTA-s (Client and Therapist) and SOATIF-s (Client and Therapist), pp. 297–299, from: Friedlander, M. L., Escudero, V., & Heatherington, L. (2006). *Therapeutic alliances in couple and family therapy: An empirically informed guide to practice.* http://dx.doi.org/10.1037/11410-000.

(continued)

	Not at all	A little	Moderately	A lot	Very much
12. Some members of the family don't agree with others about the goals of the therapy	1	2	3	4	5
13. I understand what is being done in therapy	1	2	3	4	5
14. The therapist lacks the knowledge and skills to help me	1	2	3	4	5
15. At times I feel defensive in therapy (continued)		2	3	4	5
16. Each of us in the family helps the others get what they want out of therapy	1	2	3	4	5

SOFTA-s (therapist)

Evaluate the following phrases, and indicate your level of agreement by circling the appropriate number:

	Not at all	A little	Moderately	A lot	Very much
1. What happens in therapy can solve this family's problems	1	2	3	4	5
2. I understand this family	1	2	3	4	5
3. The therapy sessions are helping family members to open up (share feelings, try new things, etc.)	1	2	3	4	5
4. All of the family members who are coming for therapy want the best for the family and to resolve their problems	1	2	3	4	5
5. It is hard for me and the family to discuss together what we should work on in therapy	1	2	3	4	5
6. I am doing everything possible to help this family	1	2	3	4	5
7. Family members feel comfortable and relaxed in the therapy sessions	1	2	3	4	5
8. All of those who come for therapy sessions value the time and effort the others put in	1	2	3	4	5
9. The family and I are working together as a team	1	2	3	4	5
10. I have become an important person in this family's life	1	2	3	4	5
11. There are some topics that the family members are afraid to discuss in therapy	1	2	3	4	5
12. Some members of the family don't agree with others about the goals of the therapy	1	2	3	4	5

(continued)

(continued)

		Not at all	A little	Moderately	A lot	Very much
13.	What this family and I are doing in therapy makes sense to me	1	2	3	4	5
14.	I lack the knowledge and skills to help this family	1	2	3	4	5
15.	At times some family members feel defensive in therapy	1	2	3	4	5
16.	Each person in the family helps the others get what they want out of therapy	1	2	3	4	5

Scoring Guide for the SOFTA-s

Item #	Score
ENGAGEMENT	
1	
*5	
9	
13	
TOTAL	
EMOTIONAL CONNECTION	
2	
6	
10	
*14	
TOTAL	
SAFETY	
3	
7	
*11	
*15	
TOTAL	
SHARED SENSE OF PURPOSE	
4	
8	
*12	
16	
TOTAL	
TOTAL SCORE	

*Items with asterisks (5, 11, 12, 14, and 15) must be inverse scored, so that:
If the client marks 5 ⇒ the score should be 1.
4 ⇒ the score should be 2.

3 ⇒ the score should be 3.
2 ⇒ the score should be 4.
1 ⇒ the score should be 5.

SOFTA-s (Shortened Versions)

Client version:
Evaluate the following phrases, and indicate your level of agreement by circling the appropriate number:

	Not at all	A little	Moderately	A lot	Very much
1. What happens in therapy can solve our problems	1	2	3	4	5
2. The therapist understands me	1	2	3	4	5
4. All my family members who come for therapy want the best for our family and to resolve our problems	1	2	3	4	5
7. I feel comfortable and relaxed in the therapy sessions	1	2	3	4	5

Therapist version:
Evaluate the following phrases, and indicate your level of agreement by circling the appropriate number:

	Not at all	A little	Moderately	A lot	Very much
1. What happens in therapy can solve this family's problems	1	2	3	4	5
2. I understand this family	1	2	3	4	5
4. All of the family members who are coming for therapy want the best for the family and to resolve their problems	1	2	3	4	5
7. Family members feel comfortable and relaxed in the therapy sessions	1	2	3	4	5

Appendix C: Rating Guidelines and Rating Sheets for the SOFTA-o (Client and Therapist)[3]

Rating Sheets

DIRECTIONS: Please read the definition of each of the following four constructs. Then, on the client rating sheets, identify the family members to be rated in the top row. As you observe the session, mark each behavior that occurs in the appropriate column. Note that items in italics reflect a lack of engagement, poor emotional connection, a lack of a shared sense of purpose, and a lack of safety. At the conclusion of the session, use these marks to make a judgment about each family member's alliance on Engagement, Emotional Connection, and Safety (client version). (Rate the entire family system on Shared Sense of Purpose). Similarly, use the therapist rating sheet to rate the therapist on each of the four dimensions. To do so, use the guidelines (which appear after the series of rating sheets) to make global (−3 to +3) ratings for each alliance dimension based on the behaviors you marked as you observed the session. Use the guidelines in the training manual to go from check marks to ratings. Note that items in italics reflect a lack of engagement, poor emotional connection, a lack of a shared sense of purpose, and a lack of safety:

+3 = extremely strong
+2 = moderately strong
+1 = somewhat strong
0 = unremarkable or neutral
−1 = somewhat problematic
−2 = moderately problematic
−3 = extremely problematic

---

[3] © Friedlander, Escudero, & Heatherington, 2001, and © Escudero, Friedlander, & Deihl, 2004. Reproduced by permission of the authors.

Appendix A: SOFTA-o (Client and Therapist) and SOATIF-o (Client and Therapist), pp. 269–280, from: Friedlander, M. L., Escudero, V., & Heatherington, L. (2006). *Therapeutic alliances in couple and family therapy: An empirically informed guide to practice.* http://dx.doi.org/10.1037/11410-000.

Engagement in the therapeutic process	Safety within the therapeutic system
The client viewing treatment as meaningful, a sense of being involved in therapy and working together with the therapist, that therapeutic goals and tasks in therapy can be discussed and negotiated with the therapist, that taking the process seriously is important, that change is possible	The client viewing therapy as a place to take risks, be open, flexible; a sense of comfort and an expectation that new experiences and learning will take place; that good can come from being in therapy; that conflict within the family can be handled without harm; that one need not be defensive

Emotional connection to the therapist	Shared sense of purpose within the family
The client viewing the therapist as an important person in her/his life, almost like a family member; a sense that the relationship is based on affiliation, trust, caring, and concern; that the therapist genuinely cares and "is there" for the client; that he/she is on the same wavelength with the therapist (e.g., similar life perspectives, values); that the therapist's wisdom and expertise are valuable	Family members seeing themselves as working collaboratively to improve family relations and achieve common family goals; a sense of solidarity in relation to the therapy ("we're in this together"); that they value their time with each other in therapy; essentially, a feeling of unity within the family in relation to therapy

RATING SHEET (CLIENTS)

FAMILY MEMBER

_____ _____ _____ _____

ENGAGEMENT IN THE THERAPEUTIC PROCESS:

Client indicates agreement with the therapist's goals

_____ _____ _____ _____

Client describes or discusses a plan for improving

the situation

_____ _____ _____ _____

Client introduces a problem for discussion

_____ _____ _____ _____

Client agrees to do homework assignments

_____ _____ _____ _____

Client indicates having done homework or seeing it

as useful

_____ _____ _____ _____

Client expresses optimism or indicates that a

positive change has taken place

_____ _____ _____ _____

Client complies with therapist's request for

an enactment

_____ _____ _____ _____

Client leans forward

_____ _____ _____ _____

Client mentions the treatment, the therapeutic process,

or a specific session

_____ _____ _____ _____

Client expresses feeling "stuck," questions the value

of therapy, or states that therapy is not / has not

been helpful

_____ _____ _____ _____

Client shows indifference about the tasks or process

of therapy (e.g., paying lip service, "I don't know,"

tuning out)

_____ _____ _____ _____

Rate Engagement in the Process	-3	-2	-1	0	+1	+2	+3
for each family member:				___	___	___	___

EMOTIONAL CONNECTION TO THE THERAPIST:

Client shares a lighthearted moment or joke with the therapist				___	___	___	___
Client verbalizes trust in the therapist				___	___	___	___
Client expresses interest in the therapist's personal life				___	___	___	___
Client indicates feeling understood or accepted by the therapist				___	___	___	___
Client expresses physical affection or caring for the therapist				___	___	___	___
Client mirrors the therapist's body posture				___	___	___	___
Client avoids eye contact with the therapist				___	___	___	___
Client refuses or is reluctant to respond to the therapist				___	___	___	___
Client has hostile or sarcastic interactions with the therapist				___	___	___	___
Client comments on the therapist's incompetence or inadequacy				___	___	___	___

Rate Emotional Connection to the Therapist	-3	-2	-1	0	+1	+2	+3
for each family member:				___	___	___	___

SAFETY WITHIN THE THERAPEUTIC SYSTEM:

Client implies or states that therapy is a safe place				___	___	___	___
Client varies his/her emotional tone during the session				___	___	___	___
Client shows vulnerability							
(e.g., discusses painful feelings, cries)				___	___	___	___

Client has an open upper body posture ＿＿＿ ＿＿＿ ＿＿＿ ＿＿＿

Client reveals a secret or something that other

    family members didn't know ＿＿＿ ＿＿＿ ＿＿＿ ＿＿＿

Client encourages another family member to

    "open up" or to tell the truth ＿＿＿ ＿＿＿ ＿＿＿ ＿＿＿

Client directly asks other family members for feedback

    about his/her behavior or about herself/himself as a person ＿＿＿ ＿＿＿ ＿＿＿ ＿＿＿

Client expresses anxiety nonverbally (e.g., taps or shakes) ＿＿＿ ＿＿＿ ＿＿＿ ＿＿＿

Client protects self in nonverbal manner (e.g., crosses arms

    over chest, doesn't take off jacket or put down purse,

    sits far away from group, etc.) ＿＿＿ ＿＿＿ ＿＿＿ ＿＿＿

Client refuses or is reluctant to respond when directly

    addressed by another family member ＿＿＿ ＿＿＿ ＿＿＿ ＿＿＿

Client responds defensively to another family member ＿＿＿ ＿＿＿ ＿＿＿ ＿＿＿

Client makes an uneasy/anxious reference to the camera,

    observation, supervisor, or research procedures ＿＿＿ ＿＿＿ ＿＿＿ ＿＿＿

Rate Safety within the Therapeutic System　　　　　**-3　　-2　　-1　　0　　+1　　+2　　+3**

for each family member:

＿＿＿ ＿＿＿ ＿＿＿ ＿＿＿

SHARED SENSE OF PURPOSE WITHIN THE FAMILY:

Family members offer to compromise ＿＿＿ ＿＿＿ ＿＿＿ ＿＿＿

Family members share a joke or a lighthearted moment

    with each other ＿＿＿ ＿＿＿ ＿＿＿ ＿＿＿

Family members ask each other for their perspective   ___ ___ ___ ___

Family members validate each other's point of view   ___ ___ ___ ___

Family members mirror each other's body posture   ___ ___ ___ ___

Family members avoid eye contact with each other   ___ ___ ___ ___

Family members blame each other   ___ ___ ___ ___

Family members devalue each other's opinions or perspective   ___ ___ ___ ___

Family members try to align with the therapist

  against each other   ___ ___ ___ ___

Client makes hostile or sarcastic comments to family members   ___ ___ ___ ___

Family members disagree with each other about the value, purpose,

  goals, or tasks of therapy or about who should be included

  in the sessions   ___ ___ ___ ___

Rate Shared Sense of Purpose within the Family   -3   -2   -1   0   +1   +2   +3

for the family as a whole:

_____

RATING SHEET (THERAPIST)

CONTRIBUTIONS TO ENGAGEMENT IN THE THERAPEUTIC PROCESS:

Therapist explains how therapy works.   _____

*Therapist asks client(s) what they want to

    talk about in the session.   _____

*Therapist encourages client(s) to articulate

    their goals for therapy.   _____

Therapist asks client(s) whether they are willing to

    do a specific in-session task (e.g., enactment).   _____

*Therapist asks client(s) whether they are willing to follow

    a specific suggestion or do a specific

    homework assignment.   _____

*Therapist asks client(s) about the impact or value

    of a prior homework assignment.   _____

*Therapist expresses optimism or notes that a positive

    change has taken place or can take place.   _____

Therapist pulls in quiet client(s) (e.g., by deliberately leaning

    forward, calling them by name,

    addressing them specifically).   _____

Therapist asks if the client(s) have any questions.   _____

Therapist praises client motivation

    for engagement or change.   _____

Therapist defines therapeutic goals or imposes tasks or

procedures without asking the client(s)

  for their collaboration.   _____

*Therapist argues with the client(s) about the nature,

  purpose, or value of therapy.   _____

Therapist shames or criticizes how clients did

  (or did not do) a prior homework assignment.   _____

Rate therapist contribution to Engagement: -3   -2   -1   0   +1   +2   +3

THERAPIST CONTRIBUTIONS TO EMOTIONAL CONNECTION:

*Therapist shares a lighthearted moment

  or joke with the client(s).   _____

*Therapist expresses confidence, trust,

  or belief in the client(s).   _____

Therapist expresses interest in the client(s) apart

  from the therapeutic discussion at hand.   _____

*Therapist expresses caring or touches client(s) affectionately

  yet appropriately (e.g., hand shake, pat on head).   _____

Therapist discloses his or her personal reactions or feelings

  toward the client(s) or the situation.   _____

*Therapist discloses some fact about

  his or her personal life.   _____

Therapist remarks on or describes how his or her values

or experiences are similar to the clients'.   _____

Therapist (verbally or nonverbally) expresses empathy

    for the clients' struggle (e.g., "I know this is hard,"

       "I feel your pain," crying with client).   _____

Therapist reassures or normalizes a client's emotional

    vulnerability (e.g., crying, hurt feelings).   _____

Therapist has hostile, sarcastic, or critical

    interactions with the client(s).   _____

Therapist does not respond to clients' expressions

    of personal interest or caring for him or her.   _____

Rate therapist contribution to

Emotional Connection: -3   -2   -1   0   +1   +2   +3

THERAPIST CONTRIBUTIONS TO SAFETY WITHIN THE THERAPEUTIC SYSTEM:

*Therapist acknowledges that therapy involves taking risks

    or discussing private matters.   _____

Therapist provides structure and guidelines for safety

    and confidentiality.   _____

*Therapist invites discussion about intimidating elements in the

    therapeutic context (e.g., recording equipment, reports to third

    parties, treatment team observation,

    one-way mirror, research, etc.).   _____

Therapist helps clients to talk truthfully and

   nondefensively with each other.   _____

Therapist attempts to contain, control, or manage

   overt hostility between clients.   _____

Therapist actively protects one family member

   from another (e.g., from blame, hostility,

   or emotional intrusiveness).   _____

Therapist changes the topic to something pleasurable

   or non-anxiety arousing (e.g., small talk about

   the weather, room decor, TV shows, etc.)

   when there seems to be tension or anxiety.   _____

Therapist asks one client (or a subgroup of clients) to leave

   the room in order to see one client alone for a

   portion of the session.   _____

Therapist allows family conflict to escalate to verbal abuse,

   threats, or intimidation.   _____

Therapist does not attend to overt expressions of client

   vulnerability (e.g., crying, defensiveness).   _____

Rate therapist contribution to Safety: -3   -2   -1   0   +1   +2   +3

THERAPIST CONTRIBUTIONS TO A SHARED SENSE OF PURPOSE WITHIN THE FAMILY:

*Therapist encourages clients to

    compromise with each other.   _____

*Therapist encourages clients to ask each

    other for their perspective.   _____

*Therapist praises clients for respecting each

    other's point of view.   _____

Therapist emphasizes commonalities among clients'

    perspectives on the problem or solution.   _____

Therapist draws attention to clients' shared values,

    experiences, needs, or feelings.   _____

Therapist encourages clients to show caring, concern,

    or support for each other.   _____

*Therapist encourages client(s) to ask each

    other for feedback.   _____

*Therapist fails to intervene when family members argue

    with each other about the goals, value, or

    need for therapy.   _____

*Therapist fails to address one client's stated concerns

    by only discussing another client's concerns.   _____

Rate therapist contribution to Shared Purpose: -3   -2   -1   0   +1   +2   +3

_____

*indicates a similar item in the client version

SOFTA-o Rating Guidelines[4]

The behavioral items are assumed to be indicators of the more global, underlying dimensions, which are defined in more subjective terms (i.e., in terms of the clients' cognitions and affect or the therapist's contributions to each dimension of the alliance). Raters need to use the check marks they made on the individual items to make their overall ratings rather than rely simply on an intuitive sense about each dimension.

It is impossible for a rater to avoid making comparisons of the strength of the alliance across family members while watching the session and marking behavioral indicators. Thus, the rating of each family member is influenced by the ratings of all the other family members. For this reason, the following guideline should be used: The rater should first look at the check marks and decide who in the family seems to be the *least* involved and connected. This person should be rated first, followed by the family member who is the *next least* involved, and so forth. In this way, the family member whose behavior suggests the greatest involvement or commitment is rated last.

To facilitate the process of going from the check marks to the ratings, judges should use the following guidelines for the *Engagement, Safety,* and *Emotional Connection* dimensions:

1) If *no* checks are made in a given dimension, the score should be *0 (unremarkable)*. This means that the therapist has made no remarks that either contribute to or detract from the alliance. In terms of the family, the client who receives a rating of *0* is viewed as at least moderately aligned (otherwise, he or she would be protesting the therapy or would leave the room). In family therapy, it sometimes occurs that a client does not speak during a given session, particularly if there are many people in the room. If there are no negative or positive indicators and the client does not speak, the rating should be *0*.
2) If *only negative* items are checked, the score *must* be less than *0*. On the client measure, rate the client as *−3 only* if it is clear that the person is antagonistic to the therapy and demonstrates that antagonism behaviorally—otherwise the score would be a *−2* or *−1* depending on a decision about how negative the behaviors seem to the judge.
3) If *only positive* items are checked, the score *must* be above *0*.
4) If the only positive item is nonverbal (open upper body posture, mirrored body language), the rating should be *+1*.

---

[4] Adapted from the *System for Observing Family Therapy Alliances* (SOFTA-o) *Training Manual—Revised,* by M. L. Friedlander, V. Escudero, L. Heatherington, L. Diehl et al., 2004, unpublished manuscript. Available from http://www.softa-soatif.net. Adapted with permission of the authors.

Also in Appendix A SOFTA-o Rating Guidelines, pp. 293–295, from: Friedlander, M. L., Escudero, V., & Heatherington, L. (2006). *Therapeutic alliances in couple and family therapy: An empirically informed guide to practice.* http://dx.doi.org/10.1037/11410-000.

5) A +3 is given *only* if it is clear that the therapist is making a great effort or if the client is *highly* invested in the therapy, as demonstrated by showing a great deal of vulnerability (Safety) or taking a very active part in the therapeutic process (Engagement), or there is clear, important caring demonstrated toward the therapist (Emotional Connection). Otherwise, the score should be a +1 or +2 depending on how positive the behaviors are judged to be. If the client is crying from the heart, for example, the score would probably be a +2.

6) If *both positive and negative* items are checked, the rating should either be −1, 0, or +1 depending on an assessment of the balance in frequency or meaningfulness of the checked behaviors.

7) -3 is given *only* when it's clear that the client is *absolutely extremely problematic* invested in the therapy.

The rater's task is, nonetheless, somewhat subjective. Some behaviors, particularly the nonverbal ones, can occur throughout the session (e.g., "Family members mirror each other's body posture"), whereas most of the other behaviors are likely to occur once or a few times. Here is where the judge needs to decide on the significance or clinical meaningfulness of the behavior. If, for example, a family member "agrees to do homework assignments" once and with minimal enthusiasm, the rating might be +1. If the family member asks for details about the assignment and talks about when, how, and under what circumstances it will be done, the rating might be +2. If the family member is particularly enthusiastic and committed to the assignment, the rating might be +3.

As another example, consider the item, "Client refuses or is reluctant to respond to the therapist." If this occurs once or minimally, the rating would be −1. If the client spends a fair amount of the session refusing to speak, the rating could be −2. If the session is entirely spent this way, the rating would be −3.

For *Shared Sense of Purpose*, client version, one rating is given for the couple or family as a unit. Raters should be aware that this dimension refers to a shared sense of purpose *about the therapy*, not about the family in general or the presenting problem. In other words, a couple might enjoy each other's company a great deal yet have very different views on the value of therapy for improving their relationship. Alternately, everyone in the family might agree that the teenage son has a problem; this agreement reflects a shared sense about what the problem is, but not necessarily a shared sense of purpose *with respect to the therapy*. The parents, for example, might indicate that the focus of therapy should be the son's misbehavior, but the teen might state that the therapy is a complete waste of time or that he thinks the therapist should focus on his parents' strictness and his father's alcoholism. In this case, the sense of unity within the family with respect to the therapy is not optimal.

On the client measure, raters should use the following guidelines to go from the behavioral ratings to the overall rating for *Shared Sense of Purpose*:

1) *Judges first need to see how many family members have positive and negative items checked.*

2) If there are *no* items checked *for any family member*, the rating should be *0*, i.e., *unremarkable*. As with the other ratings, the assumption is that there is at least a moderate sense of purpose within the family if everyone is there and is not showing any behavior indicative of a poor alliance.

3) If there is *at least one positive* item *and no negative* items checked *for every family member*, the rating should be at least *+1* and could be *+2* or *+3*, depending on the rater's judgment of the number and meaningfulness of the checked items.

4) If there is *at least one negative* item for *only one family member and no positive items checked for anyone*, the rating should be *−1* or *−2*, depending on the judgment of just how negative the behavior is in the session.

5) If *two or more family members* have *only negative* items checked, the rating should be *−3* or *−2*.

6) If there are *both positive and negative* items checked *for any one family member*, the judgment should either be *−1*, *0*, or *+1* depending on an assessment of the balance in frequency or meaningfulness of the checked behaviors.

7) If there is a major disagreement between family members expressed in the session about the value of therapy or what is going to be accomplished there, the rating should be *−3*, *even if* no other negative items are checked.

Index

© Springer International Publishing AG 2017
V. Escudero, M.L. Friedlander, *Therapeutic Alliances with Families*, Focused
Issues in Family Therapy, DOI 10.1007/978-3-319-59369-2

Made in the USA
Columbia, SC
05 August 2021